T0304288

The National Institute of Economic and Social Research is an independent, non-profit-making body founded in 1938. It always has had as its aim the promotion of realistic research, particularly in the field of economics. It conducts research by its own research staff and in co-operation with the Universities and other academic bodies. The work done under the Institute's auspices is published by the Cambridge University Press in two series: *Studies* and *Occasional Papers*.

THE NATIONAL INSTITUTE OF
ECONOMIC AND SOCIAL RESEARCH

Economic and Social Studies

X

LESSONS OF THE BRITISH WAR ECONOMY

THE NATIONAL INSTITUTE OF
ECONOMIC AND SOCIAL RESEARCH

Economic and Social Studies

The Institute assumes no responsibility for the theories and opinions
expressed in the *Studies* and *Papers* prepared under its auspices.

LESSONS OF THE
BRITISH WAR ECONOMY

EDITED BY

D. N. CHESTER

CAMBRIDGE
AT THE UNIVERSITY PRESS
1951

CAMBRIDGE UNIVERSITY PRESS
Cambridge, New York, Melbourne, Madrid, Cape Town,
Singapore, São Paulo, Delhi, Tokyo, Mexico City

Cambridge University Press
The Edinburgh Building, Cambridge CB2 8RU, UK

Published in the United States of America by Cambridge University Press, New York

www.cambridge.org
Information on this title: www.cambridge.org/9781107698208

First published 1951
First paperback edition 2011

A catalogue record for this publication is available from the British Library

ISBN 978-1-107-69820-8 Paperback

CONTENTS

THE AUTHORS

The following biographical details give the present post held by the author, followed by his position immediately prior to the outbreak of war, his official wartime experience and any relevant postwar positions he may have held.

Where the author's period in a University post overlaps with the dates when he held a government post it can be assumed that he was on leave of absence from his University for that period.

PROFESSOR G. C. ALLEN, M.Com., Ph.D. Professor of Political Economy, University of London, since 1947. Brunner Professor of Economic Science, University of Liverpool, 1933–47; Assistant Secretary, Board of Trade, 1941–4; member of the Central Price Regulation Committee since 1944; Adviser on Industrial Location to the Board of Trade, 1944–5; Counsellor, Foreign Office, October 1945–April 1946.

PROFESSOR IAN BOWEN, M.A. Professor of Economics and Commerce, University College, Hull, since 1947. Fellow of All Souls College, Oxford, 1930–7; Lecturer in Economics, Brasenose College, Oxford, 1931–40; Research Associate, Oxford University Institute of Statistics, 1936–40; Statistical Officer (later Chief Statistical Officer), Ministry of Works, 1940–5; Lecturer in Economics, Hertford College, Oxford, 1946–7.

D. N. CHESTER, C.B.E., M.A.(Admin.), M.A. Official Fellow of Nuffield College, Oxford, since 1945. Lecturer in Public Administration, University of Manchester, 1936–45; member of the Central Economic Information Service and of the Economic Section of the War Cabinet Secretariat, 1940–5.

PROFESSOR ELY DEVONS, M.A. Robert Ottley Professor of Applied Economics, University of Manchester, since 1948. Statistician, Cotton Control, Ministry of Supply, 1939–40; member of the Central Economic Information Service and then of the Central Statistical Office, War Cabinet Secretariat, 1940–1; successively Chief Statistician, Director, and Deputy Director-General, Planning, Programmes and Statistics Division, Ministry of Aircraft Production, 1941–5; Reader in Statistics, University of Manchester, 1945–8.

PROFESSOR PERCY FORD, B.Sc.(Econ.), Ph.D. Professor of Economics, University College of Southampton, since 1938. Raw Materials Department, Ministry of Supply, 1939-45.

RT. HON. SIR RICHARD V. N. HOPKINS, P.C. 1945; G.C.B., cr. 1941 (K.C.B., cr. 1920); hon. Fellow of Emmanuel College, Cambridge; Member of the Court of the University of London. Second Secretary, H.M. Treasury, 1932-42; Permanent Secretary to H.M. Treasury, 1942-5.

G. D. A. MacDOUGALL, C.B.E., M.A. Reader in International Economics and Professorial Fellow of Nuffield College, Oxford, since January 1951. Lecturer in Economics, University of Leeds, 1936-9; First Lord of the Admiralty's Statistical Branch, 1939-40; Prime Minister's Statistical Section, 1940-5; Fellow and Lecturer in Economics, Wadham College, 1945-50; Economics Director, O.E.E.C., 1948-9.

A. W. MENZIES KITCHIN, M.A., Ph.D. Agricultural Economist and Director of Farm Economics Branch, School of Agriculture, Cambridge, since 1939 and University Reader in Agricultural Economics since October 1949. Engaged on work for the Ministry of Agriculture and Fisheries, 1939-45, and Joint Secretary of the Scientific Committee on Food Policy.

PROFESSOR E. F. NASH, M.A. Professor of Agricultural Economics, University College of Wales, Aberystwyth, since 1946. Economist at the Ministry of Agriculture and Fisheries until 1939; Ministry of Food, 1939-45; Control Commission for Germany (British Element), 1945-6.

PROFESSOR RICHARD PARES, C.B.E., F.B.A., M.A. Professor of History, University of Edinburgh, since 1945. Lecturer, New College, Oxford, 1929-40; Board of Trade, 1940-5.

W. B. REDDAWAY, M.A. Fellow of Clare College, Cambridge, since 1938 and Lecturer in Economics at Cambridge University since 1939. Statistics Division, Board of Trade, 1940-7.

PROFESSOR E. A. G. ROBINSON, C.M.G., O.B.E., M.A. Professor of Economics, University of Cambridge, since 1950 and Fellow of Sidney Sussex College, Cambridge, since 1931. Lecturer (later

Reader) in Economics, University of Cambridge, 1929–49; member of the Central Economic Information Service and of the Economic Section of the War Cabinet Secretariat, 1939–42; Economic Adviser and Head of Programmes Division, Ministry of Production, 1942–5; member of the British Reparations Mission, Moscow and Berlin, 1945; Economic Adviser, Board of Trade, 1946; member of the Economic Planning Staff, 1947–8.

RICHARD STONE, C.B.E., M.A. Director, Department of Applied Economics and Fellow of King's College, Cambridge, since 1945. With C. E. Heath and Co., Lloyds Brokers, 1936–9; Ministry of Economic Warfare, 1939–40; member of the Central Economic Information Service and of the Central Statistical Office, War Cabinet Secretariat, 1940–5. Director of the National Accounts Research Unit of OE.E.C. since 1949 and Foreign Adviser to the National Income Committee of the Government of India since 1950.

HUGH T. WEEKS, C.M.G., M.A. Deputy Chairman, Trussed Concrete Steel Company Ltd. Research and Statistical Manager, Cadbury Brothers, until 1939; Director of Statistics and, later, Director-General of Statistics and Programmes and member of the Supply Council, Ministry of Supply, 1939–43; Head of Programmes Division, Ministry of Production, 1943–5; represented the Ministries of Supply and Production on various missions to North America, 1941–5; Director, J. S. Fry & Sons, 1945–7; member of the Economic Planning Board, 1947–8; Joint Controller, Colonial Development Corporation, 1948–51.

ACKNOWLEDGEMENTS

The essays collected in this volume are an outcome of the extensive use in wartime administration of economists and other academic specialists in the field of social studies. The Committee of the National Institute of Economic and Social Research thought that this innovation had a double interest; it was an interesting experiment in the improvisation of an expert administrative staff, and it offered an unusual opportunity for intimate study to professional students of public administration. They were aware that an official history of wartime administration was in preparation; but the intrinsic importance of the experiments is so great that they thought there was room also for a more limited and specialized review—limited to contributors who took part in planning and carrying out the tasks they described, and directed specially to any lessons which these experiments had for the study of administration in general. Accordingly, with the exception for obvious reasons of Sir Richard Hopkins, invitations to contribute were restricted to economists and other university teachers who had come into the Government's service during the war and had returned to their pre-war occupations subsequently.

The Committee have many obligations to acknowledge and thanks to offer—to the Permanent Secretary to the Treasury for his sympathetic response to the proposal of such a review; to the heads of the Departments concerned for the necessary permissions to publish; to the Nuffield Foundation for their interest in the scheme, and for a special grant of £1,000 towards its cost; to Sir Richard Hopkins for contributing an introduction out of his unrivalled experience; to the contributors who have made time for their contributions when most of them were struggling with the resumption of teaching in overcrowded and under-staffed universities; and, most of all, to Mr. Chester, whose patience, persistence and editorial skill have brought the book through all the obstacles which faced a co-operative enterprise in the immediate postwar years, and successfully brought to realization the hopes in which it was planned.

HENRY CLAY

President
National Institute of Economic and Social Research

January 1951

EDITORIAL NOTE

Readers of these essays may find it helpful to have a few words of explanation about the intended scope of the book and the date when the essays were written.

Though the essays cover a large part of the Government wartime activities there are obvious gaps, for example Treasury policy, Labour controls, Shipping and Exchange control. In part this is due to my failure to persuade certain economists with experience of these matters to write about them. But it was never the intention to produce a volume which aimed at covering all aspects of the wartime economy. To do this properly would have meant including contributions based on research rather than on direct personal experience; and the main aim was to enable the authors to write about their experiences in the Civil Service as frankly as the Official Secrets Acts and reasonable discretion would allow. Thus when invitations were sent out in December 1946 'temporaries' who were remaining in the Service after that date were not approached.

Most of the essays were written a considerable time ago. Many of the authors wrote their contributions during the spring and summer of 1947 and most of the remaining essays came in during 1948, but the list was kept open for some months longer in the hope, a vain hope in certain cases alas, that those who had not yet found time from their University duties to complete their contributions would still be able to do so.

This note provides me with the opportunity to express publicly my thanks: to the contributors who responded so well and yet have had to suffer such a long delay in publication; to Feodora Stone for her continual encouragement and advice; and to Miss H. M. Rogers of the staff of the National Institute for giving me so much help in getting the book through the press and for all her work on the index.

D. N. CHESTER

I

INTRODUCTORY NOTE
by
SIR RICHARD HOPKINS

It is a wide gap that separates the civil business of government in wartime from its peacetime operations. If confirmation were necessary, the first world war would have afforded it. Note of that experience was indeed taken at the end of that war, lest ever again a like disaster should befall, and in the later thirties preparations for the transformation, should it be required, were intensified.

In the later months of 1939 the aspect of the civil service was changed. A little before the outbreak of war the Ministry of Supply had been formed. On the outbreak new Ministries sprang up—the Ministry of Home Security, which was associated with the Home Office, the Ministries of Shipping, of Food, of Economic Warfare, and of Information. A little later the Ministry of Aircraft Production was established. Subsequently the Ministry of Transport and the Ministry of Shipping were amalgamated into the Ministry of War Transport, and in due time the Ministry of Production appeared. Meanwhile, changes had occurred unobserved in the peacetime departments. Few escaped the need to lend leading members of their staff to undertake urgent duties elsewhere. Subject to that, those departments whose burdens increased were reinforced, while those in which the *tempo* declined gave up all the staff that they could spare. Apart also from new departments many other new organizations were created, not a few undergoing change as experience was gained. Not least among these organizations were two associated with the War Cabinet secretariat—the Economic Section and the Central Statistical Office, both of which find frequent mention in these pages.

The wartime control of industrial production and of the whole civil economy, when added to the conduct of ordinary government business, involved a vast increase in the numbers engaged. If the Post Office and the Revenue departments are excluded, the numbers of the civil service other than industrial workers had increased at the peak of the war to more than four times the peacetime norm. This extra army of more than a quarter of a million men and women came from many parts and from many ranges of society, and they worked in many places. Most were engaged, of course, on subsidiary duties. The leaders in their several ranks came in particular from responsible positions in industry and commerce, from the professions and from all sections of the academic world.

No overall picture of this wartime activity has yet been attempted nor, in all its variety, would the picture be easy to draw. It would not be merely a picture of Whitehall and its environs. It would, for example, include the people of the Post Office maintaining the flow of mail through fair conditions and foul and encountering a flood of new functions at their counters. It would include the local officials of the Ministry of Labour overloaded with new tasks, and the Revenue officials throughout the island collecting a swelling revenue from an ever-widening circle of contributors. At the centre it would need to show the ordinary discharge of current business as well as the shouldering of immense new tasks alike in the fighting departments and in civil offices. It would include also the picture of large bodies of people working in the States, in the Middle East, and in various places elsewhere in the world.

The reader of this book will be hardly conscious of this picture for, as the title shows, the object of the book is different and more austere. Yet it may be well at the outset to make a point with which the writers of these essays will be the first to agree. However ingeniously and wisely the civil and industrial controls and rationing schemes may have been devised—and economists and statisticians (including not a few of the authors of this volume) often played a leading part in their contriving—they would not have achieved their full success but for the goodwill with which amid the strain and stress of war they were accepted by industry and by the community as a whole; a goodwill which went beyond—in my judgment much beyond—any forecast which could reasonably have been made before hostilities began.

The need for the services of economists and statisticians was felt from the outset of the war and grew as the control of the economy proceeded until the search for additional economists became difficult, and for additional recruits from the narrow field of trained statisticians at times well-nigh hopeless. This experience, save so far as it was illustrated in the first world war, was novel, for the ordered use of those professions in the conduct of government business had not proceeded far in previous periods of peace.

Even before the first war names will be recalled of economists of distinction serving in the government services, especially in the Board of Trade, but in most cases they were occupied in the management of the practical business of the departments. Between the wars, however, it was not the case that the employment of economists in their professional capacity was only sporadic or incidental. The appointment in 1925 of the Committee of Civil Research suggested a new field, for included among its functions was the duty of giving 'connected forethought from a central standpoint to the development of economic and statistical research'. Apart from the Prime Minister this Committee had no fixed personnel and its proceedings were not published, but it was replaced in 1930 by a body entitled the Economic Advisory Council with a similar but wider scope. This body, in addition to five Ministers, included economists in its membership. One of the committees of this Council—the Committee on Economic Information, which sat under the chairmanship of Lord Stamp[1]—was designed 'to supervise the preparation of periodical reports on the economic situation and to advise as to the continuous study of economic development'. Its membership included five well-known economists and two senior officials especially concerned with financial and economic questions.

This was the first body at the centre of government consisting preponderantly of economists and concerned exclusively with economic advice. It continued its work with regularity until the onset of war. Through its official members it was linked with the general administration, though it lacked the advantage of reporting directly to any one Minister primarily concerned with economic affairs.

A further development took place in the summer of 1939 when, in a body known as the Survey of Financial and Economic Plans, Lord Stamp, Sir Hubert Henderson[2] and Sir Henry Clay[3] were asked to survey the economic plans which had been prepared against the possibility

[1] Stamp, 1st Baron, cr. 1938, of Shortlands; Josiah Charles Stamp, G.C.B., cr. 1935; G.B.E., cr. 1924; K.B.E., cr. 1920. Killed in a German air raid on London, 21st April 1941. Chairman of the London, Midland and Scottish Railway and President of the Executive; Director of the Bank of England; member of the Economic Advisory Council; Chairman of the Survey of Financial and Economic Plans, 1939–41; Chairman of the Official Committee on Economic Policy, 1939–40.

[2] Sir Hubert Douglas Henderson, Kt., cr. 1942. Professor of Political Economy, Oxford, since 1945, and Fellow of All Souls College, Oxford since 1934; Joint Secretary to the Economic Advisory Council, 1930–4; member of the Survey of Financial and Economic Plans, 1939–41; Economic Adviser, H.M. Treasury, 1939–44.

[3] Sir Henry Clay, Kt., cr. 1946. Stanley Jevons Professor of Political Economy, University of Manchester, 1922–7; Professor of Social Economics, University of Manchester, 1927–30; Economic Adviser to the Bank of England, 1930–44; member of the Survey of Financial and Economic Plans, 1939–41; Warden of Nuffield College, Oxford, 1944–9. Chairman of the Executive Committee of the National Institute of Economic and Social Research, 1941–9, and President since 1949.

of war and watch for gaps or inconsistencies between them. The manner in which the Economic Section of the War Cabinet and the Central Statistical Office sprang from this and other origins is shown in later essays.

During the war, in addition to those who served on these bodies and in the Prime Minister's Statistical Section, many economists and statisticians were engaged in the various Departments of State. No department was more fortunate than the Treasury, which had the help both of Lord Keynes and of Sir Hubert Henderson and Professor Dennis Robertson[1], now Professors of Economics in Oxford and in Cambridge respectively. In other offices I imagine that a good number of these who, like other recruits from the academic world, had volunteered for service under arrangements made in the preparatory stage, were engaged at the outset in duties requiring general capacity rather than economic expertise. But they gravitated either towards advisory posts or to posts which, even if in the main administrative, called also for their professional qualifications. Thus, like the scientists, economists and statisticians were enabled to bring the principles of their profession to bear on practical problems of the day. The contribution which they made, though in the nature of things second to that of the scientists, was unquestionably of high significance.

In the period of transition from war to peace—the economic consequences of war persisting long after the thunder of the guns had ceased—many economists stayed on. And in the welfare state of the future, on whatever general principles it may be ordered, it is clear that need both for the economist and for the statistician will persist. On this I would only express agreement with the view which emerges from the concluding passages of Mr. Chester's essay. There will be room for the economist who makes government service his career. But in addition much advantage would accrue from securing the temporary sojourn in Whitehall of academic economists of distinction in mid-career. A sabbatical quinquennium would seem to be at once a misnomer and a contradiction in terms. Often it might also be difficult to arrange. In other respects it would be a very desirable aim—or must I write 'target'?—in these times.

[1] Dennis Holme Robertson, C.M.G. 1944. Professor of Political Economy in the University of Cambridge since 1944. Fellow of Trinity College, Cambridge, 1914–38 and since 1944; Sir Ernest Cassel Professor of Economics in the University of London, 1939–44; member of the Economic Advisory Council, 1936–9; an adviser to H.M. Treasury, 1939–44.

II

THE CENTRAL MACHINERY FOR ECONOMIC POLICY

by

D. N. CHESTER

This is not the place for a detailed descriptive account of the development of the central machinery for dealing with economic affairs during the war. The purpose of this essay is to comment on certain aspects of the working of that machinery, not to explain in precise detail how it worked.

THE COMMITTEE STRUCTURE

The central machinery for economic policy[1] went through three main stages between the outbreak and the end of the war:

(1) the Treasury period—September 1939-May 1940;
(2) the period of Committees—May-December 1940;
(3) the period of the Lord President's Committee—January 1941-August 1945.

The second and third of these periods overlap somewhat and probably the date of the third period should start some months later. Also towards the end of the third period the Treasury were rapidly regaining their old position, but they did not fully retrieve this until Sir Stafford Cripps became Chancellor of the Exchequer in November 1947.

Consideration had already been given to the changes necessary in Cabinet machinery and at the outbreak of war Mr. Neville Chamberlain instituted a small War Cabinet of nine members with a number of committees mainly inherited from the Committee of Imperial Defence. A month later, following criticism in the House of Commons and the Press, the Government set up an Economic Policy Committee at the official level, followed shortly afterwards by one at the Ministerial level. Presumably up till then it had been thought that economic policy could best be handled by the Treasury as in peacetime, with the occasional use of a Home Policy Committee for general issues. This Com-

---

[1] This description excludes most of the central organization concerned solely with production or with linking supply and defence policy.

B   5

mittee though it developed a strong Food Policy sub-committee was, however, mainly immersed in the normal task of the pre-war Home Affairs Committee—dealing with important draft regulations and legislation. The two Economic Policy Committees soon developed a strong existence, under the tutelage of the Treasury. The Chancellor of the Exchequer, who was in effect Minister for Economic Co-ordination, was Chairman of the Ministerial Economic Policy Committee and Sir Josiah Stamp (later Lord Stamp) was Chairman of the official Committee. Stamp and his two associates, Henry Clay and Hubert Henderson, had been called in by the Prime Minister in the summer of 1939 and worked directly under the Treasury.

When Mr. Churchill's Government took office in May 1940 the political atmosphere was definitely antagonistic to the Treasury. There was a strong feeling that finance should be put in a less dominant position; the Labour Ministers favoured the idea of the non-departmental co-ordinating Minister; and the then Permanent Secretary of the Treasury (Sir Horace Wilson) had unfortunately become associated in the public mind with Mr. Neville Chamberlain's appeasement policy. So for the first time the Chancellor of the Exchequer ceased to be a member of the Cabinet. True Mr. Churchill's War Cabinet at that time contained only five members, of whom only the Foreign Secretary was a Departmental Minister, but in Mr. Lloyd George's 1916–19 War Cabinet of five or six members the Chancellor of the Exchequer was always a member. The Chancellor returned to the Cabinet in October 1940, but only along with the Minister of Labour and National Service, and indeed, so shaken was the Treasury's position that the Chancellor was omitted again between 19th February 1942 and 28th September 1943.

Moreover, the new Government brought into being quite a different idea of Cabinet structure. The two Labour Ministers divided between them the Chairmanship of four important Cabinet committees—Mr. C. R. Attlee (Lord Privy Seal) was Chairman of the Home Policy and the Food Policy Committees and Mr. Arthur Greenwood (Minister without Portfolio) was Chairman of the Economic Policy Committee and the Production Council. As these two Ministers were members of the War Cabinet whilst the other Ministerial members of these Committees were excluded, it was clear that the Chairmen were envisaged as super, non-departmental co-ordinating Ministers. It was this feature which really marked the change; the Committees were in existence in one form or another prior to May 1940. The Production Council, for example, was largely a transformation of the Ministerial Priority Committee. The terms of reference of these Committees as announced by Mr. Attlee in June 1940[1] were as follows:

(1) Production Council:
    'will give general direction as to the organization and the priority of production for war purposes';
(2) Economic Policy Committee:
    'will concert and direct general economic policy';
(3) Food Policy Committee:
    'will deal with problems of food including food production';
(4) Home Policy Committee:
    'will deal with questions relating to the Home Front and social services; it will also be responsible for the framing of regulations and draft legislation';
(5) Lord President's Committee:
    'The work of these Committees (i.e. the four mentioned above and the Civil Defence Committee) will be concerted and directed by a Committee under the Chairmanship of the Lord President, of which the Lord Privy Seal, the Minister without Portfolio and the Chancellor of the Exchequer will be members. It will be the function of this body to ensure that the work of the five Ministerial Committees is properly co-ordinated, and that no part of the field is left uncovered.'

The other important development was the recruitment of a small group of economists by the Minister without Portfolio. As already mentioned, Lord Stamp, Sir Henry Clay and Sir Hubert Henderson had been established in the summer of 1939 as the Survey of Financial and Economic Plans. The Survey started by examining the war plans of various Government Departments, but after the outbreak of war and the creation of the Economic Policy Committee it concentrated more and more on the formulation and co-ordination of economic policy. At the end of 1939 three or four additional economists were recruited and a Central Economic Information Service was started. As the Chancellor of the Exchequer was the Minister concerned with the co-ordination of economic policy, this group worked closely with the Treasury. When, however, Mr. Greenwood became Chairman of the Economic Policy Committee he took over and considerably enlarged the staff of the Central Economic Information Service, until in the summer of 1940 the group contained a dozen or more economists, almost all of whom had been recruited from university teaching. This group was located

[1] 361 H.C. Deb., 4th June 1940, Cols. 769–70.

in the War Cabinet Offices, where under a civil service Assistant Secretary of the Cabinet it worked closely with Mr. Greenwood.

For various reasons, some due to the personalities involved and others due to the inherent weaknesses of a committee structure of this pattern, important changes were made at the beginning of January 1941.[1] The Production Council was replaced by a Production Executive whose functions included the allocation of raw materials, productive capacity and labour and the fixing of priorities where necessary. Mr. Bevin (Minister of Labour and National Service) was Chairman. A new committee called the Import Executive (under the Chairmanship of the Minister of Supply—Sir Andrew Duncan) was set up, whose duty was 'to animate and regulate the whole business of importation in accordance with the policy of the War Cabinet'. The Economic Policy Committee disappeared. Its work on imports was transferred to the Import Executive and its duties in connexion with the general issues of economic policy went to the Lord President's Committee.

Lord President's Committee

The Lord President's Committee had been set up in May 1940 with the task of ensuring that the work of the four main Committees already described was properly co-ordinated and that no part of the field was left uncovered. As the name implies the Chairman was the Lord President, first Mr. Neville Chamberlain, and then, from the 3rd October 1940, Sir John Anderson.[2] The changes in January 1941 considerably increased the power of the Committee. For one thing it now became a committee directly concerned with general policy. The Central Economic Information Service was split into two parts—one under Mr. Francis Hemming (and shortly after this under Mr. H. Campion) which formed the nucleus of the Central Statistical Office[3], and the other, under Professor John Jewkes[4], became the Economic Section.

[1] See announcement in *The Times*, 7th January 1941.

[2] Rt. Hon. Sir John Anderson, P.C. 1938; G.C.B., cr. 1923; G.C.S.I., cr. 1937; G.C.I.E., cr. 1932. Chairman, Port of London Authority; M.P. for Scottish Universities, 1938–50; Lord Privy Seal, 1938–9; Home Secretary and Minister of Home Security, 1939–40; Lord President of the Council, 1940–3; Chancellor of the Exchequer, 1943–5.

[3] It was unfortunately not found possible in this volume to cover the development and work of the Central Statistical Office, other than its important contribution to the study of the National Income and Expenditure which is dealt with in Chapter VI.

[4] Professor Jewkes moved to the Ministry of Aircraft Production at the beginning of 1942 and was succeeded by Professor Lionel Robbins.

John Jewkes, C.B.E. 1943. Professor of Economic Organization, Oxford University, since 1948; Professor of Social Economics, Manchester University, 1936–46; Stanley Jevons Professor of Political Economy, Manchester University, 1946–8;

Though this latter group was in theory available to the War Cabinet generally, it became in practice the economic staff of Sir John Anderson (Lord President of the Council) and his Committee. Moreover, it was clearly the intention that this Committee should be a 'Steering or Planning Committee . . . which deals with the larger issues, and also deals with questions of adjustment,' in the words of the Prime Minister. He went on to say: 'It is fitted to do so, because although it is not exactly the Cabinet it contains a very large proportion of its members.'[1]

On paper, however, the situation was not radically different from the 1940 organization. The Home Policy, Food Policy, and Civil Defence Committees still continued, the Production Council had changed its name and its Chairman, and though the Economic Policy Committee had disappeared the Import Executive had entered on the scene. But right from the beginning the Lord President's Committee gained in strength and stature and the other Committees either had a short life or became more and more confined to a few narrow issues. In February 1942, with the establishment of a Ministry of Production, the two Executives disappeared[2]—they had been working fitfully for some time—and their work was distributed between the Ministry of Production, Ministry of Labour (allocation of manpower) and the Lord President's Committee. The Food Policy Committee found that the main issues with which it had to deal were either ones on which it was difficult to get agreement and which therefore tended to get referred to the Lord President's Committee or ones which raised large general issues of economic policy and were therefore more properly within the terms of reference of this other Committee. So the Food Policy Committee declined and disappeared.[3] By the end of 1941 the Lord President's Committee dominated the whole field of home and economic policy, so that in February 1942 Mr. Churchill could say of it: 'The Lord President of the Council presides over what is, in certain aspects, almost a parallel Cabinet concerned with home affairs. Of this body a number of Ministers of Cabinet rank are members, and others are invited as may be convenient. An immense mass of business is dis-

Director, Economic Section of the Offices of the War Cabinet, 1941; Director-General of Statistics and Programmes, Ministry of Aircraft Production, 1943; Principal Assistant Secretary, Office of the Ministry of Reconstruction, 1944.

Lionel Charles Robbins, C.B. 1944. Professor of Economics in the University of London since 1929; Director of the Economic Section of the Offices of the War Cabinet, 1941–5.

[1] See statement by Mr. Churchill, 22nd January 1941, 368 H.C. Deb., Col. 264.
[2] The Import Executive continued until May 1942.
[3] The Lord President became Chairman of the Food Policy Committee in February 1942, but the Committee seldom needed to meet and it was abolished later that year.

charged at their frequent meetings, and it is only in the case of serious difference or in very large questions that the War Cabinet as such is concerned.'[1]

The reasons for the emergence of the Lord President's Committee to this supreme position are many and complex. I am inclined to suggest there were four main reasons. First and foremost I would put the personality and abilities of Sir John Anderson. No matter how many statements in the House of Commons, or how imposing are the terms of reference given to a Cabinet committee, whether the committee is a success or even functions depends very largely on the Chairman. Sir John Anderson had a great many qualifications for this most difficult task of presiding as a non-departmental Minister over a home-front Cabinet. He had had a long experience of the Whitehall machine. He had a great capacity for digesting the mass of paper, could remember details, and yet sort out the main issues. Moreover, he devoted all his time to the job of being Chairman and spent very little time in the House of Commons. Perhaps even more important, he was trusted and respected by the leaders of the Parties in the Coalition and had the full confidence of the Prime Minister. He had not been involved in the bitter party controversies of the interwar period which did not make it any easier for Labour Ministers to work under a Conservative Chairman or Conservative Ministers to work under a Labour Chairman. Not being a party politician he did not arouse the same jealousies which on occasions mar the relations between leading Ministers, even (or perhaps particularly) of the same party. And so as the Prime Minister concentrated on the military and supply sides of the war, Sir John Anderson attracted to himself great prestige, authority and an increasing amount of work. It was not merely that the Committee over which he presided became so important. Frequently when the Prime Minister wanted an urgent and thorough inquiry into some issue of topical importance he asked Sir John Anderson to undertake it either personally or as Chairman of an *ad hoc* committee. On other occasions a particular function would be given to Sir John Anderson because the departmental Minister concerned preferred him to handle it rather than it fall within the province of some other War Cabinet Minister. And so Sir John Anderson gradually acquired a dominant position in home policy and interdepartmental issues. By the time he became Chancellor of the Exchequer, at the end of September 1943, the Lord President's Committee was firmly established.

Second, the Lord President was undoubtedly helped by having at

[1] 378 H.C. Deb., 24th February 1942, Col. 38.

his disposal the services and advice of the Economic Section. Usually, non-departmental Ministers are confined to one or two private secretaries with perhaps a more senior civil servant as adviser and personal assistant. Sir John Anderson had an excellent staff of this kind who must be given a deal of the credit for fitting the Economic Section so well into the Whitehall machine. But however able such a staff is, it is not likely to have either the time or the range of expert knowledge to service the Minister for the wide range of topics which come before the Chairman of a general-purpose committee such as was the Lord President's Committee during this period. And a Chairman to be fully effective must be very much more than a Speaker or Judge; he must be ready to give a lead, be capable of surveying the field of economic affairs and drawing attention to gaps in Government policy; he must be looking ahead, foreseeing the next problem and arranging for preparatory work to be done in connexion with it. In other words, to be a kind of Minister for Home and Economic Affairs the Minister must have the necessary staff, a staff seldom available to the non-departmental Minister.

Third, the 1940 Committee structure was much too complex and subdivided. The field of home and economic policy did not easily divide itself into watertight compartments which could be handled conveniently within the limits of tightly worded terms of reference. Food policy could not be separated from economic policy nor from imports, at least not in such a way as to be convenient for discussion at the highest Ministerial level. Hence either the discussion of a topic in one of these committees became stilted and unreal because the Chairman was trying to keep within narrow limits or else spread over a very wide field and in doing so overlapped and infringed upon the discussions taking place in other committees. In such circumstances it is not always clear on which committee's agenda the topic should be placed, and here an inverted Gresham's law of committees operated, for Ministers and officials directed their topics to the committees where they were likely to get an adequate and firm decision and so the more powerful and able chairman attracted items to his agenda.

Fourth, the development of a Ministry of Production in 1942 undoubtedly helped to clear up a particularly awkward and untidy aspect of the non-military side of the war. Neither the Lord President nor the Economic Section had become effectively concerned with the production of military weapons and supplies. Questions concerning the allocation of manpower were an important part of the responsibility of the Lord President, and from time to time a major raw material or the building programme would fall to be handled by him. But the field of military supplies is so vast and requires such a constant attention to detail that it is doubtful whether it could have been handled by the same Minister who was exercising a general supervision over the home and economic policy generally. This was certainly true in 1943–4, when on the one hand preparations for D-day and the need for constant and close consultation with the Americans demanded a full-time Minister for Production, whilst on the other the Lord President had an increasing amount of his time taken up with questions of postwar reconstruction.

The decision in May 1940 that the same Minister should be Chairman both of the Economic Policy Committee and of the Production Council had something to commend it, at least in theory. In so far as production policy is concerned with the allocation of resources between broad classes of claimants it clearly must go hand in hand with economic policy. For a change in the allocation of resources, for example between home and military production, will have repercussions on, say, the inflationary position; whilst economic policy can be directed so as to facilitate, even bring about, changes in production and in the distribution of resources. Moreover, decisions as to the allocations of resources cannot very well be left to the contending departments. The power to make such decisions is best given to some non-departmental Minister and this may place him in a stronger position than that of a Minister whose power has to be derived from being chairman of a committee for discussing broad issues of economic policy. Nevertheless, there is a big step between this broad conception of the job of a Production Committee and a conception involving an intimate and detailed knowledge of the production programmes of the supply departments, including the relation between the progress of the production of particular, perhaps highly specialized, weapons in this programme and the military plans. Allocations between broad classes of uses— military, home, export, etc., can be discussed without a knowledge of the present supply position of a particular mark of tank or size of ammunition. But within the broad allocation for, say, military supplies, a whole host of questions will arise which can only be adequately handled by those familiar with the detail. Thus a Production Committee—whether called a Council or an Executive—found itself in a dilemma. On the one hand the more it confined itself to broad issues of allocation or production policy the more it was discussing questions which could be most conveniently dealt with by the Lord President's Committee, which could take into consideration questions of general home, economic and social policy. On the other hand, the more it tried to handle the detail of the military production programmes the more it found itself handicapped by shortage both of time and of a specialized secretariat. The appointment of a Minister of Production with a staff handled the second part of the dilemma and the clear position of the Lord President's Committee in the sphere of general home and economic policy dealt with the first. On the whole, the division worked very well, but there were obvious possibilities of over-lapping jurisdictions, and towards the end of the war the Minister of Production may have extended his activities into fields which earlier had been clearly within the jurisdiction of the Lord President's Committee.

Some Conclusions

Thus during the latter years of the war the pattern of central policy organization was broadly as follows:

(1) The Prime Minister as Minister of Defence handled with the Service Ministers and Chiefs of Staff all military operations and actively concerned himself with any issue of foreign affairs, production, imports, shipping and internal economic or social policy which appeared to him to be of major importance.

(2) The Lord President and his Committee handled issues of home and economic policy.

(3) The Minister of Production along with the Supply Ministers and their joint staffs handled the general issues of the supply programmes with the Defence (Supply) Committee coming in on major issues.

(4) The War Cabinet discussed foreign policy, major issues of military policy and such social, economic and production questions as could not be dealt with by either the Lord President or the Minister of Production.

This is an oversimplified, indeed perhaps an idealized, picture of the central organization and the distribution of responsibilities as existing at any one time. It ignores the many special interdepartmental questions always arising which did not fit easily into any simple pattern and which were handled by one or other senior Ministers or by an existing or newly created committee according to their importance and the view of the moment. The detail is, however, perhaps less significant than the general features revealed. I would summarize these in this way:

(1) There were clear advantages in freeing the small War Cabinet

and in particular the Prime Minister from having to handle questions or data not of a direct bearing on the course of military and foreign affairs.

(2) In devising a system of committees, to which the War Cabinet could delegate some of its work, the experience of 1939–45 showed considerable advantage in having a single major committee—a kind of sub-Cabinet for home affairs—providing a full-time non-departmental chairman of the highest calibre and political acceptability could be found and given an adequate secretariat.

(3) The field of home economic policy does not readily lend itself to any neat division. This does not exclude the possible use of subordinate committees on special topics, working under the general direction of a major committee, but it does make it difficult to run a series of committees of apparently equal status under different chairmen.

(4) In so far as a division of the field outside the main interests of the War Cabinet proved necessary on the ground of its being beyond the capacity of any one Minister, the division developed between the Lord President and his staff and the Minister of Production and his staff appeared to have the most justification.

In the subsequent pages I propose first to make a few comments upon the place of the Economic Section in the work of this central policy machinery and second to reflect more generally on certain impressions which remain with me after watching it at close hand for over five years.

THE PLACE OF THE ECONOMIC SECTION

The great value of the Whitehall process with its numerous inter-departmental committees and its stress on clearing matters at all levels with interested departments is that any course of action finally agreed upon is usually practicable, at least it is practicable in the eyes of Whitehall. Included in the term practicable is the acceptance of the policy by all the departments who will have some part in its administration. The danger inherent in the process, indeed in any process in which a large number of interests and considerations have to be taken into account, is that the ideal course of action may be completely lost sight of in the discussion of departmental difficulties and objections.

It always seemed to me that one of the important jobs which the academic 'temporary' could perform was not to be afraid of stating what he thought to be the ideal or proper course of conduct, without too much regard in the first instance to all the probable objections which other people were likely to think up. A big difference between the academic approach and the approach of the official immersed in day-to-day administration is in their sense of long-term values. The university teacher is practised in presenting issues to students in their clearest and most elementary form and in searching for long-term trends in his data; the administrator is concerned with achieving practical results. Yet up to a point the administrator will gain by having put before him an analysis of the situation and an indication of lines of policy, unhampered by much consideration for practical difficulties. Help of this kind should enable him to take a broader view of his actions and may well give these actions a coherence which it is always difficult to achieve in a mass of decisions on detailed issues. I do not think the academic temporary is making his best contribution if he regards himself purely as a departmental administrator. These remarks, of course, apply mainly to an academic economist not engaged in an ordinary departmental administrative job. In the latter post he is likely to become as immersed in detail of practical problems as his 'permanent' colleagues. My interpretation of the experience of the war years is that Ministers and the administrative class gained immeasurably by having in Whitehall a number of 'temporaries' whose approach to the process of policy formation was wider, less orthodox and less concerned with the practical difficulties involved.

At the same time it is clear that no group of back-room boys writing memoranda embodying ideal policies is likely to have much influence. Indeed, I am now going to appear to contradict myself by saying that such a body is likely to succeed only in so far as it has the chance and the ability to take full part in the ordinary Whitehall machinery, is aware of departmental views and takes account of departmental difficulties. In the early days of the Economic Section (the Central Economic Information Service as it then was) it became clear that an important part of the work of its members must be attendance at inter-departmental committees and that indeed members must be prepared to be secretaries (sometimes jointly with an administrative class officer) in the case of some committees. This development was not without its dangers. It meant that the economist found himself using his time in all the normal processes of running a committee, arranging meetings, and writing the minutes of such meetings, etc. It might mean his becoming very much immersed in the details of the work and so in danger of losing his wider viewpoint. But the result was well worth it taking all in all. It brought the members of the Economic Section into close touch with an ever-widening range of departmental officials, and in a way which appeared to such officials most natural. It enabled them to get a clearer idea of departmental difficulties and to appreciate the meaning and strength of the reaction of different departments to particular lines of policy. They were able to expound their ideas to officials in the atmosphere of comrades in the same cause and not through the less potent method of the circulation of remote, impersonal memoranda. And though the work of these committees could be very detailed this was seldom a disadvantage, for a major problem in central economic policy is to see that the main ideas accepted formally by some Ministerial committee are applied in the everyday work of the departments concerned.

In these circumstances two advantages should accrue to any group of Government economists concerned with the formation of policy. On the one hand they can influence departmental action by methods other than the formal submission of memoranda to a Minister or to a committee of Ministers or of senior civil servants. On the other hand, such advice as they have to tender in respect of economic policy will be more realistic and therefore more likely to be acceptable if tendered with a reasonable knowledge of what are departmental views and difficulties. It is also likely to be better timed. But they have still a different function to perform from the ordinary departmental official in that they should be less impressed by such views and difficulties and be prepared to analyse the situation and present their policy according to their training and knowledge of the subject.

Perhaps I should add two riders to my remarks on this aspect of the process of government. First, there may be some difficulty in finding economists who can fulfil the two roles. It is not sufficient to be a reasonably good economist, the person concerned must be able to hold his own in committee work and not be too far behind in understanding and taking part in the administrative process. The difficulty is increased by reason of the fact that many of the committees concerned with economic policy must necessarily be at a high level—Assistant Secretary and upwards—and that the economist must have the capacity to handle people at the highest level. This tends to rule out the very young man, unless he has exceptional qualities, even though he may be perfectly able to analyse the economic situation and propose proper lines of policy on paper and indeed may be a brilliant theorist. Undoubtedly one of the sources of strength of the Section during the war was that it contained several economists who were distinguished academically and who were already well known for their published writings. The same was true of many of the economists in the various departments. Such members were in a stronger position to influence departmental opinion than the youngster who, however brilliant, had still to receive public recognition. And in the field of economic policy where, as in other fields of government policy, the final decision involves a large element of personal judgment, the public reputation of one of the persons tendering advice may well tip the final decision in his favour. An Economic Section recruited wholly or mainly from young graduates would not have this advantage.

Relations with the Treasury

Second, there is the difficult problem in central administration of the location of such a Section. During the war the Economic Section was part of the War Cabinet Secretariat. To some extent this was a chance decision due to the Minister for whom it primarily worked being a non-departmental Minister. Also the Treasury was under a cloud and not very powerful during the period when the Section was growing to strength. Being a branch of the War Cabinet secretariat it was comparatively easy for one of its members to be Secretary, usually Joint or Assistant Secretary, of a Cabinet committee. But this was not without its problems. For the tradition of the Cabinet secretariat, certainly on its civil side, was that the duties of its members were to keep minutes, arrange for the circulation of papers and generally to assist the smooth working of the Cabinet and its committees; they were not formulators of policy, whereas members of the Economic Section were definitely associated with policy formation over a wide field of economic affairs. Was there not a danger that the traditional neutrality of the secretariat might be lost or that the policy side of the Economic Section be weakened and confined? I do not think these dangers materialized and for several reasons. Members of the Section were only used in a secretarial capacity for committees on whose agenda technical economic issues bulked large: they were not, for example, part of the secretariat of the Lord President's Committee. Moreover, in most cases they acted jointly with a member of the ordinary civil staff of the Cabinet secretariat. Finally, in so far as the Lord President was either chairman of or responsible for the field covered by the committee in question members of the Section were in effect briefing their own Minister.

Not all the departments, however, liked the arrangements and the alternative in the minds of some people was to place the Economic Section in the Treasury. This had the merit of appearing logical, for financial policy can hardly be separated from general economic policy.

It appeared more attractive after the revival, perhaps renaissance is the better word, of the Treasury towards the end of the war. Yet I am not at all happy that this would have been the best solution. Certain consequences follow if the Economic Section is part of the Treasury. Administratively the Section would have to be fitted into the departmental hierarchy. The views of the Section on policy would probably have reached the Chancellor only after being sifted through the general Treasury machine. There would indeed have been a strong inclination to put before the Chancellor one official view. The normal arrangement is for the expert to advise the Administrative Class and for them to take such advice into account in their advice to the Minister. To paraphrase Sièyes—if the Section agreed with the 'official' view it would be superfluous, if it disagreed it would be mischievous. There is something in the argument that it was better for the Treasury to be influenced by the viewpoint of the economist expressed within the department than to rely upon external influence through interdepartmental committees. As against this there were merits in having the views of the Economic Section placed before Ministers in addition to the Treasury view. The Treasury, though concerned with general financial and economic policy, was nevertheless still a department, and like all departments had a particular interest to further or protect. The Economic Section, on the other hand, if it were doing its job properly, should be taking a very general view and should be free of particularized departmental loyalties and also free of the suspicion that in interdepartmental disputes it was permanently biased in favour of one of the contestants. An Economic Section within the Treasury, working on current policy mainly with other Treasury officials, would in time have come to be regarded as but one branch of the Treasury. It is difficult to see how the Treasury could have been represented by two voices in interdepartmental discussions. It would have required somebody as powerful and as influential as was, for example, Maynard Keynes to have maintained any marked degree of independence. Furthermore, though the Treasury is a department pre-eminent in the field of economic policy, a number of other powerful departments are concerned, principally the Board of Trade. Indeed, having regard to the wide interpretation given to the term 'economic policy' during the war there were probably some ten to fifteen departments directly involved. It would appear reasonable therefore that these departments should hear the views of the Economic Section at first hand and not as merged into a general Treasury view.

During the war there were occasions on which there were definite differences of opinion between the Economic Section and the Treasury, and if the Section had not been working through its own Minister but through the Chancellor of the Exchequer some ideas, including many subsequently taken up by the Treasury, would have been unlikely to be given a wider hearing. And at least Ministers had the advantage of hearing two general views on the important issues of economic policy. My experience indicates that this was worth something, even at the expense of some apparent untidiness in Government machinery.

There is also another consideration. It is unlikely that there will be many Ministers mentally and physically capable of being both Chancellor of the Exchequer and also co-ordinator of economic and production policy. Where no such Minister is available the Prime Minister may well have to have a non-departmental Minister concerned with general economic policy, and in such a case the Economic Section clearly would have to work closely with that Minister and not inside the Treasury. Personal considerations of this kind are very important. It is possible to argue that the Economic Section was rightly placed during the war because a series of personal considerations favoured that particular arrangement. But one could imagine a different set of personal circumstances in which it would have been desirable to place the Section in the Treasury.

CHARACTERISTICS AND PROBLEMS OF THE WHITEHALL MACHINE

I now wish to comment upon certain characteristics of the Whitehall machine which have important implications for those who wish to use it as an instrument of economic policy. The characteristics which struck me most forcibly were: the great weight and vastness of the machine which on occasion almost amounted to an immovable object, if you were against it, but was an irresistible force if you were on its side; the tremendous power which lay in the hands of Ministers and in the hands of their nearest personal advisers; the heavy burden borne by a small number of people and their ability to act irrespective of the formal machinery through which they had to operate; and the remoteness of all the apparatus from most of everyday life and happenings except in so far as these could be translated into statistics or a general report. Let me say something of each in turn.

The Whitehall machine during the war consisted of some thirty departments, several of which had a staff of more than 30,000 and branches in many parts of the country. Some were conducting operations in different parts of the world, others were dealing with many countries and keeping British policy in line with that agreed with those countries. The problem always was to get a policy decision which fitted into the total jig-saw puzzle. Few things affected only one department, most affected many departments and might even have to be cleared with other countries. At the top was a small War Cabinet which, however, confined itself to major issues of the war and foreign policy, and now and again some important issue on the home front, e.g. the introduction of a new rationing scheme. Under the War Cabinet there were at varying times a dozen or so ministerial and official committees and beyond these several hundred interdepartmental committees of varying degrees of importance mostly serviced by the departments concerned.

In so far as the decision required fitted readily into the current pattern and had no peculiar difficulties or newness the machine dealt with it efficiently and reasonably expeditiously. It dealt best with cases which could be decided in the light of general principles already laid down, especially if these were clear and well known. But great difficulties arose when a marked change in the situation or in attitude at the highest level required a revision and therefore a re-learning of the general principles. The machine would work best if it could be given one or two clear leads—such as everything must be done to economize refrigerated shipping space or drop-forgings or bricklayers. More usually the central criteria by which departments had to make their day-to-day decisions were much less exact, but vague rules—such as departments must get the most out of their available resources—would seldom have secured coherence in the action of different departments or facilitated the making of interdepartmental decisions.

It was never easy for such a vast machine to deal quickly and readily with small adjustments and slight shifts of emphasis. Some dramatic decision in clear quantitative terms—such as '1,000 additional heavy bombers are required by such and such a date' or 'The manufacture of tanks has been given the highest priority by a Prime Minister's directive'—could usually get a clear response from the machine. But the more one moved into the realms of a little more of this or of that or of securing a slightly freer attitude towards the use of a particular material, especially where such matters required an interdepartmental decision, the less perfectly the machine responded.

The general problem was really twofold—how to get clear, definite decisions out of the top committee machinery and how to keep everybody in touch with such decisions and any changes which took place in them. In certain fields the application of quantitative methods enabled quite precise decisions to be handed down, e.g. in respect of the allocation of manpower or of imports. But even here the difficulties were not altogether overcome, for within any departmental allocation there was often room for use of the allocation on several differing activities. Moreover, the situation might change dramatically or imperceptibly, and so make adherence to the existing allocation unwise, yet a fresh decision took time to make.

Communication

Communication was the main problem here. By communication I mean not merely an awareness that such a decision had been taken, but also an understanding of the principles on which the department should act. There was also the need for an awareness of the current attitude of the key Ministers and of any tendencies towards a new attitude. The formal apparatus of communication was the minutes of committee meetings from the War Cabinet downwards; and in addition, when Mr. Churchill was Prime Minister, a series of directives. But the most effective method was the close personal contact which existed between a comparatively small number of Ministers and civil servants—permanents and temporaries. From their daily attendance at this or that committee they took back to their departments the current attitude. By lunching, dining, even breakfasting together, during the long days worked during the war they not merely kept in touch with what was happening—and the situation was always changing—but also developed a corporate thought which was more effective than any series of minuted decisions. Indeed, I should imagine the war historians will have difficulty in tracing changes of policy merely from a study of Cabinet or Cabinet committee decisions: some such decisions were a dead letter very shortly after being made because the situation or atmosphere changed yet no new decisions were formally put in their place. Indeed, formal committee decisions were perhaps among the least important of the devices of the central machine, save on purely statistical matters. Of primary importance was keeping all the top people in touch with the current situation—the facts of the military, economic and production situation and in particular with any important changes of emphasis—such as shipping is now tighter than dollars. In the phrase 'current situation' must be included any changes in the attitude of the Cabinet and of the few people who counted in the formulation of major decisions of policy—and the earlier such changes could be foreseen or forecast the better. Some of this was gossip or pure speculation, but from it all emerged important pointers to individual departmental policy. It might be only that X—a powerful Minister —was known to have expressed a view that a line of policy—say con-

c

scription of women—to which he had hitherto been opposed had become inevitable; or that at a meeting of Ministers held yesterday there was a clear view that something would have to be done quickly about a particular matter even though no formal decision was recorded; or that there was the likelihood of more steel or timber from this or that country. In the committee room, in corridors, over the phone, over a meal at the club, or in the many other ways of human contact, so the process of communication, of sifting, of formulation went on and from it emerged—sometimes clearly, sometimes rather muddled—the current attitude in Whitehall. It was this attitude which gave cohesion to the vast mass of daily departmental decisions.

Though this process worked reasonably well for the small number of top level and centrally placed people, it was obviously less effective as a device for keeping informed the lower levels of the administration in the many departments. Departments differed in their capacity to keep their large staffs in touch with changes in the situation or in policy. On matters which bore directly on the work of a particular Principal or Assistant Secretary in a department, the departmental machine usually worked all right; indeed, it was most likely that the official concerned would have been in the decision from the earliest stage. But in respect of general matters where the bearing on any particular job was indirect or less obvious it was not uncommon to find some officials completely unaware of the change, even some weeks later. Indeed, so vast was the machine that I suspect that in various comparatively minor fields of Government activity a policy continued to be followed long after it had been replaced by quite a different Government policy of general application. Sometimes the fault could have been avoided had the Permanent Secretary's office been able to circulate more widely the key documents; for example, some Cabinet committee minutes or papers. But even had they wished to do so they were unlikely to have sufficient copies to circulate widely and quickly, for it was the general policy on security and other grounds to restrict to a bare minimum the number of copies of Cabinet documents circulated to departments. Moreover, the reading of papers could take up a large part of one's day, however clever one became at picking out the essential bits, and though this may have been a worthwhile use of the time of a person whose main concern was with general policy its value was less apparent to the official dealing with a vast number of actual problems and indeed might be incompatible with his getting through his other work.

At various times the suggestion was made that some kind of official periodical should be circulated internally designed to keep a wide range of civil servants in touch with the economic situation[1], the main lines of policy and the changes which might occur from time to time. The suggestion was not taken up, at least during the war years. It would have been an interesting and probably worthwhile experiment and might have gone a long way to speed up the process of communication and of securing a consistent policy at all levels. But it would not have been an easy undertaking and it certainly could not have removed the need for an efficient system of internal communication within departments or for those personal and informal explorations which I have described earlier.

One final point needs to be made on this important question of communication. The existence of a small group of economists who were closely in touch with the situation and with current lines of central policy and who had close contacts with the departments and with the main interdepartmental committees was undoubtedly an important element in securing the spread of information and ideas. Freed from the rigidities which come from rank and status and as yet untrammelled by the formalities of departmental procedure, they could act, sometimes most irregularly, in forging a closer link between central policy and departmental action. This rather roving commission was one of the most important continuous functions and one which again emphasized the importance of such a group being in close practical touch with the departments but not too formalized inside a department.

Positions of Power

Notwithstanding the vastness of the machine and the many stages which might have to be gone through before a decision could be reached, it could be galvanized into sudden action or the course of policy dramatically changed by the actions of a comparatively small number of people. In the sphere of general economic policy there were probably twenty to fifty people in Whitehall who if their views coincided could do almost anything. In case this statement should give an exaggerated impression, perhaps I should add that most of these people were usually closely in touch with the views of other Ministers and officials, perhaps working more remotely from the central machinery, and on occasion may have been the interpreters rather than the originators of policy. Nevertheless, in the final instance it was this very small group which really determined economic policy. Of primary importance in the group were the small number of Ministers who had to make final

[1] The Economic Section prepared a survey of the economic situation from time to time which was circulated to Ministers and senior officials.

decisions on any matter of major or political importance. This was the last hurdle confronting all important matters, and whatever might be the power of officials or the cogency or otherwise of their advice, in the end the decision could be taken only by the Ministers (Ministers and officials do not, of course, ever mix so far as voting at a committee is concerned). Even the most powerful official committee could never give a decision which had the definiteness or finality of a committee of their Ministers.

It follows from this that among officials the most powerful, in the sense of influencing policy, were those who saw most of or had the confidence of a Minister. No Minister, however gifted, could examine and decide for himself the correct line to be taken on the hundreds of matters which come before him during the year. The most he could do would be to satisfy himself on a small number of major issues and for the rest see that he had the kind of advisers whom he could trust. Under this system, inevitable though it may be nowadays in view of the wide range and complexity of government functions, there is a tendency for all but the most able and energetic Ministers to become but mouthpieces of their advisers.

It might appear at first sight that the power of the officials concerned would be the greater the less capable their Minister. For he might rely on their advice for almost everything and so they would always get their own way. In actual practice, however, the reverse is usually the case. For the Minister who accepts readily and without question the advice of his officials is unlikely to be good at getting this advice through a hostile or critical committee. He may read his brief very well, but he is unlikely to be prepared for matters which come up unexpectedly and are not covered in the brief. Moreover, not having taken a personal part in the formation of the policy of his department he is less likely to fight tenaciously for it in committee. Whereas the powerful Minister who dominates the policy of his department raises the status of his immediate advisers, for he is likely to be the kind of Minister who gets his Ministerial colleagues to accept the views of his department, views to which he has made a major contribution. In the long run, and not very long either, no official however senior or however able can be in a stronger position in the interdepartmental struggle than would his Minister be if the struggle were taking place in a Ministerial committee. When I entered the civil service I was inclined to believe the view sometimes expressed that power had now passed from Ministers to the permanent civil service. Experience showed this to be quite untrue—one had only to see the Ministry of Labour, for example, during Mr. Bevin's period as Minister there and contrast it with the period before and after to appreciate the vast change a dynamic powerful Minister could make not merely in his department's policy, but in the power and prestige of his officials. The official with a strong Minister as his head goes to an official committee knowing that if the decision goes against him there he has every chance of winning it at the Ministerial level, whereas the official serving under a weak Minister knows that he is likely to lose the fight in the end. And officials know this of each other's position—the ups and downs caused by a change of Minister can be most striking.

Ventriloquist dummies never get very far or wield much power, nor do the officials who serve them. A strong Minister may, of course, be handicapped by a weak set of officials, for a major part of the interdepartmental discussion and agreement must necessarily be conducted at the official level. And, however able he may be, a Minister must rely a good deal on departmental advice. When you get a good Minister and a good Permanent Secretary working closely and enthusiastically together, as was the case at the Ministry of Agriculture during the war, then the department and the interests which it handles are very fortunate.

The position of those who were not part of the normal departmental machine but who were near one or more Ministers, as was, for example, the Economic Section, was powerful but sometimes delicate. The Economic Section normally worked to the Lord President of the Council, who from the beginning of 1941 onwards was in a strategic position so far as decisions affecting economic policy and the home front were concerned. Some departments, at least when they were in opposition to the advice they knew was being given by the Economic Section, felt that the position of the Section gave its members too much power. I think this criticism, which subsequently declined in volume, was partly due to the early inexperience of the members of the Section in handling interdepartmental matters. Usually issues come up to Ministers only at the end of a process of clearing at the official level. During this process misunderstandings are cleared out of the way, issues on which all are agreed are sorted out leaving for Ministerial consideration those matters on which agreement cannot be reached at the lower level. At least, that is how it works when done properly. If, however, there is introduced into this tidy system a small group who without taking part in the earlier processes can at the final stage brief a Minister to raise issues not considered earlier or, if considered, dealt with or rejected, in these circumstances departments may justifiably get angry or complain. This is really another aspect of the back-room/front-room boys issue. If the academic economists are shut away from departmental discussions, but nevertheless are asked to brief a particular non-departmental Minister on matters coming before him there will always be exasperation. For if their views are good departments will be annoyed that they had not had a chance to consider them earlier, whilst if their views are unsound or impracticable departments will be annoyed at having to deal with matters which had already or should have been cleared at an earlier stage. Here again the solution must lie in bringing in such a group into the discussions at the earliest stage; this would not exclude their disagreeing with the decisions reached at the official level or in briefing their Minister accordingly (a right enjoyed by any departmental official), but it would ensure that the views they expressed to their Minister were made in the light of all the previous discussions and that departments had clear notice of these views. This was actually how the Economic Section operated as it rapidly acquired experience during 1940–1 and, towards the end of the war, my impression is that it was well integrated into the normal Whitehall process.

Significance of Committee Structure

At the top it is personal ability and power rather than any arrangement of offices or of committees which really matters. During the war there were from time to time discussions in the House and the Press about the structure of the Cabinet committees, and now and again the Government felt it necessary to give a list of the main committees and their functions. Much of this public discussion appeared to proceed on the assumption that committees could be discussed without regard to the character of their membership, and in particular, of their chairman. Yet time and time again committees which appeared well on paper and to the public, which had clear terms of reference and well-balanced membership, would splutter out after a short, uneasy and unfruitful life, whilst other committees would go from strength to strength. It was almost uncanny on occasion to see the rise and fall of particular committees, almost as though they had a life of their own. Some would start out with apparently rosy prospects, with a flourish of announcements, perhaps even with a public statement; they would have several regular meetings, minutes and papers would be circulated, and then even though the work for which they were originally set up still continued they would become less active, they would cease to meet, to all intents and purposes they were dead even though not formally wound up.

Decisions in this field would still be taken, but probably in another committee or in the Cabinet, or might even be largely working understandings without any formal committee decision. Broadly speaking if the Ministers (and their advisers) who really held the power were in agreement, the precise committee machinery was of little importance: if they were not in agreement, then the committee would not work anyhow. There is, of course, much more in the arrangement of Cabinet committees than this, but I have purposely oversimplified the issue because in its final form it is so simplified. The committee structure of 1940–1 in the sphere of economic and production policy failed partly because it was too complicated, but mainly because it did not coincide with political and personal realities. Yet the establishment of a Shipping Committee in 1942, with limited terms of reference, by providing a formal forum and point of focus undoubtedly added something to Government efficiency.

Burden of Responsibility

It follows from what I have been saying earlier that this small group of Ministers and officials carried a heavy burden not only of responsibility but also of sheer hard work. During the years with which I am concerned there was never a period in which events and policy stood still and those concerned with policy formation could take a breather and mark time. Even when the major decisions as regards military preparations and production of armaments had been made, indeed even before that, there started the pressure of preparations for the peace. All through 1944, for example, winning the war and planning the peace went hand in hand, and it was largely the same group of officials which was concerned in each. The preparation of a policy of full employment was going on and taking the time of Ministers and senior officials even before the invasion of Europe had started. There can hardly have been such a strenuous time in the history of British government.

Few of the issues which came up in those years were clear or the answers obvious. A good deal of the work was pioneering and involved new techniques of government, new attitudes of mind. So far as I can see there was no method whereby most of these major decisions could be made other than by the small group of Ministers and their immediate advisers. Sometimes the attempt was made to give important tasks to, say, a committee of Parliamentary Secretaries or of middle layer officials chosen by their departments to specialize in a particular aspect of their work, e.g. reconstruction studies. But while such experiments did sometimes lead to useful preparatory work being done, the results achieved were often thin and tentative. Such committees carried little weight, and the mere fact that leading Ministers and their senior officials were prepared to delegate consideration of these issues to them usually showed that the issues were not at that time considered of real importance. As soon as they became important the earlier committees vanished almost overnight and much of the work was done over again. Sometimes, however, committees of this kind, though not of first-class quality, might find themselves taking a major hand in policy because events had moved too rapidly or because departments had failed to appreciate the urgency of the subject.

There are, of course, devices for reducing the load of work on the small number of key Ministers and officials. But the fact remains that during the war there were so many decisions to be made, of such importance and affecting such a wide range of interests—in Whitehall and overseas—and the number of people in the position to make or capable of making such decisions was so limited that no devices other than an outright rejection of responsibility could have relieved these persons of a very heavy load. Only people of a strong physique could stand for long the strain involved; indeed, it is doubtful whether any ordinary human being could stand the strain for more than a few years without his health being impaired and his losing efficiency through sheer loss of staying power. Any government machine which continued at such a pace year after year could only maintain its initial vigour and freshness by replacing this small key group at regular intervals.

Whilst on this point I would like to mention the contrast which is usually made between the position of a departmental and of a non-departmental Minister. It is popular to assume that the former is heavily burdened with day-to-day work which exhausts him, whereas the latter is free to deal with a succession of problems which in some way or other is considered an easier task than running a department. My general impression is that the burden of the non-departmental Minister who is acting as chairman of various Cabinet committees can be much heavier than that of a Minister in charge of a department. It is the constant succession of widely differing issues which have to be understood and their details mastered which makes the task of the non-departmental Minister more heavy. Some departments were, of course, so large and covered such a wide range of activities as to put their Ministers in the category I have just described. But a departmental Minister has a large and well-established staff under him, whereas the non-departmental Minister is usually given but meagre assistance. The departmental Minister can without appearing to be lazy or irresponsible confine his attention to matters of immediate concern to his department, whereas the non-departmental Minister must concern himself with matters covering a wide range of departments. If the Lord President had to deal with a problem during the war one could be certain that it was both important and difficult—when things were going well he was not brought in. Finally, the non-departmental Minister is always in danger of being in a lonely or delicate position in the committee. The departmental Minister speaks with the authority and experience of his department behind him; unless his views directly affect other departments the Ministers concerned may not be greatly interested or may confine themselves to their own departmental viewpoints. Or on occasion there may be a strong conflict of interests between Ministers. The non-departmental Minister acting as chairman is faced with the difficult problems of achieving results without estranging personal relations and of influencing departmental policy without taking responsibility out of the hands of the departmental Minister. And for all this hard and difficult work he gets little or no direct Parliamentary credit. It can be done, but only by a Minister whose authority and standing are not open to question, who has a great capacity for mastering a series of problems and who has the services of a small but qualified staff. Sir John Anderson during his period as Lord President of the Council raised the position of the non-departmental Minister and Cabinet committee chairman to a remarkably high level—but then he had a unique combination of qualities for the task.

Dangers of Remoteness

My final point concerns the remoteness of all this policy-making machinery from the everyday life of the people and therefore from the effects of many of its decisions. It is only necessary to recall the kind of life led by most of those concerned to appreciate this point. If one includes lunch-time, as lunch was usually consumed while talking shop, most of the senior Ministers and officials spent at least ten to twelve hours a day in Whitehall and would frequently take home a bag of papers to read in the evening or during the week-end. Many slept in or near their office for many of the war years. But even without these rather exceptional circumstances the life of Ministers and particularly of senior civil servants is hardly characteristic of the lives of the people their decisions affect. Seldom are they dealing with the persons actually affected, almost inevitably their decisions are based on memoranda and statistics, on impersonal rather than on personal factors. They read official minutes and memoranda, reports of committees, Hansard and *The Times* and probably *The Economist* and anything in the main national dailies which deals with Government policy. The people they deal with in other occupations are usually national leaders or the secretaries of national organizations having their headquarters in London, people equally in danger of being remote from what is actually happening in areas away from London.

In such surroundings there is always a danger of a lack of reality. What can come to be important, if one is not careful, is not how decisions affect people, but how they are thought to operate by people in the Whitehall circle. The leader or letter in *The Times* or *Economist* can become the reality by which one's actions are judged. Quite small snippets of technical or local knowledge can pass for expertness. The important thing is not to offend against the conception of events and action which is accepted as real by one's colleagues. This, of course, is an exaggeration, but there is sufficient truth in it to be disquieting.

Any occupation has its own little world and set of values. An Oxford college, a mining village, the City—all have accepted modes of thought, taboos and customs—sometimes harmless, sometimes dangerous, but all making it difficult to accept new ideas. If the wartime process were reversed and permanent civil servants found themselves temporary academics or stockbrokers, no doubt they would be aghast at many things they found and their fresh outlook would undoubtedly have a good influence on the institutions they entered. But it is doubtful whether in any of these institutions they would find any great gulf between their decisions and the immediate personal consequences. As college tutors, for example, they could not but be quickly aware of the effect of changes in teaching methods, curricula, and frequency of examinations, etc., on their own lives, or on the lives of their immediate colleagues and pupils.

A similar personal impact is, of course, experienced by those responsible for many government decisions. Ministers and civil servants cannot but be painfully aware of the effect of raising the rate of income tax. I well remember one Minister coming in on a Monday morning burning with his wife's indignation at the high price of lettuces and greengroceries generally and writing a most powerful Cabinet paper in consequence. And once when discussing the question of a joint sweets-tobacco rationing scheme I remember watching the look of doubt grow on the face of a senior official when he was told what the weekly tobacco ration would be under the proposed scheme—to me, a non-smoker, it seemed a very satisfactory amount, but for him, a heavy smoker, it was well below normal consumption. But, mercifully so in many respects, most of the major decisions could be made in an impersonal, dispassionate manner and there was seldom any apparent clash between the decision taken and personal feelings or experience. Many decisions of Government are only possible if made in the most impersonal way: decisions to call up men in particular occupations, to curtail production in particular industries or to requisition certain properties are not taken lightheartedly, but they would be less easy to make, and infinitely more painful if the Ministers and officials concerned knew the personal circumstances of all the people who would be affected or were they themselves directly affected. Statistics are the great help here, statistics of manpower, of production, etc., which can be discussed and used as a basis for a decision in the most impersonal way. So impersonal, for example, that a decision to call up, say, an extra half-million men can appear as a change in a few figures in the manpower budget; as a transfer between columns on a piece of paper. Here again there is exaggeration, but again it is sufficiently near the truth to be rather frightening.

SOME IMPLICATIONS

This analysis has, I suggest, three implications for central government machinery. First, it stresses the importance of departments in the policy-making process as against the tendency in some theoretical discussions to treat departments as being mainly there to carry out decisions made by some super central body of Ministers and officials. Even in a department most decisions have to be impersonal, but at least the officials in the department do come into direct touch with many of the immediate results. To a department such as the Ministry of Labour, for example, with its exchanges spread over the whole country, its regional staffs, and its many headquarters links with employers and trade unionists, the manpower figures are not just statistics; they represent people with whom the staff are in daily contact, to whom they have to explain things, and whom they must satisfy and live with. The tendency in recent years has been to shift power away from those parts of the government machine in direct touch with affairs. The growth of central planning machinery, with its emphasis on statistics and overall decisions, has weakened the sovereignty of the individual departments and within the departments has probably opened up a gulf between those officials who spend their time dealing with the central allocations and plans and the officials who are actually administering the decisions in the field. This is an important problem in the machinery of economic planning. There are some who have stressed the merits of a central planning body situated in the Cabinet offices, or in the Treasury, a department almost equally remote from the public. Such people usually tend to regard the departments as being mere executives, carriers-out of a policy dictated by this centrally placed body. During the war the emphasis shifted from time to time. During the second half of 1940, for example, the arrangements were undoubtedly based on the idea of central policy direction, but Sir John Anderson as Lord President had a very sure sense of the importance of bringing departments fully into all policy decisions and yet at the same time he was able to make effective use of Cabinet committees. His emphasis on departments in the planning process was, I feel sure, due to his appreciation of the facts that economic policy decisions which did not make the fullest use of departmental experience would be unrealistic and, in any case, decisions taken without the clearly expressed support of the department which had to administer them might well be ineffective.

Second, there is the danger that the heavy burden carried by most Ministers is likely to reduce their value as interpreters of public opinion. Senior Ministers have to do a very large amount of reading of papers and memoranda and attend very many committees, and certainly during the war there was a danger that so far as their contact with politics and the man in the street was concerned they would be in very little different position from their official advisers. This is particularly the danger with the non-departmental Minister with a heavy load as chairman or member of Cabinet committees. The departmental Minister is brought into close contact with the day-to-day affairs of his department. He has a large correspondence with M.P.s and he meets numerous delegations. The non-departmental Minister, however, has none of these aids, and therefore unless he spends a deal of his time in the House of Commons, or makes a special effort to keep himself in touch with what is happening up and down the country he may well become but a super civil servant. This is the danger in the Prime Minister ceasing to be Leader of the House of Commons, however desirable such a development may be in allowing him to concentrate on guiding policy and major issues of political difficulty.

Third, it is now clear, looking back, that one of the great benefits which the academic and business temporaries brought to the Government service during the war was a fresh outlook. Had the Government, for example, started the war with a body of economic advisers who had been in their service for, say, ten or more years, it is doubtful whether such a body would have been anything like as useful. The temporary recruitment was due to the accident of war, yet can it be doubted that this new blood would have benefited the service even had there been no war? I think it is also true that by the end of 1945 the temporaries were beginning to lose their value in this respect; their earlier experiences had become heavily overladen with their civil service experience and they were in danger of losing their different outlook.

III

THE OVERALL ALLOCATION OF RESOURCES

by

E. A. G. ROBINSON

THE PROBLEM

The economic direction of a nation at war must be judged by one relatively simple criterion—the concentration of the nation's maximum effort against the enemy, so as to bring the fullest possible force to bear upon him at the appropriate moments within the period of hostilities. The practical problems are wholly concerned with how that shall be done.

In a democratic country the point of departure is the economic system as it exists in peacetime, modified only to the extent that may have been implied by rearmament and by the measures which it may have been thought proper to impose immediately at the outbreak of hostilities. The existing economic incentives will depend upon the political complexion of the country concerned, but at least in the case of the United Kingdom both in 1914 and in 1939 they were primarily those of a free enterprise system, with monetary rewards as the guides both to the entrepreneur in the choice of his activities and to the worker in the selection of his occupation.

Such a system may or may not be the most appropriate to the conditions of peace; that is not a matter that concerns this essay. It has certain obvious defects from the point of view of the conduct of war. In war, time is of paramount importance. In the early stages, speed is necessary to build up the war effort quickly enough to escape defeat in the perilous moments of military nakedness. In the later stages, speed is equally necessary to redirect the effort, so as to ward off new threats or to make it possible to seize great opportunities. Under pressure of time it would not be practicable to wait for the ordinary economic incentives to redistribute the labour force, to secure the best use of factory space, or to provide the most appropriate allocations of materials. Some direct intervention by the government machine is inevitable if the necessary results are to be obtained quickly enough.

It is necessary also for a further reason. In wartime the whole eco-

34

nomic and political system is, whether we like it or not, inevitably subordinated to the objectives of war. By 1945 over two-thirds of the national resources were directly employed on work for the Government. The choice between different employments of the nation's resources is therefore in large measure a choice between different uses of those resources by the Government itself. The more nearly does civil consumption approach an irreducible minimum, the more truly do the practical alternatives become choices by the Government of the way that resources can best be used by itself to achieve its own objectives. The ordinary economic criteria do not apply, though other statistically measurable criteria may take their place.

There is thus apt to be a process of development of the war economy as conscious allocation of resources progressively replaces the less conscious systems of peacetime. The development in the years 1939 to 1945 was wholly empirical. There was no conscious thought in the early stages of a definite goal in the form of the perfect war economy towards which we were moving. At each stage we relied on the working of the normal incentives so far as they were practicable, and replaced them only to the extent that they appeared at a particular moment to be working badly in a particular field.

The Four Phases

Nor would it be right to think of an ideal war economy as something which can be described quite independently of the functions to be performed at a particular stage of the war. The economic effort, if no large stocks of arms are held waiting for mobilization, is almost bound to fall into four main phases. In the first phase, which may partly antedate the actual outbreak of war, the main effort is devoted to the creation of the capital equipment of the munitions industry itself: the building of new factories and the installation of special tools and equipment in them. In the second phase the capacity so created is employed to build up the initial equipment of the forces. In the third phase the military requirements are reduced to those necessary to maintain the forces and cover the wastage. In the last phase, when the end of the war is within sight, it is possible to reduce output still further and live partly on the stocks which have been built up. In the last two phases the munitions effort can be reduced and manpower made available to increase the direct military effort.

It need not be said that in practice these four phases overlap and coalesce, that they are not of equal length for all weapons, that they are affected by changes of technique and the need to build up capital equipment of new weapons, that they are much more obvious and significant in the case of Army requirements than those of the Royal Navy or Royal Air Force. There remains, nevertheless, a broad sense in which it can be said that in the case of the United Kingdom in the last war the period down to the autumn of 1941 was in the main a period of building the new aircraft and ordnance factories, and that output down to that time was limited by factory capacity. There followed a period when new factory construction declined, but there was a large absorption of manpower into munitions production and a great increase of output. During 1942 output of ground munitions was about 75 per cent higher than in 1941 and aircraft production, measured in structure weight, increased by about 50 per cent. By the end of 1942 the initial equipment of the Army was within sight of completion, and from then on the problem was increasingly one of maintenance, combined with production of new weapons and equipment to meet new needs. The peak of the munitions effort was reached in terms of manpower by mid-1943 and in terms of output by the spring of 1944. From then on the contraction was progressive. Each of these stages involved a major redeployment of the nation's manpower and other resources, and to each of them a somewhat different organization was appropriate.

But to those who lived with these problems the history of the war years was rather a series of episodes, and the progress from stage to stage was apt to be obscured by the violence of these episodic changes —the urgent perils of the days after Dunkirk, the calls for fighters during the Battle of Britain, the diversion of manpower to house repairs during the blitz of 1940–1 and again in 1944, the expansion of the bomber programme in 1941, the Battle of the Atlantic with its need for a greatly increased programme of merchant ships, escort vessels and carriers, the recurrent problems of tank design and supply, the provision of camps, accommodation, aerodromes and countless minor services and supplies for the American forces, the landing-craft programmes and the special weapons and equipments for the Normandy landings, the fears in the last months of possible ammunition shortage. All these emphasized again and again that the power to make rapid change in the disposition of the nation's resources was the greatest war-winning weapon of all. The power to step-up quickly the production of a new weapon, to exploit a success, to make good unexpected losses, or to retrieve a difficult situation, was of first importance. The administrative tasks fell primarily on to the supply departments and on to the actual factories concerned. But a central organization had to ensure that the system as a whole was fully loaded yet not overloaded and that resources could be set free as required and absorbed into the employments of greatest urgency.

The Limiting Factors

At the different stages of the war, and indeed in the course of the different episodes of the war, the limiting factors were different. Throughout the war there were four main limits: materials, manpower, shipping, capacity. In the early stages of the war there was a fifth limit, the reserves of gold, dollars and other currencies and assets which could command the aid of foreign producers and maintain our essential imports without equivalent exports. This last limit disappeared with the coming of Lend-Lease and mutual aid and, from then on, it was the general limits and division of allied production rather than our power to pay for them which were at issue.

These various limits were effective in different degrees at different stages of the war. In 1940 and 1941 it was capacity that was the chief limiting factor. At important moments throughout the war, and particularly during the crisis of the Battle of the Atlantic, it was shipping, and thus more directly materials, which in effect set the limits. From the end of 1942 onwards the problems of manpower supply became paramount. But right through the war there were particular sectors where limits of materials were always dominant. And right through the war there were particular sectors also where shortages of special skills always set a limit to output.

Thus, at least until 1942, there was no single limiting factor that was so dominant that planning could safely neglect all the others. And even after 1942 there was so narrow a balance between the scarcity of manpower and the scarcity of materials (and particularly that of steel which was all-pervasive in its effects) that planning had always to take account of both limits simultaneously.

For these reasons, even had we possessed in 1939 the experience, knowledge and statistical equipment which we had in 1945, it is very doubtful whether it would have been right to build up immediately the precise system of control which circumstances led us to operate in 1945.

THE DEVELOPMENT OF THE CENTRAL ORGANIZATION

At the outbreak of war the central organization was relatively weak and, by the standards of the end of the war, ill-equipped to handle the tasks of the overall allocation of the nation's resources. The first tasks, indeed, were to improve the organization itself. Some time before the

D

outbreak of war Sir Josiah Stamp, Mr. Henry Clay and Mr. Hubert Henderson[1] were entrusted with the task of surveying the national preparations for war in the economic field, and early in the war Sir Josiah Stamp was made economic co-ordinator. The Economic Survey, as the three-man committee was called, made use of the secretariat and organization of the Economic Advisory Council, which formed a part of the office of the War Cabinet. It contributed greatly both in detail and in broad policy to the avoidance of major dislocations in the transition from peace to war. But anything like a complete and effective control over the various economic resources of every kind was not yet practicable.

Already before war broke out the nucleus of one very important system of allocation of resources had been brought into existence. The experience of 1914–18 had shown the dangers of shortages of raw materials and a small Raw Materials Department in the Ministry of Supply had been created to handle the problems of import and allocation of materials. This was, indeed, in essence a function of a central organization. Its attachment to the Ministry of Supply which, as things turned out, was primarily the supply department for the Army, was due partly to the lack in 1939 of any strong central body to which it could properly be attached; the Cabinet Office was at that stage no more than a handful of officials and Service officers who provided the secretariat for the Cabinet and its committees. It was in part due to an expectation, that was never fulfilled, that the Ministry of Supply would grow into an all-embracing Ministry of Munitions, with as wide a field of responsibility as that Ministry possessed in 1918. Thus, in its earlier stages, the Ministry of Supply acquired various functions which, as things turned out, more properly belonged to an interdepartmental central organization.

The Raw Materials Department got quickly into its stride and built up within a few months a system of administration and the Controls themselves. Rather more slowly it built up also the body of statistical knowledge and experience which was essential to its work. The progress with other forms of economic co-ordination was far less rapid. This was only in part because the problems were less urgent. It was in part because the statistical material to measure and appraise the problems scarcely existed. Much of the effort of the early months of the war had to be put into creating a statistical system capable of bearing the burdens of war.

In 1939 the limits of our reserves of foreign assets appeared to be

[1] See page 3.

more fundamental than they proved in the event. One of the first tasks of the Economic Survey in the later months of 1939 was to measure the available reserves and the rate of their exhaustion. Since forecasts of the balance of payments had not previously been made, this involved the building up of a new body of statistical material. The estimates and forecasts, once made, were revised at intervals until the introduction of Lend-Lease made them less significant. It was far more difficult to judge what policy should be adopted in relation to the reserves. In 1939 and the early months of 1940, when the shape of the future war was very obscure and 'cash and carry' was the prevailing rule, it seemed wiser than it now appears in retrospect to husband the foreign assets, develop an export drive, and provide for the maintenance of imports of food, materials and munitions over a period of two to three years. Events proved the error of this judgment.

The problems of manpower obtruded themselves almost from the first. The system of reservations which had been worked out before the outbreak of war prevented some of the more disastrous consequences of the denuding of industries of their skilled workers which had occurred in 1914–18. But already in the early months of 1940 certain difficulties began to appear. The expansions of the munitions industries were being made on too haphazard a basis. In choosing locations for new plants preference had been given to particular regions. Sometimes, as in the case of the North-West Region, it was because strategic advantages of remoteness from bombing risks were allied to the economic advantages of surplus labour. Sometimes, as in the case of the Birmingham-Coventry area, it was because the resources of management and skill could most readily be made available close to already existing plants. But whatever the cause there was far too great a concentration of the planned munitions production in certain areas, almost certainly in excess of the possible manpower resources of those areas.

In the very early stage of the war any detailed discussion of manpower problems was made impossible by the lack of sufficiently frequent statistics of employment. The quarterly census of employment which provided the basis for the whole control of manpower in the later stages of the war was introduced only in the middle of 1940. Thereafter it became possible to exercise a much more accurate and detailed supervision. And since the census included information as to the proportion of workers engaged on government work for the various departments concerned, it became possible to measure the expansion of the war effort and the volume of manpower resources devoted to particular sectors, and to see whether the desired changes were taking place or not. The figures were never wholly accurate, and inevitably depended on personal judgments of how a firm's production was divided between departments. Their accuracy was apt to be affected by views as to which departmental aegis was most likely to result in a generous supply of manpower. They were, nevertheless, sufficiently accurate to afford some guide for policy.

The statistical information about the use of shipping and the tonnage of imports was in the early stages of the war almost equally rudimentary. There were no satisfactory pre-war bases of comparison and when it first became necessary in 1940 to set limits to the imports of food, raw materials and other categories, the adequacy or inadequacy of the several allocations in relation to the needs could be based on no really firm statistical foundation.

For the wider problems of the overall use of resources there was an almost equal deficiency of national income statistics. The national income estimates made before 1939 were entirely due to the enterprise of individual private scholars. The resources and, what was more important, the immense fund of existing or potential statistical information in government departments had never been fully harnessed to the building up of official national estimates. When the need for such estimates had been shown, more particularly by Lord Keynes' brilliant pamphlet *How to Pay for the War* (London, 1940), a small section was created in the War Cabinet Office charged with this task. Its work is described elsewhere in this volume by Mr. Stone.[1] Two things must be emphasized here.

First, the work of putting the national income estimates on a firm basis and of making use, by wholly new techniques, of all the knowledge and opportunities for cross-checking which could be devised was a large and laborious one. Results could not quickly be expected, and in practice were available only just in time for the budget of 1941. Thus in the very early phases of the war only limited and uncertain guesses existed in this field.

Second, in the planning of the British war economy the national income calculations had a very important but in some senses a limited function. They were of absolutely first importance in relation to budgetary, savings and consumption policy and to the essential task of preventing inflation. But they did not play a central part, either then or later, in the actual planning of the war effort. That was done almost wholly in terms of the physical resources, and to an increasing extent as the war went on it was done in terms of manpower.

[1] See pages 83–101.

It is difficult in retrospect to assess the consequences of the lack of statistical information in the early years of the war. In one sense it was at that stage less disastrous than it would have been at later stages. In this first phase of the war the scale of the war effort was largely determined, as has been said above, by the available capacity in the engineering industries, and particularly by the available supplies of certain key equipment, such as extrusion presses, drop-forges and gun-boring and gun-turning lathes. The manpower problems were in the main problems of skill, training and dilution. The necessary supplies of untrained or semi-trained manpower could be, and were, found by contraction of output for civil consumption, and particularly by the process of concentration of industry which was so important a factor in speeding up the transfer to munitions production. A greater knowledge of the potential resources could not at this stage greatly have increased the immediate levels of production.

On the other hand, greater knowledge and a more detailed analysis of the potential resources in the years ahead could almost certainly have prevented some waste and misdirection of resources in these early years. Reference has already been made to the lack of any sufficiently clear view of the manpower problems underlying the location of munitions production. It is very easy to be wise after the event. There was an urgent necessity to make decisions as quickly as possible. To have held up important decisions to start new factories until there might be available a voluminous manpower study, based as it probably would have been on an unrealistic view of the potential war, might have been disastrous. And it must be remembered that even in the autumn of 1939 the picture of the shape of the forthcoming war was very misty. The possibilities of huge land forces all over the world, maintained by a large British munitions industry, were scarcely yet envisaged. The continued participation of France in the war was treated as axiomatic. The power of an air force to secure a decision in war was quite unknown and largely overestimated, at least in lay circles. It is by no means certain that more careful pre-war analysis of an economico-statistical character would have produced substantially better results than the empirical methods which were in fact adopted. Indeed, in the field of the requirements of materials, pre-war estimates sadly underestimated the actual use. Nevertheless, it is legitimate to think that a more highly developed pre-war study of the use and deployment of manpower on the same lines as that which was actually made by Dr. H. W. Robinson and Miss H. Makower in the *Economic Journal* of December 1939, if it had used all the material available to Government departments, might have helped to avert some of the errors of those years.

Principal Errors

The principal errors that we made in that period fall into three broad categories. First, we took too little account of the limits of local labour supply and labour mobility in planning the locations of munitions production; it was insufficiently appreciated that a total war must mean the full employment of the nation's manpower resources chiefly in the places where that manpower has its homes; that in a short period, when house building must be reduced to a minimum, movements can only be marginal and will in any case be difficult. A clearer appreciation of this in the early days would have saved many headaches in later years.

Second, partly because the limits of the ultimate resources of operative manpower were too little appreciated, partly because of the inevitable pressures to save time in building up the initial equipments of forces, the scale of planning of new capacity was in very many cases excessive. Many of the projects never got beyond the paper stage. But in some cases resources were wasted in preparatory work or in the initial stages of building work which had to be abandoned when a more realistic view had been formed of what was practicable. Thus both in the crisis of the summer of 1940 and at the inauguration of the big bomber programme in the autumn of 1941 there was a review and a wholesale slaughter of overambitious factory building projects. Not all of the slaughter on either occasion was the consequence of a changed strategic concept of the war. And right through the war there is no question that plants were actually built and completed which would never have been undertaken if the manpower situation of 1944–5 had been better appreciated in advance.

Third, and in some ways another aspect of the second type of mistake, there was in the early years of the war far too little appreciation of the possibilities of subcontracting, and far too little use of the potential resources in the small undertakings. This was partly because those who were planning production were largely drawn from the large and efficient firms, thought naturally in the techniques of such firms, and feared that scarce resources of skill and machinery would be wasted if they were dissipated in the small workshops. It was partly also that the administrative problems of tooling up, inspection, supply of materials and transport of products to these small outlying workshops were difficult and tiresome, and the necessities did not yet compel firms to solve them. The regional organizations were as yet weak, and the efforts of the Industrial Capacity Committee to stimulate fuller use of such resources took time to bear fruit. Because of this, there was waste in creating new capacity where it was already available if more trouble had been taken to find it. The difficulty was that by and large managements were desperately overburdened and additional trouble was precisely what they were in no position to take.

How far could these errors have been avoided by better planning? It is very difficult to say. A better knowledge of the basic data would have been invaluable. We knew very little indeed about the available factory space of the country or of what amounts might be made available by concentrating particular industries. The machine tool resources of the country were largely a closed book until after the results of a census became available in 1941.

With better statistical equipment the problems, as they arose, could have been handled very much more quickly and effectively. As it was they nearly always involved a major piece of statistical or semi-statistical research for their solution. Indeed, in retrospect the war is apt to appear as a series of crises, each leading up to a new body of statistics, subsequently maintained as part of a new administrative set-up to handle the problems which we had been forced to solve. Certainly we started in a state of almost complete statistical nakedness and ended in a state where almost every administrative official was the master and originator of some set of figures, often regarded as private or semi-private. Their central collection and co-ordination was in itself a major problem.

THE APPROACH TO THE PEAK OF THE WAR EFFORT

The emergence of the problems of full employment was not, it need scarcely be said, a sudden phenomenon. In one sense there had been something approaching full employment ever since mid-1940, by which time the total of unemployed had fallen from about 1,900,000 in 1938 to about 700,000. But in a more significant sense the autumn of 1941 saw the beginnings of a new situation. Unemployment had fallen well below 200,000. What was more important, the manpower in some of the less essential industries was beginning to approach the more or less irreducible levels needed to maintain even a wartime civilian economy. Thus for the first time those responsible for the further development of the war economy were brought hard up against the problems of alternatives within the war economy itself. Hitherto the expansions of the war economy had been made by imposing further sacrifices on the civil population. These were by no means at an end; indeed, far further from an end than most of us then imagined. But the need to scrutinize new projects and to ask where the resources were to be found remained a central preoccupation until the end of the war, as it has remained since the war.

The turning-point in this respect came when the Prime Minister called for an expansion of the big bomber programme in the autumn of 1941. This involved, first, a large increase in the Ministry of Aircraft Production factory building programme. Second, it involved the examination of the questions of location of the new factories and their manning up. To superimpose this programme on all the existing programmes was obviously impossible. A general review of the factory building programmes was hurriedly made and severe cuts were made by the supply departments concerned of all projects which were not of the very first urgency or which were unlikely to be able to recruit manpower when the new aircraft programme was in full swing.

But this was only a makeshift arrangement to deal with a particular problem. The underlying forces required a more permanent and more extensive change in the administrative set-up. This took a variety of forms. First, the central organizations of the supply departments were themselves strengthened. In the Ministry of Supply there had already been brought into existence a small organization under the Director-General of Programmes which was concerned with the receipt of requirements from the War Office, with the centralization of statistical information regarding production programmes and their fulfilment, and with the co-ordination of United Kingdom production with that of the United States. A somewhat similar organization was brought into existence in the Ministry of Aircraft Production, and Professor Jewkes, by then head of the Economic Section of the War Cabinet Office, became the first Director-General, and collected round him a powerful group of economists and statisticians. While no exactly parallel body was created in the Admiralty, the functions of the Principal Priority Officer were gradually extended to include some of the same functions as those performed by the programmes departments of the other Ministries.

The next step, taken in the spring of 1942, was the appointment—rather reluctantly and in deference to Parliamentary pressure—of a Minister of Production with certain somewhat ill-defined co-ordinating functions. These had hitherto been performed by a series of Cabinet committees and their common secretariat. Differences of view had had to be hammered out in committee or resolved by the Cabinet. The extent of effective co-ordination had depended very much on personalities. It was not an ideal arrangement. On the other hand, the Ministers concerned were responsible to Parliament for their departments, and there was a real difficulty, never wholly resolved in the subsequent years, as to how far a co-ordinating Minister could do more than exercise a certain moral suasion over the Ministers and Ministries that it was his responsibility to co-ordinate.

Lord Beaverbrook was initially appointed Minister of Production, but he held the office only for a few days and was almost immediately succeeded by Mr. Oliver Lyttelton.[1] The office of the Minister was, in the first months, a minute and intimate body, composed of no more than some fifteen or twenty officials and experts. It was housed in the War Cabinet Office and able to draw on its resources. If the Ministry of Production grew monstrously in its later days, it lost appreciably in cohesion and in that first essential of a co-ordinating body, an exact knowledge of what all its highly individualist fingers were doing in all the pies into which they had been inserted.

As part of the original set-up of the new organization, Lord Beaverbrook brought with him Sir Walter Layton, who had been his Director-General of Programmes at the Ministry of Supply, and Mr. Geoffrey Crowther[2] and a few others who had been on the staff of the department. The Programmes Department of that Ministry had, indeed, undertaken, in the absence of any alternative, some of the general economic and statistical functions which more properly belonged to any central co-ordinating body in the field of munitions production, and they brought with them much of the experience not only of the previous years but also of the Ministry of Munitions of 1914–18. The present author joined them almost immediately to give a link with the earlier work in this field done by the Economic Section of the War Cabinet Office.

Under the aegis of the Minister of Production there were gradually collected some of the main functions of co-ordination of the economic war effort, more particularly in the field of munitions production. But co-ordination is meaningless unless the co-ordinator has certain powers and sanctions. He must ideally be the ultimate source of authority to

[1] Capt. Rt. Hon. Oliver Lyttelton, P.C. 1940. Member of Parliament for the Aldershot Division since 1940; Managing Director, British Metal Corporation, Ltd.; Controller of Non-Ferrous Metals, 1939–40; President of the Board of Trade, 1940–1; Minister of State, 1941–2; Minister of Production, 1942–5; Member of the War Cabinet, 1941–5; President of the Board of Trade and Minister of Production, May–July, 1945.

[2] Geoffrey Crowther. Editor of *The Economist* since 1938. On the staff of the Ministry of Supply, 1940–1, and of the Ministry of Information, 1941–3; Deputy Head of Joint War Production Staff, Ministry of Production, 1942–3.

use the resources that are in such scarce supply that they form the basis of programming. In practice to appoint a new Minister and to arm him with such overriding powers in the face of existing departmental set-ups would have been difficult; indeed, in view of the clashes of personalities within a Cabinet and the problems of Parliamentary responsibility, it was almost certainly impossible. Thus the task of co-ordination had to be carried through by a curious and wholly illogical mixture of power and persuasion. It was most necessary and most possible of achievement in four fields: those of raw materials, of man-power, of new building, and of joint planning with the United States and other allied countries.

The allocation of materials had been from the beginning of the war a central function. It was performed by a committee which included officials representing the claimant departments and was served by a small secretariat in the War Cabinet Office headed from 1941 onwards by Professor Arnold Plant.[1] The Committee had as its chairman a junior Minister who, with the assistance of the secretariat, took the leading part in framing the allocations and getting them accepted by departments. After the appointment of the Minister of Production the same procedure was maintained; but the secretariat of the committee passed into the Ministry of Production, and the work of the Ministerial chairman was carried out on behalf of, and often after some consulta-tion with, the Minister of Production. Through the secretariat touch was kept constantly with the raw material situation, and it was possible to ensure that, so far as the overall position permitted, the manpower and other allocations were in line with the possible raw material sup-plies. On the other hand, there was at no stage any sustained attempt to calculate the precise raw material requirements of particular pro-grammes and to translate them into proposed raw material allocations. In very few cases (ammunition was a possible exception) were the co-efficients so accurately known that very precise estimates could be built upon them. The system depended rather on the judgments of the expert central secretariat as to the most effective disposal of the limited sup-plies, taking account of stocks of materials, the probable effects of other factors in holding up programmes, and so on. Certainly they performed

---

[1] Sir Arnold Plant, Kt., cr. 1947. Sir Ernest Cassel Professor of Commerce (with special reference to business administration), University of London, since 1932. Organiser, for Ministry of Information, and first Director of Wartime Social Survey, 1940; Adviser to Ministerial Chairmen of interdepartmental Materials Committee and Central Priority Committee under Production Council (1940), Production Execu-tive (1941), Ministry of Production (1942–5), and on special duties in the Cabinet Office, 1945–6.

miracles in enabling exiguous material supplies to produce improbably large totals of output.

The broader policies of import of raw materials were also fundamental to general economic co-ordination. The responsibility for these had been given to the Ministry of Supply in the early stage of pre-war planning, when it had been expected that the Ministry of Supply functions would be more general and less particularly those of Army supply than they ultimately became. They formed in effect part of the general functions of raw material supply and control for which that Ministry had been responsible since the outbreak of war. It was decided to bring the general import policy within the ambit of the Minister of Production, while leaving the detailed control and licensing of materials to the Ministry of Supply. The reasons were practical rather than logical. The Raw Materials Department was by 1942 a large and busy organization, mainly concerned with detail, and its absorption, even if that had been desirable, would have swamped the small office of the Minister of Production.

Joint planning with the United States is the subject of another essay in this book[1]. Its particular problems will not be dealt with here. They formed, however, a large part of the activities of the co-ordinating bodies. Decisions as to what should be produced by each of the allies and in what types of production help could most usefully be given from each to each were in the main taken on pragmatic grounds. The decisions were necessarily dependent chiefly on the existence of, or easy creation of, productive capacity and the availability of skilled manpower and materials; they rested mainly within the individual supply departments. In the latter stages of preparation for the Normandy invasion attempts were made, it is true, by the Ministry of Production and American officials in London to work out the criteria for more rational decisions: some calculations of considerable academic interest were made which showed the saving in shipping tonnage which might result from different alternative uses of a given amount of British manpower devoted to reverse Lend-Lease. But while these calculations may have made some small marginal contribution to the solution of those problems, they had little or no major influence on the broader planning.

MANPOWER ALLOCATIONS

The detailed administrative responsibility for manpower rested almost wholly on the Minister of Labour. The Minister of Production from

[1] See Chapter V, 'Anglo-American Supply Relationships'.

1942 onwards was given some limited responsibility for the allocation of manpower between the competing claims of the various departments responsible for munitions supply. The supply departments had a large responsibility for the use of manpower by their factories and contractors. This division of responsibility mattered less in practice than in theory. For by 1942 the problems of manpower had become so much a part of the central direction of the war that, whatever Minister might or might not be nominally responsible, the final decisions had to be made by the Cabinet itself in relation to a general appreciation of the course of the war. Its decisions were guided by a committee of Ministers[1] under the chairmanship of Sir John Anderson, first as Lord President and later as Chancellor of the Exchequer. He was uniquely placed to see the full range of the issues involved and the successful solution of the manpower problems of the last three years of war was very largely due to his personal efforts and interventions. It was in the field of manpower policy that the problems of military operations, of munitions output, of civil standards and of the control of inflation all came together and demanded simultaneous solution.

The techniques of manpower budgets and allocations developed and improved as the war proceeded. The call-up had, of course, been a matter of careful policy since the beginning of the war. The setting of manpower ceilings for the supply departments was first introduced in the autumn of 1942. The system was extended progressively to other sectors of the economy and became both more detailed and more precise as the years went on. No useful purpose would be served by rehearsing all the many changes. It will be more interesting to give some account of the system as it operated at the end of the war.

At intervals that were dictated more by circumstances than by the calendar, but were usually between six months and a year, the Ministry of Labour was asked to prepare a manpower survey. The main purpose of this was to estimate the resources of manpower, both in total and in the age-groups suitable for military service, which might become available for a year or so ahead. This survey had to make the best estimates that could be made of the wastage that might be expected from industry, the potential supplies of new manpower and womanpower from the rising age-groups, from further attempts to draw on the unoccupied, and from transfers from less essential occupations.

At the same time an attempt was made to forecast the calls upon the probably available manpower resources. The Service departments built up their estimates of the sizes of the forces that they wished to see

[1] The Man-Power Committee. There was a similar Committee at the official level.

deployed to perform the strategic tasks that lay ahead of them in the period under review. Taking account of the wastage rates that they considered appropriate, they were able to estimate the intakes that would be necessary to fulfil these objectives. At the same time the munitions requirements in relation to these tasks and deployment were estimated. In the case of the Army, where the procedure was most formalized, requirements were calculated and submitted to the Ministry of Supply. In the case of the Royal Air Force an aircraft programme prepared by the Ministry of Aircraft Production was agreed, and this, together with the assumed wastage and training rates, formed the basis of the calculation. The translation of the requirements into production programmes and ultimately into manpower requirements was the infinitely complex task of the supply departments.

From these calculations and from discussions with the Board of Trade about the needs of civil production the secretariat of the War Cabinet Office thus built up a picture of the demands for additional manpower to set against the Ministry of Labour's estimates of manpower supplies. It need not be said that demand always very greatly exceeded supply. It was then the task, first of a small committee of officials and finally of Sir John Anderson, with the Ministers of Labour and of Production, to find ways and means of getting something near a balance. Since the achievement of the balance almost always meant fundamental changes of policy and the abandonment of cherished objectives, neither the Service nor the supply departments would lightly abandon the struggle until the issue had been fought through to the highest levels.

The manpower allocations, as such, were only a first stage in the real underlying task of seeing that the nation's manpower resources should be redistributed in accordance with current intentions. Both in the field of munitions production and in that of civil production their efficacy depended very largely on the measures taken by the Departments to give effect to the decisions.

First, it was necessary to make the best estimate that could be provided of the manpower necessary to fulfil the programmes on which they were hoping to work. The statistical difficulties of making such an estimate were very formidable. There was no easy method of measuring the total programme. In the case of the aircraft programme, for example, it might be measured in total structure weight, in terms of a rather uncertain set of target man-hours for different types of aircraft, in terms of horse-power. It was never easy to know what allowance should be made for spares and for a huge range of other stores and equipment. It was equally uncertain, in making comparison with past achievement, what time-lag should be used in associating output of completed aircraft with manpower available to the department, or what correction should be made to the manpower figure to cover the period of training before labour became effective. The methods of making departmental estimates (at least so it seemed to one in a co-ordinating capacity) were changed with bewildering and kaleidoscopic frequency and all the ingenuities of at least one statistical department were devoted to misleading the would-be co-ordinator. He could himself only hope to use rather cruder methods of checking and a certain amount of common sense as to which of the supply departments was crying 'wolf' with least necessity. One wonders in retrospect whether one was more often deluded by the statistical ingenuities of the Ministry of Aircraft Production, by the 'cards on the table' techniques of the Ministry of Supply, or by the apparent (but almost certainly unreal) statistical incapacities of the Admiralty.

Second, when the allocations had been made, the cuts that had been imposed on the supply departments' manpower (in every case they asked for more manpower than could ultimately be given them) had to be made effective by modification of their programmes. If this were not done the whole system broke down, for it depended ultimately on labour exchange managers not being asked, by firms working for given departments, for more manpower than would cover wastage and give the permitted increase (or decrease) in the department's total manpower. The translation of a cut in the allocation into a cut in the programmes was therefore absolutely essential, but it was never easy to measure or to police. The political consequences to a Minister and his Ministry of failing to achieve a programme were not infrequently more serious than the political consequences of failing to achieve a manpower cut. One could never, therefore, be wholly certain of the full co-operation of a department in giving effect to a given manpower decision.

Even when the necessary programme adjustments had been made the fulfilment of the allocations presented many difficulties. The call-up was, of course, within the control of the Government. But the filling even of first-preference vacancies was never so completely subject to control. While the powers to direct labour were in name very great, in practice they were used with reluctance. The withdrawal of labour from actual employment was at the best of times difficult, and usually quite impossible. The redeployment of the labour force was in the main a matter of securing that, as manpower became available for new employment, it was steered towards the work of greatest urgency for which it happened to be suitable.

The main instruments in this redeployment were a system of preferences of different grades. Under the Restriction on Engagement Order
no labour in the munitions industries or in building could be engaged
except through the exchanges. An exchange manager was expected to
submit labour to first or second preference work before letting it go to
work of lower urgency. In practice the managers succeeded to a surprising degree in steering labour towards the work that was most
urgently needed while preventing any wholesale breakdown of work
of lower urgency through undermanning in particular sections. But by
the end of the war the delays in filling even first-preference vacancies
had become very long. The average delay in the spring of 1944 was
about seven weeks.

The logical beauty of the system of manpower allocations, supported
but not distorted by preferences, was, however, from time to time
obscured. When the planned expansion of aircraft output was falling
behind in the middle of 1943 an overriding preference was given to the
manpower requirements of the Ministry of Aircraft Production. The
repercussions of this on other programmes might well have been disastrous if they had not been mitigated almost immediately by giving
the Minister of Production powers to designate for similar priority a
small number of products of other departments. These powers could
be used to step up laggard production and to fill urgent needs. They
proved very valuable in the period before the Normandy landings,
when the completion of equipment was of great importance. The
general preference to the aircraft programme was fortunately not of
long duration, and after a period of some six months aircraft and equipment were made to require designation, just as did other products, if
they were to enjoy a first preference.

There was another consideration also which required a certain
amount of central supervision and planning. There was from time to
time an excessive concentration of orders in particular areas, so that
manpower demands ran far ahead both of local manpower supplies and
of all possibilities of transfer; the limit to the latter was often set by
accommodation and possibilities of obtaining lodgings. In such cases
the power existed to designate that area and to require supply departments to refrain from placing new orders within it, save to the extent
that orders might be removed from it. By this means, and by more
ordinary methods of persuasion, it was possible to secure a geographical
pattern of demand which accorded sufficiently well with the geographical pattern of manpower supply. But it meant in some cases
that departments were unable to use to the full the capacity which they

had developed. It was naturally in the interest of departments to seek out areas where firms were relatively underloaded, and as the war went on Regional Organizations were greatly strengthened and were able to do more and more to help in this respect. They built up and maintained registers of available capacity and could assist both supply departments and main contractors to find subcontractors to undertake work that they could not carry themselves. By the end of the war the Regional Organization of the Ministry of Production represented a very large and important part of its functions. One lesson the war certainly taught us—that if quick results are needed in the short period it is necessary to take the work to the workers rather than wait for the worker to come to the work.

The manpower survey and the manpower allocations were the backbone of the central planning in the later phases of the war. The plans were never fulfilled exactly as we had expected. Sometimes the reason was that there had been second thoughts of some kind or other in the course of the period covered by the survey. More often it was merely that events did not accord with our predictions. The errors varied naturally from time to time. They were on occasions large because the changes that we were seeking to make in a short period of time were themselves large. Where changes were programmed, as they often were, which involved an increase or decrease of a Ministry's total labour force by something of the order of 10 per cent within a year, the achievement occasionally fell short of the target by as much as a quarter. On a few occasions the actual changes even exceeded by appreciable amounts those which we had programmed.

While the errors involved were by no means negligible, and while they might result in shortages which multiplied themselves in terms of loss of output, the last were not as a rule so great as to result in very serious dislocations. The failures of overall manpower supplies were not in general so serious as the failures due to technical hold-ups or to shortages of particular kinds of skill.

That the manpower pattern did in fact accord as nearly as it did with the manpower allocation was, I think, to be ascribed to a number of factors. First, the call-up could (so far as the needs of age and fitness permitted) be related to the shortages or surpluses of manpower in particular sectors; designation of a product was in the later stages a ground for reservation. Second, the main allocations were made on a national basis to the large supply departments: if their most urgent jobs were not in fact manned-up as they would have liked, they were often in a position to absorb, and to be glad to absorb, more manpower into other jobs where labour could be got. Third, the departments were always conscious of their manpower problems and the placing of their orders was increasingly done with manpower problems in mind. Fourth, in the Army at least, the scales of equipment were not by their nature immutable; the ratios of particular weapons could be, and were, varied within certain limits to take account of the ease or difficulty of supply. Fifth, and I believe most important of all, under the guidance of the Ministry of Labour those of us who served on the official committee which had to draw up the initial proposals gradually learned what changes were and were not within the realms of practicability; the targets that were set were related not only to potential demands, but also to potential supplies and potential transfers.

It is interesting to contrast the control through manpower that prevailed in the United Kingdom with the control in monetary terms which prevailed in the United States. At first glance there appears to be an advantage in using the generalized control over all resources, which money represents, rather than the limited control through one form of resources, which manpower allocations represent. That is, however, in important ways misleading. A monetary control includes a provision for the use of capital resources. In peacetime the period over which capital should be amortized is, if not unambiguous, at least a matter of reasonable agreement. In wartime the period over which capital should be amortized is almost impossibly difficult to define. For purposes of finance and contract making the period may be several years. But in relation to strategy the period may be very short indeed. At different stages of the war it was thought desirable to set out for guidance the moment of maximum effort to which production should be geared, and it was also indicated that new production should not be planned if it could not be available before a given date. In addition there was also in the later stage an assumed end for the war (which had from time to time to be modified) so that stocks of equipment and ammunition might be run down. In many cases this period of maximum effort was so short that if an investment could not be amortized within two years it should not, in theory at least, have been made. In this situation it was more realistic and more practical to plan on the basis of the use of manpower than to attempt to work out artificial rates of amortization, which might well have been different from those included in financial contracts. If it was right to create new facilities even in the face of the current assumptions of maximum effort and of the end of the war, it meant in effect that it was believed to be one of the right means of using the limited manpower resources.

E

But even more important was the fact that wartime planning in monetary terms was in danger of leading one into the major error of treating all resources as uniform and mobile. In fact, in relation to the very rapid changes that were constantly being required, resources were extremely specific and extremely immobile. Even attempts to plan in terms of manpower were in danger of treating manpower as homogeneous and mobile to an extent that was unrealistic. But if you were engaged in cutting the Ensa allocation in order to increase the supply of shipbuilding labour, you were at least under pressure to ask by what concatenation of intermediate transfers, both geographical and occupational, an actress might be transmogrified into a rivet boy. And the dangers of thinking in terms of homogeneous and mobile resources were not confined to manpower. The capital of the munitions industry was highly specific. There was no possible reason to think that £10 millions per annum of resources withdrawn from making explosives could be readily converted into £10 millions more of resources making aircraft.

THE DEFECTS OF THE MANPOWER PLANNING

It would be wrong to judge the success or failure of our manpower planning by the success or failure in making the actual manpower at the disposal of the supply or Service departments at particular moments correspond to the targets set some six months or a year before. That is not the ultimate criterion. The true criterion is whether by this instrument we were able to secure that the greatest possible effort was made against the enemy and the least possible volume of potential resources was wasted, in the sense that it was not effectively brought to bear on the enemy.

Measured by these more fundamental criteria it is by no means so clear that the wartime economic planning at all consistently achieved its objectives. Effective planning ought to have secured two things: first, that over comparatively short periods the resources were deployed as usefully as possible, so that there was the best possible division between the use of manpower, materials and capacity, on the one hand, to produce different kinds of munitions, and the employment of manpower, on the other hand, in the various Forces, to bring the weapons to bear on the enemy; second, that the development of new capacities and the planning of expansions of output should be properly related to the resources likely to be available for its operation when the capacity should become available. The manpower planning was on the whole reasonably well done in relation to the first of these two purposes. But it was always done for comparatively short periods only. There was no official and agreed long-term appreciation of the manpower position two years or more ahead. The departments had to use their own judgment about the planning of extensions of capacity, in almost complete darkness as to the likelihood that a sufficient proportion of the progressively diminishing manpower resources would come their way.

While this is a valid criticism, it would not be true to say that it was a criticism often advanced during the actual course of the war. It may be that departments, irked by central control, did not wish to add yet another link to their fetters. It remains that I have no recollection of actual demands for longer-term manpower forecasts or of refusals to undertake them. That does not, of course, imply that, if good reason can be shown for such a procedure, we ought not to have seen it and to have developed such a longer-term appreciation of our resources.

It is more difficult to say whether we could have undertaken this task sufficiently well to have been able to afford useful guidance to departments. The answer turns on whether we could or could not have foreseen the military course of the war two to three years ahead with sufficient clarity to have been able to predict the best division of our resources between the three Services and between their three supply departments. I think it would be true to say that, even at the end of the war, there was too little contact and exchange of ideas between the military planners on the one hand and those who were charged with thinking about the use of our total resources on the other hand. In the later stages these contacts were very considerably strengthened, but it so happened that they were much more effective in relation to shorter-term problems of the development of particular weapons and equipment than in relation to these wider and longer-term issues of the use of resources. In the earlier stages any exchange of views on longer-term problems was comparatively rare.

A clearer appreciation on all sides of the long-term limits would obviously have been valuable. But it is a very different thing to say that we could by 1941 or 1942 have foreseen with any accuracy the best balance of the use of our resources in the latter half of 1944 or 1945. The pattern necessarily depended on many things which at that time were wholly unknowable: the outcome of the Battle of the Atlantic; the efficacy of heavy bombing; the success or failure of our attempts to land in France; the casualty rates that were to be expected in all the forthcoming operations. Great accuracy was clearly out of the question. A long-term appreciation progressively modified would, none the less, have made clearer the limits of our resources and would have discouraged both overambitious developments by the supply departments and overambitious requirements by the Service departments.

The first real attempt at a longer-term appreciation of this sort was undertaken in relation to the Japanese war. In 1944 it was expected that, when the Germans had been defeated, the war against the Japanese would require some two to three years to complete. It was not, however, expected that it would require, or that the limits of shipping would permit, the full deployment of the military resources of all the allies. At the same time the problems of Lend-Lease and mutual aid required special reconsideration in this context. Thus the broader economic problems and the general deployment of all resources were more fully examined in relation to the expected Japanese war than they had been in relation to the earlier phases. That the problems we foresaw were wholly belied by events and the transition, when it came, had to be handled at a vastly increased *tempo*, is perhaps the best commentary on such attempts. The most that can be said is that we were far better equipped to handle the problems as they actually emerged than if we never exercised our brains at all.

The conclusion, I think, is that we probably ought to have attempted this task, but that we could scarcely have hoped to have achieved such certainty that a very large element of judgment would not still have had to be exercised by departments in planning particular expansions of capacity.

SOME CONCLUSIONS

The main purpose of economic planning, in war as in peace, is to foresee difficulties sufficiently in advance for it to be possible to diminish their impact and, if practicable, to avert them entirely. Some catastrophes, in war as in peace, are almost unpredictable. But many dangers can be foreseen, even if not with accuracy or so as to be able to measure them precisely. Sometimes the power to glimpse through the mists of the future depends on seeing the likely trends of particular factors. More often it depends on the certainty that whatever may be true about the various parts of the economic system there are fairly predictable limits to the total of achievements: there is a fairly predictable limit to the total resources of manpower, to the practicable trend of productivity and even to the practicable rates of change.

No amount of statistical investigation could have yielded, in our present state of knowledge, forecasts of the accuracy that some laymen would like to believe possible. Pre-war estimates would, I suspect, have underrated the willingness that emergency elicited to submit to hardships and reductions of consumption levels. None the less, I am myself convinced that there was nothing like sufficient background study in peacetime of the economic problems and limitations of conducting a total war.

As the war developed the need for central allocation of resources increased progressively. The central problem in regard to this—though I have no recollection that it was so formulated at the time—was how this central control should be exercised. The golden rule of all planning is that it must be done in terms of the scarcest of the resources. By the end of the war there was little doubt that, in general, manpower was the scarcest of our resources. But in regard to many particular problems there were other bottlenecks at least as severe. For some of our problems it was shipping space; for some it was supplies of particular raw materials; for some it was internal transport; for some it was building resources or building accommodation; for some it was very specialized skills. Thus any attempt to work out an overriding allocation in terms either of manpower as the scarcest of all resources or of money as a general common measure of all resources was foredoomed to failure. It was necessary to work simultaneously in terms of all the scarce resources, to give each its paramountcy in the field in which it particularly applied, and to see that, so far as human intelligence was capable of providing, the decisions made under one head were reasonably consistent with the decisions made under other heads.

That the system as it ultimately emerged was perfect no one who was intimate with its complexities and with its dependence on the give and take of rival allocators of different resources would for one moment claim. But it is almost certain that any simpler alternative would have been no better, and indeed almost certainly less effective than the machine that was built up out of experience.

IV

THE PRIME MINISTER'S STATISTICAL SECTION

by

G. D. A. MACDOUGALL

ORIGINS AND DUTIES

Soon after the outbreak of war in September Mr. Winston Churchill, then First Lord of the Admiralty, appointed Professor Lindemann,[1] the Oxford physicist, as his personal adviser. At first he was intended to advise mainly on scientific matters, but in October the First Lord asked him to form a statistical branch as well, and within a month or so some half a dozen economists, nearly all in their twenties, had been collected from the universities. 'S Branch', as it was called, was to collect and co-ordinate Admiralty and cognate statistics for the First Lord and also to advise him on wider matters with which he was concerned as a member of the War Cabinet. When Mr. Churchill became Prime Minister in May 1940 the Branch was transformed into the Prime Minister's Statistical Section and the scope of its work greatly enlarged. It remained in being until the change of Government in July 1945. In December 1942 Professor Lindemann (now Lord Cherwell) was appointed Paymaster-General, and the Section was sometimes known thereafter as the Office of the Paymaster-General. An important part of its work was now to advise Lord Cherwell in his personal capacity as a member of the House of Lords, a Minister, an attender at meetings of the War Cabinet and a member of several Cabinet committees. Individual members of the Section also undertook work from time to time, on interdepartmental committees or otherwise, that had only an indirect bearing on their work for the Prime Minister. But the Section continued to be primarily the Prime Minister's personal section, acting through Lord Cherwell as his personal adviser, and it is with this aspect of its work that the present chapter deals.

The total establishment was in the neighbourhood of twenty. On the

[1] Cherwell, 1st Baron, cr. 1941, of Oxford; Frederick Alexander Lindemann; P.C. 1943; F.R.S. Professor of Experimental Philosophy, Oxford; Fellow of Wadham College since 1919; Student of Christ Church since 1921; Personal assistant to the Prime Minister, 1940; Paymaster-General, 1942-5.

average there were perhaps half a dozen economists; one scientific officer; one established civil servant (with economic training) to help keep the amateurs on the rails; some half a dozen computers; two or three typists and clerks; and last, but not least, a number of what were called 'chartists'—about four were fully employed in the early period when there was much drawing of new charts and diagrams.

The staff had contacts with nearly every Ministry, most of all with the Service and supply departments, the Ministries of War Transport, Fuel and Power, Food, Labour and Economic Warfare, the Treasury and the Board of Trade. They dealt with departmental officers at all levels, and Lord Cherwell had much conversation and correspondence with the various Ministers. Work was informal and intimate, and Lord Cherwell spent much of his time in discussion with his staff.

The main method of communication with the Prime Minister, apart from tables and charts submitted regularly, was through minutes from Lord Cherwell supplemented by his frequent discussions with the Prime Minister. There was a steady flow of these minutes, which totalled some 2,000 over the whole period of nearly six years, or an average of roughly one per day.

One of their main characteristics was brevity, a quality on which the Prime Minister insisted. This at times meant some sacrifice of accuracy and perhaps undue emphasis of one side of the case. But to members of his staff who had delved deeply in the problem and whose inclination, both as academics and as temporary civil servants, was to tell the whole story, Lord Cherwell's reply was always, 'l'art d'être ennuyeux c'est tout dire'. Brevity was an essential quality of minutes addressed to so burdened a man as the Prime Minister, and I believe that the minutes, while less complete, were often more readable than official reports composed to please every member of an interdepartmental committee or all the interested parties within a Ministry.

Some of the minutes were comments on official papers circulated to the Cabinet or Cabinet committees; some commented on minutes sent by other Ministers to the Prime Minister; many were written in response to requests by the Prime Minister for information and an opinion on specific topics; many raised matters which Lord Cherwell, on his own initiative, wished to bring to the Prime Minister's attention.

The Section was thus much more than a purely statistical one. It was concerned not merely with the collection and presentation of statistics but with the conclusions to be drawn from them, and it also made frequent recommendations on general economic policy. Except at the Prime Minister's request minutes were seldom submitted unless they recommended action. Lord Cherwell was loth to add minutes that were only for information to the pile of papers always in the Prime Minister's box.

A minute from Lord Cherwell recommending action might occasionally form the basis of a directive by the Prime Minister, after consultation with the Ministers concerned. More often the Prime Minister would address an inquiry to the appropriate departmental Minister or Ministers, or ask a Minister without departmental responsibility to conduct an inquiry and report. The Ministerial reply would normally be passed to Lord Cherwell for comment. When a new line of policy was settled the Prime Minister would sometimes ask for periodic progress reports which would in turn be examined by the Section. As these were normally of a statistical nature the obligation to make returns might occasionally encourage action, undesirable in itself, simply to boost the figures, but this was unusual. The progress report was in general a useful method of ensuring that decisions were implemented or at least, when this was impracticable, not forgotten.

CHARACTER OF THE WORK

Part of Lord Cherwell's work was in the scientific field and concerned with the technical details of instruments of war, their development, production and use. An analysis of the minutes he submitted to Mr. Churchill shows that nearly one-third were mainly on such scientific matters. It is impossible, however, to draw a hard and fast line between minutes on 'scientific', and minutes on statistical and economic, matters, and it would be a mistake to think that these two aspects of Lord Cherwell's work were in wholly watertight compartments. In the development of new weapons, for example, questions of manpower and materials were often as important as the more technical details. When weapons reached the stage of production and use there was obvious scope for statistical treatment to test their effectiveness, the adequacy or superfluity of stocks, and the like. The technical details of the war at sea had an obvious bearing on the shipping and import position. We are concerned here with the statistical and economic side of the work, but the fact that Lord Cherwell was also deeply concerned with 'scientific' matters is a characteristic of the Section that must be emphasized.

On what may be called the non-scientific side of the work the range of subjects covered was wide. Of the 'non-scientific' minutes sent to the Prime Minister perhaps 30 per cent were mainly concerned with the armed forces, 20 per cent mainly with shipping, 15 per cent with food, agriculture and raw materials, about 10 per cent with postwar problems, and the remaining 25 per cent with miscellaneous topics ranging widely from the building programme to the shortage of matches, from economic warfare to the supply of doctors, from Russia and India to export policy, rationing, inflation and austerity. These proportions varied, of course, from time to time. The emphasis on postwar problems naturally increased during the last few years, and the proportion of minutes dealing with the armed forces tended to decline. The proportions are very rough and ready, since many of the minutes covered a number of fields. A characteristic of the Section was indeed the breadth of its interests. I think it fair to say that this facilitated a breadth of vision as well, although an excessive range of interests may also lead to amateurish dabbling. The Section cannot be wholly acquitted of this, at least in the early period, but as time went on it gained much from its continuity and from the comparative freedom of its members from routine administrative duties. This enabled them to acquire some expert knowledge in a fair number of subjects and to gain in the end the confidence of most departments concerned.

It will be seen that much of the work related to the armed forces, of which the Section kept copious records. This interest, together with Lord Cherwell's work on more technical matters, differentiated the Section in an important respect from the Economic Section of the War Cabinet secretariat. The latter body was more concerned with the maximization of the war effort as a whole than with the use made of resources once they had been set aside for war purposes. The maximization of the total war effort may be a problem that can be considered from the civilian side alone. We know that, after a point, cuts in civilian transport, medical services, food, or consumer goods in general will affect the ability and willingness of the civilian population to produce warlike goods. The problem is to transfer resources from civilian to warlike uses up to the point where a further transfer will bring no *net* gain to the war effort. But in practice, where particular adjustments at the margin are under consideration, it may be useful to have some idea of what would happen to resources if they were transferred to the military sector. The total effect of the transfer might be to increase a less urgent, at the expense of a more urgent, part of the war effort. For example, to cut bus services in order to release oil tankers for military use might, where the extra oil demanded by the armed forces was not 'really necessary', add little to their effectiveness while it held up production of essential weapons through the indirect effect on the workers involved. Then again some knowledge of the state of the armed forces is required when advising on the allocation of, say, manpower between the various Services, their respective production departments, and the building programme.

Use of Statistics

We have seen that the Section was much more than a purely statistical one, but a considerable part of the work was, of course, of a statistical nature. In the early days of the war many government statistics were extremely confusing, conflicting and incomplete. It was extraordinarily difficult to get a simple, overall picture of what was happening. The Section devoted much energy to the collection of statistics, to the reconciliation of apparent discrepancies, and to the simple presentation of the facts, especially in the form of charts. Such simple presentation was required for the use of the Section itself, for the information of the Prime Minister, and also, on occasion, for the information, through the Prime Minister, of President Roosevelt and other Americans. The development of the Central Statistical Office, and of central statistical departments in the various Ministries, reduced the burden of collection and reconciliation as time went on; and as the general statistical picture, and the more important orders of magnitude, became better known, the need for simple table, charts and exposition was diminished. But the Section continued to keep many detailed statistical records in the form required for its particular purposes, and until the end it provided Mr. Churchill with statistical summaries for use at his conferences with allied leaders.

The Section was also statistical in that it was interested primarily in the quantitative aspect of problems. Few of Lord Cherwell's minutes to the Prime Minister were free from figures. An argument was hardly considered respectable unless backed by statistics. An attempt to establish a prima facie case for action by the Prime Minister had at least to be illustrated by appropriate orders of magnitude.

The establishment of such orders of magnitude sometimes involved much work, especially when a major change in Government policy was being recommended. Before proposing to the Prime Minister that, say, the building programme should be curtailed, it would be necessary to show, by some simple quantitative measures, that further building on the current scale was relatively unnecessary, and that the saving of imports and manpower to be achieved was large. A proposal that military vehicles should be dismantled before shipment, despite the inconvenience involved, would have to be backed by a demonstration that the shipping to be saved was substantial. The Section would also have to examine carefully many of the detailed technical problems involved and if possible to secure the support and agreement of departmental officers. All this meant that weeks of work might lie behind a half-page minute to the Prime Minister.

The collection and clarification of statistics relating to the past was a necessary preliminary to work on estimates of the future. Much of the Section's time was devoted to such work. Being responsible for warning the Prime Minister of impending shortages, it had to make independent forecasts of its own; and it often had to make critical analyses of forecasts and requirements submitted by departments. In the early years especially, a finding of undue pessimism was as common as one of excessive optimism. The Section often reached the conclusion that departments were exaggerating the demands likely to be placed upon them and underestimating what could be done with the resources at their disposal. The detection in this way of excessive 'requirements' can often be as important in avoiding waste and maldistribution of resources as the forecasting of a shortage that will cause a bottleneck. The rather rudimentary statistical organization of some departments in the earlier part of the war, coupled with a natural desire to be 'on the safe side', provided scope for a non-departmental body prepared both to examine critically the details of departmental calculations and to apply broad, common-sense tests to the conclusions reached. As statistical departments were strengthened throughout the government service, and as more and more experience was gained of war conditions, estimates of the future improved greatly; and with the formation of bodies like the Ministry of Production the need for scrutiny by the Section was diminished. But the natural tendency of departments to take a departmental rather than a national view continued, and the criticism of departmental estimates remained an important part of the Section's work until the end.

When it comes to forecasting shortages the ability of an organization like the Prime Minister's Statistical Section is limited. It may be able to give an opinion on, for example, the likelihood of a coal shortage, or a general appraisal of the shipping or manpower position in the near or more distant future. It may possibly, by keeping detailed statistics of weapons of war, be able to forecast a likely lack of balance. But it will seldom, except by accident or by personal contact with those immediately responsible, be able to foresee a bottleneck in, for example, drop-forgings, alloy steel or some aircraft component, unless it is large enough to duplicate much of the detailed work of production departments.

It was necessary on occasion to call the Prime Minister's attention to impending shortages that were clear for all to see, but on which sufficiently urgent action was not being taken. The Section would then also propose what it considered to be the least harmful methods of adequately meeting the shortage. This might involve quite disproportionate cuts in some sectors—a drastic reduction in military shipments to theatres overseas, but little or no cut in imports; a drastic cut in raw material imports, but little reduction in imports of food. Such proposals were at times different from those that might have emerged from normal interdepartmental negotiations. An acceptable compromise is then normally the object. The measures agreed may sometimes, too, be inadequate to meet the case, leaving the final incidence of the shortage unsettled, with possibly disastrous effects on some sector of the economy. Whether or not such compromises and half-measures would have been better policy, it is necessary to record that the Prime Minister did on occasion make proposals, or issue directives, based on the apparently less 'reasonable' recommendations of Lord Cherwell and his staff.

When reviewing the various possible methods of meeting a shortage the Section always attempted to evaluate their relative importance. This helped to concentrate attention on those that really mattered and to avoid useless discussions of the trivial. It was desired to increase imports or to balance the coal budget; this measure might contribute several million tons, that several hundred thousand, another a mere hundred or so. Such indications, however rough and ready, may be invaluable to the Prime Minister when conducting a meeting. They serve as a useful reminder that success in dealing with a problem is not to be gauged by the *number* of measures taken. As Lord Cherwell, with his flair for orders of magnitude, never tired of insisting, a small change in a big thing may often be more effective, and is usually more desirable, than a lot of big changes in a lot of small things.

SOME LESSONS

The foregoing pages have described in very general terms what the Prime Minister's Statistical Section was, how it worked and what it did. It is hard to assess its accomplishments or to strike a balance between its merits and defects. One who was a member of the Section from its first day till its last is hardly qualified to deliver judgment.

Whatever the verdict the success or failure of Mr. Churchill's Statistical Section under Lord Cherwell during these six years would neither establish nor disprove the case for a Prime Minister's statistical or economic section in general. The character of the Section depended greatly on these two personalities, on the nature of the problems that arose during the second world war, and on the general organization of the government service during the period. It may nevertheless be useful to outline some considerations that will be relevant if the establishment of such a body is ever again considered.

Much will depend on the personality of the Prime Minister. In the first place, some Prime Ministers may not be greatly interested in the quantitative aspect of problems. They may prefer, in making a decision, to rely on personal discussion with the Ministers concerned. They may not, in addition, feel the need for a simple, independent, overall appraisal in quantitative terms. Such Prime Ministers will have little need of a statistical section of any kind.

In the second place, an organization of this type can easily arouse the opposition of departmental officers and of their Ministers. Some Prime Ministers may not be prepared to risk this opposition. Even if they are, it may be hard for members of the section to co-operate successfully with departmental officers if they lack the backing of a strong Prime Minister. This difficulty applies to most organizations without a departmental minister. Except in cases of collusion between the section and departmental officers, the latter may often be reluctant, and very naturally so, to divulge information that may be used to criticize their Ministry, or to spare the time needed to provide information in the form requested. They may fear that figures given will be misinterpreted. They may be reluctant to confirm calculations of a type to which they are unaccustomed in their departmental work, but which are essential for a section which has to paint with a broad brush. Averages, they will argue, are misleading because of the dispersion about them. How can you possibly say what tonnage of imports is sacrificed for every extra soldier sent to the Middle East? And so on.

The experience of the Section during the war showed, however, that these difficulties are not insuperable. Given understanding on both sides good relations can be built up. It is an advantage to have in the section some members who have worked in a department. The fundamental remedy is for the section to become sufficiently expert to gain the confidence of departmental officers. For this purpose the staff must be large enough to make some specialization possible, and the turnover must not be too rapid. The section must be absolutely confident of any facts and figures supplied by it that are likely to be quoted outside. In framing estimates and making calculations even more care is required than is expended by departmental experts who are, after all, the recognized authorities. Whenever possible the agreement of the latter should be secured in advance. A sense of proportion must, of course, be preserved. A large collection of unduly cautious specialists of long standing might be of even less value than a few careless, tactless amateurs. A little irresponsibility is desirable in a section intended partly as an irritant.

A possible criticism of an organization like the Prime Minister's Statistical Section in the recent war is that it may give undue influence to people who develop prejudices. It is inevitable that such a section, and its head, will come to take a certain line on a number of matters— it could hardly fail to do so and avoid inconsistency. The question is whether these lines are sound or otherwise, a matter on which opinion will not always be unanimous. There is no doubt that the Section did develop views—or prejudices, if you will. Lord Cherwell held views on the correct distribution of our war effort between land, air and sea; on the importance of feeding the people; on postwar problems; and on many other matters. But such views were not inflexible. Opinions based on continuous study of the relevant facts and figures naturally changed from time to time as circumstances altered. The opinion of the Section that the coal shortage in the earlier years of the war was not quite so disturbing as sometimes supposed had changed, long before the end, to an equally firm conviction that the outlook was more serious than commonly imagined. Both views, I believe, were right. Despite a general emphasis on the vital need to maintain imports at a minimum level, even at the expense of military shipping requirements, it was felt necessary to insist at various times that the estimates of import requirements were exaggerated, and that more shipping might be diverted to military use. A tendency, after about 1942, to stress the dangers of false economy in imposing austerity on the people followed an equally strong disposition, earlier in the war, to doubt whether our war-making plans were sufficiently ambitious.

Whether the views of the Prime Minister's advisers are right or wrong it is impossible to advise without them; and, as we have seen, advice can sometimes be too well-balanced.

A Prime Minister's statistical section could, of course, be a less ambitious affair. It could be relieved of the responsibility of giving advice. As a minimum it could act as little more than a post office for transmitting the Prime Minister's requests for statistical information to the appropriate departments. This would not be quite so pointless as it sounds. It may often be better to obtain information in this way than by a direct request from the Prime Minister to the Minister concerned. The Prime Minister's statisticians, knowing what was in his mind, could help to frame the question in a precise statistical form that admitted of an answer. They might assist the departmental statisticians in any calculations required, if these were outside their normal line of country. They might also perhaps help to 'serve up' the reply in a form that would be readily understood by the Prime Minister and consistent with other statistics with which he was familiar.

Slightly more ambitious would be a section that collected and marshalled statistics from various sources when asked by the Prime Minister for general information on some fairly wide topic. The section might also keep its own records and prepare tables and charts for regular submission to the Prime Minister; it might draw his attention to the more important changes and tendencies from time to time; it might even give a balanced summary of the arguments for and against particular lines of action. All this was done by the Prime Minister's Statistical Section during the war. But if, as was the case, it goes further, if it recommends lines of action, either on its own initiative or at the Prime Minister's request, it becomes an advisory body with the advantages and disadvantages mentioned above.

A Prime Minister's statistical section might thus take various forms, so that even if a body of the 1939–45 variety were ruled out there would be other possibilities.

It may be thought that other bodies, such as the Central Statistical Office and the Economic Section of the Cabinet secretariat, could perform many of these duties. This may be so, but it is worth recording that during the last war, while there was close and cordial co-operation between these bodies and the Prime Minister's Statistical Section, there was little overlapping. Nor, I think, did members of the three bodies have any feeling that effort was being duplicated in a wasteful manner.

The function of the Economic Section was to advise the War Cabinet, and the Lord President in particular, on economic matters. That of the Central Statistical Office was to serve Ministers and departments generally by the collection, reconciliation and presentation of statistics. When the Central Statistical Office was established in January 1941, and separated from what then became the Economic Section of the War Cabinet secretariat, one of the main objects was to provide at least one source of authoritative statistical information which was entirely divorced from the business of advising, and so free from any suspicion of tendentious bias.

The Prime Minister's Section differed from the Central Statistical Office in being an advisory body; it was established, moreover, some time before the services of the Central Statistical Office became available; and the range of interests of the two bodies did not wholly coincide. It differed from the Economic Section, as has been said, in its much more detailed work on the military side; it also laid greater emphasis on quantitative studies and on the keeping of statistical records. Most important of all, it was essentially personal to the Prime Minister; it worked continuously for him; it had some idea of what was in his mind; it knew the sort of thing he wanted to know and how he liked to have it presented; its loyalty was to him and to no one else. This is the crux of the matter. The desirability or otherwise of a staff of this sort depends largely on how strongly the Prime Minister of the day feels the need for such a staff—a staff entirely his own. Some of the possible dangers have already been mentioned. It may be that the Prime Minister should be advised by the responsible Ministers and by no one else; that once Ministers have been appointed they should be allowed to get on with the job. On the other hand, the Prime Minister must see that they do get on with the job. He must decide, too, what job they are to get on with, both when there is a clash of departmental interests and also when a fundamental change is required in the policy of the Government. How far should the Prime Minister be assisted in these duties by personal advisers? The question is really one of degree. All Prime Ministers have a personal staff. They have private secretaries and a Parliamentary Private Secretary; they are assisted by the Secretary to the Cabinet; if Minister of Defence, they have military advisers; and so on. The question at issue here is whether, since so many of the problems with which Prime Ministers must deal have economic and quantitative aspects, their staff should also include economists and statisticians. Is it right that, when Ministers meet to discuss such matters, the Prime Minister alone should be largely unsupported by expert advice?

V

ANGLO-AMERICAN SUPPLY RELATIONSHIPS
by

HUGH WEEKS

The supply of material of war from the United States—the arsenal of democracy—to the British forces during the war was always an issue of the greatest importance. The basic problem—how much America should produce for British forces—was always the same. But the nature of the problem and the machinery for its solution changed greatly between the first two years, when the outputs from the British and French contracts were the sole source of armament supply from America, and the peak of combined production in 1944. By this time the total volume of American production was several times that of the whole British Empire and a quarter of the armaments accruing to British forces came from the U.S.A. There were also fundamental changes of attitude between the time when the British forces were the only ones engaged and that when the American troops became an increasing majority in the field.

To secure supplies from America the British were involved in two distinct types of negotiation which from time to time appeared to merge, but which usually were separated later by the machinery which developed.

The first type of negotiation was to ensure that the necessary production would take place in the States. Such arrangements were often made without any implied decision about the ultimate transfer which was the subject of the second type of negotiation. Throughout the period slightly different arrangements applied to equipment for naval, land and air forces, though the broad principles were sufficiently close for them to be treated together. In general the Navy negotiations were simplest (and reliance on American supplies was least) and the Army negotiations were most complex (and reliance was greatest). Negotiations became increasingly complex, the worst time naturally being the first year after American entry into the war. They were at all levels; mainly between the permanent military and civil staffs in Washington, but special missions from the United Kingdom, Ministers and Chiefs of Staff, were called into play as the occasion demanded. They were complicated by the fact that the British and American machinery for the control of war production was not organized on parallel lines.

STAGES OF DEVELOPMENT

This is the general background. The methods and lessons of this period can best be seen by taking an historical view in five different periods which might be defined as follows:

(1) British contracts up to Lend-Lease.
(2) Lend-Lease without war—up to Pearl Harbour.
(3) The early days of war—from Pearl Harbour to the middle of 1942.
(4) Combined Boards from the middle of 1942 onwards.
(5) 'Stage II' discussions, 1944 and 1945.

These periods, of course, are not self-contained and any time division is arbitrary. For example, in the early period before Lend-Lease, British contracts were being placed and deliveries were pathetically small, but the main deliveries of these contracts came after Lend-Lease was in operation and by arrangements made under the Act were sometimes financed by Lend-Lease funds. Nevertheless, it is round these major periods that the story of Anglo-American supply relationships must develop.

The British contracts were first organized by a small mission in Ottawa which later moved to New York and finally (with a few important exceptions) transferred to Washington. The first problem was that our dollar reserves and earnings were limited and a basic decision had to be made between spending on contracts for finished material or for the creation of manufacturing facilities for munitions, which were very limited at that time in America. This second choice implied that ways and means would be found at a later stage to finance the product of these facilities. The compromise reached had a definite tendency towards the creation of facilities and in the light of what followed it is clear this decision was right; and indeed it is possible we ought to have gone further, for some of the quick start which American production was able to make after Pearl Harbour was due to the fact that British contracts had been developing production facilities in the States for the previous two years.

The second problem was the question of which types of weapons were to be made, an issue which raised strong feelings on both sides and repeatedly threatened the general harmony of Anglo-American relations. At first the main field of battle was between the soldiers, where the merits of the 25-pounder and the 105-millimetre field guns, the 3·7-inch and the 90-millimetre heavy anti-aircraft guns and the Valentine and the M.3 tanks were hotly debated. In the end few British type munitions were made in the States, the main exception being the Merlin engine and the .303 rifle. One compromise was the 6-pounder anti-tank gun, which with some slight modification became the American standard weapon under the name of 57-millimetre.

The happiest conclusion was the production of tanks. The Canadians were called in to manufacture a tank of mixed parentage, using the American chassis modified to take the British-type turret. From this tank grew the successful Sherman tank which with various developments was the standard weapon of the American forces.

British dependence on American production tended to become specialized. The changes in the need for particular types of equipment, as well as convenience of manufacturing capacity, meant that American supplies were of outstanding importance in certain particular classes of material, such as R.D.X.,[1] transport aircraft, heavy vehicles, tanks and their transporters, heavy engineering equipment. Apart from this specialized reliance which developed during the war, the supply problems were a reflection of the basic fact that the British forces during the war were built up to a total which was greater than could be supported by the manufacturing capacity under British control. This fact sprang from decisions reached during that period in 1941 when American supply promised to be of significant dimensions, though American participation in the war was still in doubt. Why that policy did not change is a large question outside the field of this paper.

The fact that we drew munitions heavily from the United States must not be taken to imply any criticism of the intensity of the British war effort. The States were able to produce with greater efficiency than we were, partly because her plants were exceptionally well-tooled, and partly because the freedom from bombing—and the threat of bombing—meant that munition production could be concentrated in an uninterrupted flow from very large plants.

At a much later stage in the war attempts were made to measure the proportion of the resources of the United Kingdom and the United States which were being devoted to war. There were differences of opinion on the method of calculation and on the precise answer, but there was no doubt that a larger proportion of the British economy was devoted to warlike purposes than in the United States—and, of course, for a longer period.

[1] A more powerful form of explosive than T.N.T.

By the autumn of 1940 the running out of British funds and the military situation forced a fresh approach on the financing of contracts. Layton[1] visited the States in the latter months of 1940 and from his visit arose a new conception which was of tremendous importance as being a forerunner of Lend-Lease. This was what was known as the 'B' Programme. The plan was that the American War Department itself would place orders for the complete equipment and reserves (all in American types) for ten divisions over and above the programme for the projected American forces. There was no decision and no commitment on how the equipment was to be used. It would be available either for American forces if sufficient had been trained and if the need arose, or for British and other allied forces which might be available. The value to the American programme was that heavier orders were justified which led to great benefits at a later stage. In the event little of this equipment was taken by the British and most of it was used to equip the Free French.

The next step was taken when Arthur Purvis[2] laid before the President in January 1941 what was known as the 'Purvis Balance Sheet'. This showed the needs in 1941 and 1942 of the British forces which were being raised and the maximum possible supplies from all sources other than the States. The deficiencies which appeared on the balance sheet were the first indication of the dimensions of American production which were required.

It must be remembered that these broad steps towards the concept of integrating American production with that of the British Empire were taken before America was at war.

And then in March of 1941 came Lend-Lease which entirely shifted the nature of the supply problem from the British point of view. The Act included various categories each of which had a predetermined allocation of funds. There was, it is true, some possible *virement*, but basically the British needs had to be tailored to those categories of

[1] Layton, 1st Baron, cr. 1947, of Danehill; Walter Thomas Layton; C.H. 1919; Kt., cr. 1930. Chairman of News Chronicle, Ltd., and of The Economist Newspaper, Ltd., etc. Director-General of Programmes, Ministry of Supply, 1940–2; Chairman of Executive Committee, Ministry of Supply, 1941–2; Chief Adviser on Programmes and Planning, Ministry of Production, 1942–3; Head of Joint War Production Staff, 1942–3.

[2] Arthur Blaikie Purvis. Killed in an air accident, 14th August 1941. With I.C.I.; President of Canadian Explosives, Ltd., 1924; Head of the Anglo-French Purchasing Commission in the U.S.A., 1939; Director-General of the British Purchasing Mission, 1941; Chairman of the British Supply Council, 1941; was to have been sworn a member of the Privy Council on 15th August 1941, but embarked upon a return to the United States sooner than he had expected.

so much for aircraft, so much for tanks, for explosives, etc. The first appropriation was followed by supplementals. Successive programmes to fill these supplementals were called for at very short notice, but the co-ordination between the character of the British needs and the financial provisions made for them was one of slow development.

Lend-Lease, of course, covered more than purely military supplies, and the number and complexity of the forms required to claim for civilian stores is still a legend and a nightmare among those who had to prepare them.

The next step in the munitions field was the compilation of the document known as the 'Consolidated Statement'—a statistical summary of the production of the more important munitions in America and in the British Empire. This was an essential background to all future planning, but knowledge of American plans was very vague—for a great part confined to cryptic messages from the President to the 'Former Naval Person'. On the British side the next move towards the problem of expanding and guiding American production to meet British needs was the preparation, in the fall of 1941, of the heroically named 'Victory Programme' which, as did the Purvis balance sheet, led to the conclusion that victory was only possible with greatly increased American supplies.

ESTABLISHMENT OF THE COMBINED BOARDS

The entry of America into the war led to a rapid and complete change in supply arrangements. The first effects were indeed alarming, for ships were stopped loading munitions for Britain and munition ships at sea were for a short period called back. But the visit of Churchill and Beaverbrook and the Chiefs of Staff at the end of December 1941 led to a complete change of attitude and the creation of a complex system of combined machinery. The most important decision in the munitions supply field was the creation of the Combined Munitions Assignment Board (C.M.A.B.) under the chairmanship of Harry Hopkins which, from then until the end of the war, proceeded each month to allocate the supplies of finished munitions coming forward between America, Britain and the other claimant countries. This, and the other combined organizations[1]—the Chiefs of Staff, the Raw Materials Board (C.R.M.B.), the Shipping and Food Boards and later the Production and Resources Board (C.P.R.B.)—all had to face the problem

[1] See W. K. Hancock and M. M. Gowing, *British War Economy*, H.M. Stationery Office, 1949, pp. 389–404, for the establishment and organization of these Combined Boards.

of where the centre of direction was to lie. In each case efforts were made to develop a double-headed organization, but in every case the final result was the same—that the real centre of operation was in Washington. The devices to overcome this somewhat unpalatable lowering of the prestige of London were various. Occasionally meetings of a Combined Board would be held in London. In the case of the Production Board a London Committee was formed, which was to a large degree a face-saver. For Munitions Assignment a London Board was created with restricted powers of action.

Combined Boards were formed for Munitions Assignment and Raw Materials—basically also an assignment machine—but the other essential part, a combined body to determine production plans, was postponed although it was pressed strongly at the time, particularly by Jean Monnet.[1] One of the contributing reasons was that it was only at this time that the President decided to place the control of American production under a single head in the person of Don Nelson as head of the War Production Board. But though the official formation of the Combined Production and Resources Board did not take place until the following June, there had been considerable interchange of views on programmes among officials even before America came into the war, and British influence affected the size of the Presidential objectives for production in 1941 and 1942 which were issued early in January 1941.

On the military side the formation of the Assignment Board and the development of large programmes for the American forces began a long series of arguments at the two stages at which British needs were taken into account.

The first stage was the acceptance of British requirements as an addition to, or a part of, the American production programme. To secure these acceptances the basic military plans were agreed, complicated statistical calculations on the scale of provisioning and wastage were tabled, arguments developed on the virtues of types of equipment, and the British military staffs in Washington grew to impressive proportions. But this was only to the stage of inclusion in a programme. As production was completed a similar series of arguments based on immediate plans, immediate deficiencies and shipping possibilities was fought out in the Assignment Board, where the British were the largest but by no means the only claimant for American munitions.

---

[1] Jean Monnet. Hon. G.B.E., 1946. Commissioner for the French National Plan since 1946; Chairman, Franco-British Economic Co-ordination Committee, 1939–40; Commissioner for Armament, Supplies and Reconstruction, French Committee for National Liberation, 1943–4.

At a slightly later stage—in 1943 and 1944—a similar situation arose in reverse. The American forces in Britain required a wide range of materials from British manufacture and stocks in amounts which were comparable in proportion to the British demands in America. A far simpler procedure was evolved with wide delegated powers of local action and with practically no appeal against the allocations—all the more creditable in that the British officer in charge had been through the most trying periods of similar negotiation in Washington.

Between these two stages lay the long period of production, and during 1941 there were periods of fear that the British needs were not being looked after to the same degree as the accepted needs of the American forces. In the early part of that year the authorities of the various American agencies were confused. Just as the W.P.B., for example, was giving thought to the creation of priority classification in connection with the British, it was suddenly discovered that the A.N.M.B.[1] had issued a priority directive, which had been communicated to all manufacturers by the American supply departments, which gave the British element in the American programme a much lower priority than was given to the corresponding American equipment. These and other problems were settled by lengthy and gruelling, but on the whole amicable, discussion.

Already thought was being given by the Americans to the character of the British production programme, such as repeated suggestions, not always at this stage very acceptable, that as British tanks were so bad their production should be greatly reduced and the British should rely largely on the improved American tank. It was in this atmosphere that in the middle of 1942 the Combined Production and Resources Board was born as a result of a mission headed by Oliver Lyttelton, who for the rest of the war was the British Minister most closely concerned with Anglo-American supply questions. This was in effect a liaison organization between the British Ministry of Production, which had recently been formed, and the American War Production Board, which was only a few months older. Like other boards, the main headquarters were in Washington and Anglo-American staff was seconded from the two departments concerned. As with other combined organizations, the staff rapidly began to lose their individual nationalist points of view and began to reflect the point of view of the new organism.

The line of demarcation between the C.P.R.B. and the C.R.M.B. was at certain points somewhat blurred, but this did not prevent agreement on the handling of individual problems which fell within territory

[1] Army and Navy Munitions Assignment Board.

that on paper might be held to be common to both Boards. It was not an easy task for the British staff of these Boards to establish good working relations with their opposite numbers on the American side, but in large measure they succeeded. Much of the credit for this must lie with the British representatives on these two Boards (Sir Robert Sinclair[1] and Sir Clive Baillieu[2]), who in many ways had a harder task than their American counterparts. It was their job to let America benefit from the longer experience of wartime planning which Britain had undergone. They, in common with the Chiefs of Staff, Salter[3] on the Shipping Board, and Brand[4] on the Food Board, and with all their successors, had to play the difficult part of operating as equals but with a minority shareholding which was steadily declining. In the early period they were greatly helped by the good personal relations established by the visits of people such as Sir Ronald Weeks[5] and Sir William Rootes[6].

[1] Sir Robert John Sinclair, K.C.B., cr. 1946; K.B.E., cr. 1941. Chairman, Imperial Tobacco Company, Ltd. Director-General of Army Requirements, War Office, and member of Supply Council, 1939–42; Deputy for Minister of Production on Combined Production and Resources Board, 1942–3; Chief Executive, Ministry of Production, 1943, and subsequently with the Board of Trade until November 1945.

[2] Sir Clive Latham Baillieu, K.B.E., cr. 1938. Chairman, Dunlop Rubber Company, Ltd. Executive member of the Export Council, 1940; Director-General, British Purchasing Commission, Washington, 1941; Head of British Raw Materials Mission, Washington, 1942–3; British representative on Combined Raw Materials Board, Washington, 1942–3; Member of British Supply Council in North America, 1941–3.

[3] Rt. Hon. Sir (James) Arthur Salter, P.C. 1941; G.B.E., cr. 1944; K.C.B., cr. 1922. M.P. for Oxford University, 1937–50. Gladstone Professor of Political Theory and Institutions, Oxford, 1934–44; Parliamentary Secretary to the Minister of Shipping, 1939–41; Joint Parliamentary Secretary to the Minister of War Transport, 1941; Head of British Merchant Shipping Mission, Washington, 1941–3; Senior Deputy Director-General of U.N.R.R.A., 1944; Chancellor of the Duchy of Lancaster, 1945.

[4] Brand, 1st Baron, cr. 1946, of Eydon; Robert Henry Brand. Managing Director of Lazard Bros. & Co. till May 1944. Head of British Food Mission, Washington, March 1941–May 1944; representative of H.M. Treasury in Washington, May 1944–May 1946; Chairman, British Supply Council in North America, April–Nov. 1942 and June 1945–March 1946; U.K. Delegate at Bretton Woods and Savannah Conferences.

[5] Lt.-Gen. Sir Ronald Morce Weeks, K.C.B., cr. 1943; C.B.E. 1939. Chairman of Vickers, Ltd.; and of English Steel Corporation, Ltd.; Director, Pilkington Bros., Ltd., etc. Chief of Staff, Territorial Division, 1939; B.G.S. Home Forces, 1940; Major-General; Director-General of Army Equipment, 1941; Lt.-Gen. D.C.I.G.S., 1942–5; Deputy Military Governor and Chief of Staff, British Zone, C.C.G., June–August, 1945; retired from the Army, 1945.

[6] Sir William Edward Rootes, K.B.E., cr. 1942. Chairman, Rootes Securities, Ltd., Rootes, Ltd., and associate companies. Member, Board of Trade Advisory Council, 1931–4 and 1939–40; Chairman, Joint Aero Engine Committee (Shadow Industry), 1940–1; Chairman, Supply Council, Ministry of Supply, 1941–2; President, Society of Motor Manufacturers and Traders, 1939–42.

The effectiveness of the C.P.R.B. is difficult to determine and is generally undervalued. In a situation in which the military negotiators for supplies were for the most part suppliants in a queue, it was invaluable to have an organization on the supply side in which the British were constitutionally able to argue as equals. Some of the weaknesses of the C.P.R.B. sprang from the weaknesses of the two organizations from which it was composed. On the British side the Ministry of Production was formed too late in the war. Its authority developed and was greatest in the period when, from the middle of 1943 onwards, manpower shortages dictated adjustments in various departmental programmes. But in London the Ministry of Production had the strength that Oliver Lyttelton was a member of the War Cabinet and especially in the early days its staff, in both London and Washington, was more closely in touch with the strategic direction of the war than its American opposites. Its field of responsibilities covered, as well as the supply side of the Admiralty, two largely civilian departments, the Ministry of Supply and the Ministry of Aircraft Production, both of which were catering for Service departments; so it was strengthened by the inevitable tendency for civilian organizations to present a front against unreasonable demands from those in uniform.

The relations of the Ministry of Production with the Admiralty were far less clear, for in the Admiralty both Service control and the control of supplies lay under a single head. This was, indeed, the position in the States, where the War Production Board (outside its responsibility in the field of raw materials) had to deal on procurement and programme matters with departments which were wholly in uniform—the U.S. War Department covered most of the ground of four separate British Ministries.

On the whole, the influence of the W.P.B. upon the American munitions programme appeared to be appreciably less than that of the Ministry of Production upon the British programmes.

The activities of both Ministries and the Combined Production Board itself were largely devoted to the undramatic task of marginal adjustments in programmes. In the early days of the C.P.R.B. it was realized that it was impracticable to follow its literal terms of reference, and in practice the main purpose of the Board was to focus attention on the things which mattered most in making the best use of production facilities in both countries. By the time the organization had settled down and was able to exercise some influence the broad pattern of munitions production had been determined. It was the job of the C.P.R.B. to press for more of one thing as opposed to less of another, and it was something of a happy surprise to the officials of the two countries to realize that in 1944 the list of high priorities for munitions in short supply had become almost identical in both countries. By a slow process the machinery had secured a position of equilibrium. And within the list of important items were many—escort vessels and frigates, heavy tanks, 20-millimetre guns, and ammunition, to name a few examples—in which the C.P.R.B. had secured an acceleration of production in both countries.

Within three months of its formation it was realized that Canada, by virtue of the importance of its output, ought to become a full member of the Board. Mr. C. D. Howe[1] and Mr. E. P. Taylor[2] added greatly to the value of the Board. They provided a bridge between opposing views, and in Ottawa had a simple and direct organization which was envied by those in London and Washington.

By discussion and interchange of views and plans the Board succeeded in getting a clearer assessment in all three countries of the available resources in material, manpower and facilities; a better forecasting of where the bottlenecks to greater output would be and more direct action to remove them or limit their effects.

But munition programme determination was not the only function of the C.P.R.B. It was concerned with the production and distribution of certain civilian supplies and it also served as a channel for the exchange of research, both scientific and technical, and of manufacturing and planning techniques.

STAGE II DISCUSSIONS

At the beginning of 1944 a new problem of great delicacy appeared to be ripe for discussion. This was the question of the level of munition supplies to be obtained from the United States in what became known as Stage II; that is, the period after the defeat of Germany but before the defeat of Japan. The problem arose because both British and American forces would require supplies of equipment at a far lower rate at this period than during the two-front war. Indeed, the total

---

[1] Rt. Hon. Clarence Decatur Howe. P.C. 1946. Minister of Trade and Commerce, Canada, since 1948. Minister of Munitions and Supply, Canada, 1940–6.

[2] Edward Plunket Taylor, C.M.G. 1946. President, Argus Corporation, Ltd., Chairman, Canadian Breweries, Ltd., Canadian Food Products, Ltd., etc. Among his various wartime appointments are: appointed President and Vice-Chairman, British Supply Council in North America, September 1941; Director-General, Ministry of Supply Mission, February 1942; Canadian Deputy Member on Combined Production and Resources Board, November 1942; Canadian Chairman, Joint War Aid Committee, U.S.-Canada, September 1943.

volume of supplies estimated to be required was reduced to a level which (apart from particular problems of types) lay well within the capacity of munitions production which had been developed in the U.K. But if Britain were to attempt (or were forced) to become self-sufficient, the consequence of maintaining such a high level of munitions output at the time when the United States production would be doubly cut, because of both a fall in U.S. forces requirements and the cessation of British munition needs, would be most serious. It would have meant that the essential reconversion of British industry from war to peace, and in particular the first postwar steps towards the expansion of export trade, would have been greatly delayed. So a proposal developed that during this period the United States should continue to accept the responsibility for providing part of the British munition needs and that an attempt should be made to secure comparable reductions to the munitions programmes of the two countries. And it was felt that a similar arrangement should be made with the third member of the C.P.R.B.—Canada. The negotiations took a considerable period of time and developed in a manner which illustrated the way in which a major problem of supply of this kind was tackled at this period when the machinery of collaboration had reached its highest level.

The first stage was an informal exploratory discussion between the members of the C.P.R.B. in Washington, supported by a representative from London. This first approach led to agreement in principle to the reasonableness of the proposal, though with no further commitment. The Ministry of Production then proceeded to develop the case in London between the Service and supply departments, and after Cabinet approval arrangements were made that the subject should be discussed between Roosevelt and Churchill at the Octagon Conference held in Quebec in September 1944. The outcome of this discussion was that further agreement in principle was reached and representatives from both sides were appointed to carry discussions a stage further. Throughout this phase guidance was being obtained on the basic assumptions about levels of activity and duration of fighting from the Chiefs of Staff who were at that time assembled at Quebec. This gave the 'all-clear' for the visit of a special mission headed by Keynes and Sinclair, which was perhaps the largest and best of any of the large-scale missions which visited the States during the war on supply questions. The field to be covered was wide, ranging from military strategy to economics. The problem which had first seemed to be largely theoretical became increasingly practical as time went on, for by this time Anglo-American production had become so closely interrelated that most of the material

that the British would require from the United States under any pro
posed formula would in fact be made up of actual equipment—very
long-range aircraft, transport aircraft, specialized tropical fighting
equipment, etc., of various kinds—which the British were making on a
small scale and for which they would continue to be largely dependent
upon American output. After protracted discussions (which included
a visit to Ottawa to develop the same approach and to secure Canadian
agreement) final understanding was reached and signed by the various
parties.

Then came the end of the European war and in the first shocks of
partial reconversion the question of implementing the agreement arose
and with it a new crop of theoretical troubles, for though the agreement
had been signed between officials it had not been ratified by the President or Prime Minister, and Roosevelt, who had supported the whole
approach, was now dead. Problems arose, too, in Ottawa, where it was
felt that the continued munitions programme which the British required was unfairly high. This was a simpler question to solve, for after
certain adjustments the Canadian Mutual Aid Board accepted the
British statistical demonstration that equity between the three countries
was being preserved. The American situation was more difficult, but
was on the way to partial solution when VJ-Day came.

CONCLUSIONS

From this wide field of Anglo-American co-operation it is possible to
draw some conclusions—many of them obvious, but still worth re-stating.

There was great value in frequent visits to the other side for those
dealing in these problems. The permanent staffs in the other capital
found great difficulty in following changes in policy and emphasis, and
tended, the longer they were away, the more to see problems through
the eyes of their temporary hosts. British staffs in Washington were apt
to forget that their job was more to present the British view to Americans than the American point of view to London.

The quality of staff was of supreme importance. The large numbers
of British in Washington, and of Americans in London, became a
source of slight irritation for different reasons—the British were thought
to waste dollars, the Americans to live in a private island of plenty. The
first-class man who was acceptable to the other side could generally be
more effective away than at home, for he could influence opinion and
improve relations as well as negotiate and plan.

One recurrent problem was the level at which to negotiate. The
temptation was to call in Ministers or the very highest authority. But

this was a dangerous weapon. The final conclusion of the highest authorities might defy editing to make it a workable basis, and even if it was crystal clear it was apt to cause some resentment among those with whom the usual negotiations and discussions were carried on. And since a surprisingly high proportion of American administrators were lawyers, ways of escaping the intended decision were not hard to find. Professional honour being satisfied, however, some similar solution could usually be found. But the appeal to Caesar more often wasted than saved time.

Perhaps of greatest interest was the effect of the Combined Boards on those working in them—the sensible lessening of national feeling, the growth of association with the combined organization, and the combined front against other organizations. Some of this came from the professional solidarity which again overrode national feelings—the way the two Navies stood firm against the other Services; the common support statisticians and economists would, to a lesser degree, give each other when attacked. But this was not always the case, for professional pride could override professional solidarity. The soldiers could not bear criticisms or doubts of their favourite weapons, and the different method of approach to calculations of requirements caused endless discussions; indeed, to the end few British soldiers appeared to know how the American requirements were calculated, while most Americans knew how the British were and disagreed with the method.

Such points were important, for the American departments had a great appetite for statistical presentations, and at times it seemed that though the material was on Lend-Lease the real payment was with statistics.

But throughout the essential difficulty was to realize how great are the differences masked by an apparently common language. The mental approach of most Americans to a new problem was different—a process of 'thinking out loud' which was usually the first thought given to the subject, followed by bewildering changes of opinion which at times seemed like a double-cross. American officials did not seem to be pinned down by the decisions of their superiors as the British were. On any complex problem various American departments would openly and loudly state divergent views; consequently the British approach—the line thought out in private and followed in public—seemed constrained and suspicious. But in the innumerable discussions and meetings which made up the sum of a single negotiation, the solid presentation of the British case was not without success.

In this short survey of a most complex subject I have tried to describe how the organization for joint supply developed and worked. I have

limited myself to those developments of which I have first-hand knowledge, and my views on the success and failure of different parts of the
organization are entirely personal. This period was fascinating in itself,
but the interest is far from being historical. Very similar problems of
co-ordination and assimilation are arising now from the postwar problems—particularly on the Marshall Plan.

It is obvious that in many ways collaboration in peacetime presents
greater difficulty than in war. The objectives of wartime were comparatively simple ones to state. Both countries were working against a
common danger, and in the States there was an acute realization of
the perils and discomforts of life in the United Kingdom.

British negotiators were supported by the fact that this country was
the only one fighting the Germans in the dark days of 1940 and 1941.
Although America was in the end the largest producer and the largest
military power, it was always possible to maintain a sense of real
equality. The United Kingdom could help the United States. It could
give as well as receive.

The peacetime situation is very different. The United Kingdom is
now one of many European countries—all urgently requiring help to see
them through their economic problems. British negotiators may take
the lead in international discussions, but they feel, unavoidably, that
they are one of a queue.

But, clearly, such difficulties have to be overcome, for collaboration
in the future is vital. It would be foolish to attempt to re-create the
machinery of the past, but it is essential to remember that the human
problems behind the organization that is formed will be repeated in
peacetime—and in war or in peace are of the greatest importance.

VI

THE USE AND DEVELOPMENT OF NATIONAL INCOME AND EXPENDITURE ESTIMATES

by

RICHARD STONE

THE BEGINNING

In attempting to describe the wartime development of national income estimates in this country it is convenient to take a brief look at the state of affairs before the war broke out. At that time, hardly a decade ago, the investigators in this field were all private individuals and the works of the most celebrated of them in this country, Bowley, Stamp and Colin Clark, are well known to all economists. For, from humble beginnings, they raised a subject which, despite some brave attempts such as that of Baxter in 1867, had largely been neglected since the original *tour de force* of Gregory King, to a position of great theoretical and practical interest. From the point of view of what I have to say here the work of Colin Clark, and particularly his *National Income and Outlay* (1937), is especially stimulating. For in this book the emphasis is not exclusively or even mainly on the national *income*, but on this in relation to other economic flows, such as consumers' expenditure, government revenue and expenditure, asset formation, saving and the balance of payments. Most of the effort that has been put into this whole subject since the war began has been directed to a satisfactory workable integration of all these magnitudes into a single picture of economic change and in tracing their relationships to one another and to the different parts of the economy from which they arise.

In November 1939 three articles by Keynes appeared in *The Times*, and early in the next year these were expanded into a classical discussion of the problems of war economy and finance in *How to Pay for the War* (1940). This book is essentially quantitative, and in it much use was made of estimates of the national income and expenditure for 1938–9 prepared by Rothbarth. In the following month Keynes had privately printed a small paper entitled *The Budget of Resources*, and at this time was urging the importance of our financial problems in quantitative terms.

83

Early in 1940 an official estimate of the national income was presented to the eminent committee presided over by Stamp which was
charged with watching economic developments. This committee decided that a full financial survey was needed and the task of preparing
one went to the Central Economic Information Service of the Offices
of the War Cabinet which, in December 1940, was subdivided into the
Economic Section and the Central Statistical Office where the official
work on national income and expenditure has been continued ever
since. When I first met him, in the summer of 1940, James Meade[1] was
engaged in drawing up the plans for such a survey in the form of a
complicated system of balancing tables. I joined him in September o:
that year.

By early December Meade and I had prepared our first draft o:
what was later to become the second part of the first Budget White
Paper on national income and expenditure. There was still plenty to
be done, but at least we had a rough quantitative picture for 1938
and 1940 that made sense. We had not made ourselves universally
popular among the purveyors of facts and figures in our search for
knowledge, but on the whole people had been sympathetic and helpful
Some had been sceptical, a few thought we were mad and said so, and
one man found time to wonder on paper whether we could not find
some more useful employment in our country's darkest hour.

Meanwhile, the discussion on national finances and inflation con
tinued. Late in September Keynes had administered over the wireless
a dose of soothing syrup and by so doing he seems to have succeeded
in upsetting the financial journalists if anything more than usual. His
general line had been that while drastic financial measures would
become necessary to finance the level of the war effort we should
eventually have to make, all this was a problem for next year: this year
things were all right financially because the real effort was yet to come
The debate continued. Early in the new year the idea began to circulat
in Whitehall that something would have to be done to close the gap
that had been developing between the inside and outside views of the
financial position. Our survey of the national income and expenditur
told a story which it was felt should be more widely known and variou
proposals were made to achieve this end. The last straw was an articl

[1] James Edward Meade, C.B. 1947. Professor of Commerce (with special reference
to International Trade), London School of Economics and Political Science, since
1947; Member, Economic Section, League of Nations, Geneva, 1938–40; Econom
Assistant (1940–5) and Director (1946–7) of the Economic Section of the Offic
of the War Cabinet.

in *The Economist* early in February 1941 in which the current annual rate of the national income was put at £8,120 millions and a level of £9,000 millions was predicted for the financial year 1941–2. Preposterous, everyone said, ridiculously too high: the national income cannot be running at more than a little over £6,000 millions at the present time. 'I really think', wrote Hopkins to Keynes shortly afterwards, 'that something must be done both about the national income and about the gap. Perhaps we could talk.' They did, and before long the matter was referred to higher quarters. In a few days the Chancellor was considering a new form of Budget White Paper and Keynes was drafting the account of our financial position which subsequently appeared as the first part of Cmd. 6261.

From this point on things began to move fast. The Chancellor was prepared to take a bold step. Hopkins put his powers of persuasion at the service of the new venture of which he thoroughly approved. Keynes, on whom the principal task fell, gave of his best. A draft was prepared. Soon the comments of the pundits started to come in. Clay at the Bank recognized the revolutionary character of the document, but welcomed it wholeheartedly from the start. Robertson at the Treasury was also favourable but, as always, careful and cautious, bristling with fine points and Alice-in-Wonderland examples. Henderson reacted with strong doubts about quantitative economics in general and the procedure of obtaining items by difference in particular. Others added their meed of praise or blame and we settled down to the game of reconciling views through drafting amendments. It took a long time, but in the end it was done. On 7th April the Chancellor opened his Budget and amongst the papers that accompanied it was a new one entitled *An Analysis of the Sources of War Finance and an Estimate of the National Income and Expenditure in 1938 and 1940*. It was a great day. We drank champagne that night and felt we had accomplished something.

But I have not quite finished this account of our beginnings. Having explained the strategic role played by *The Economist* in these proceedings I must now try to make amends. This is easy, for a reference to 'The Future of Spending', the article in question, shows that the figures related to the 'gross national income'. This, it will be remembered, was Colin Clark's phrase for what is now called the gross national product, i.e. the national income plus depreciation allowances plus indirect taxes net of subsidies. From the latest figures in the *Annual Abstract of Statistics*, No. 85 (1948), we may calculate this total for the beginning of 1941 by taking the average of the figures for 1940 and 1941, and we may calculate the level in the financial year 1941–2 by

G

taking three-quarters of 1941 and one-quarter of 1942. We obtain
£7,990 millions and £8,780 millions for the two periods. Preposterous
At least £2,000 millions too high? Well, well! Such is the tyranny o
words and the depth of the conceptual muddle from which we wer
emerging, for no one took the point at the time.

USES DURING THE WAR

Any comprehensive quantitative survey of economic change require
the re-working of existing statistical sources and will usually assist i
bringing new ones into being. For example, the farm-operating serie
compiled in part to replace the wholly inadequate returns of farn
'income' assessed under Schedule B proved of considerable value i
connexion with agricultural policy and price fixing, as well as in com
piling statistics of income. Again, it was in connexion with the nationa
income and expenditure study that the regular series of the advers
balance viewed from the capital side was developed. Also, the ver
complexity of the survey will mean that it finds innumerable uses othe
than the main one for which it was principally devised. For example
the material assembled on consumers' expenditure and retail price
proved of the greatest value in the civilian consumption study begu
in 1944 to provide comparative material on the impact of the war o
standards of living in the United Kingdom, the United States an
Canada. This investigation was subsequently published as *The Impac
of the War on Civilian Consumption* (1945).

The main use of the work on national income and expenditure wa
to throw light on the magnitude of the problems of war finance, an
for this purpose it was used both in discussions before the Budget an
in the Chancellor's Financial Statement. The main burden of allocatin
resources in the war economy rested, of course, on physical controls c
one sort or another; allocation of materials, direction of labour, ration
ing, concentration of industry, exchange and capital issues control, an
so on. Equally obviously the proper management of the national fin
ances was also important. Not only was there the purely budgetar
aspect, the need to meet as much as possible of the vast war expenditur
by taxation so as to avoid undue increases in the national debt, but i
addition it was essential that financial measures should be on a scal
sufficient to prevent the tremendous pressure of demand from leadin
to a runaway rise in prices and a collapse of the value of money. Fror
the point of view of the Government, war needs greatly increased th
amount of expenditure to be financed. From the point of view of indivi
dual families, war needs greatly increased employment and hours c

work and therefore incomes of all kinds, while physical controls ensured that the quantity of consumers' goods available was greatly diminished. Consequently if substantial price increases in the free sector of goods and services and endless queues and confusion in the controlled sector were to be avoided, something had to be done to reduce the pressure of demand either by increasing taxation or by stimulating saving. To have done nothing would have led to demands for higher incomes to meet rising prices and to an immense waste of energy in the mere effort of shopping. The question was: How much had to be done? What was the order of magnitude of the problem? Furthermore, although in one way it made the attainment of equilibrium more difficult, it was also necessary to prevent price increases in the field of rationed goods and other necessaries, brought about, for example, by the increased prices of imported food, from being wholly passed on to the consumer, thus leading to a general demand for higher incomes. Hence the development of cost of living subsidies designed to stabilize the price of a wide range of necessary foods. As a result of these difficulties fiscal policy came to be directed not merely to the internal problems of financing government expenditure, but to the broader question of maintaining price and income stability throughout the economy.

This whole question was discussed in Sir Kingsley Wood's celebrated Budget Speech of 1941 in the context of the 'inflationary gap'. Starting with an estimate of £4,207 millions for total central government expenditure in 1941–2, the Chancellor deducted a little over £500 millions in respect of loans from abroad and the realization of overseas assets. This source of finance is not inflationary from a domestic point of view, since it provides funds out of the saving of other countries. Of the remaining £3,700 millions requiring domestic finance, some £1,636 millions were expected to be met from existing taxation, leaving about £2,064 millions to be met from the saving of individuals, businesses, local authorities and extra-budgetary funds which would in any case be made without the stimulus of rising incomes, and from sums set aside for depreciation and obsolescence which could not be currently spent on real assets because of wartime restrictions. The Chancellor put this part at £1,600 millions, assuming private saving at the current rate as then estimated. This left rather less than £500 millions to be financed from 'inflationary' sources such as saving induced by further increases in existing incomes and further depletion of the dwindling stocks of goods available in the shops. To mitigate this pressure of demand the Chancellor proposed new taxation expected to yield £150 millions in the coming financial year, thus reducing the gap to a little less than £350 millions, a level which was felt not to endanger economic stability.

This approach involves two things. First, the existence of a comprehensive statistical investigation which enables the budgetary position to be related quantitatively to the position of the whole economy. Second, the exercise of judgment to assess how numerous bits of economic behaviour are likely to change under new conditions. For, as is evident, the way of thinking just outlined is not tautological; it is not based on the fact that in the event the accounts will balance. On the contrary, it assumes that unless adequate steps are taken the way in which the accounts are brought into balance will be in a greater or less degree unpleasant or even dangerous. In theory, no doubt, the laws of human behaviour, so far as they concern these problems, could be reduced to tolerable exactness, but in the novel conditions of wartime and with our present knowledge this was impossible. What *was* needed was a blend of quantitative information and judgment. It was Keynes, equally at home with statistical economists and men of affairs, who in large measure provided that blend.

DEVELOPMENTS SINCE 1941

The regular use of national income and expenditure studies for the purposes of government policy raised a number of problems. In the first place, as already mentioned, the field covered had to be widened beyond the calculation of mere aggregates like the national income itself, so as to show quantitatively how the main parts of the whole economy fitted together. Second, speed of preparation became an important factor, since out-of-date figures would obviously be of little use. These requirements meant that a large mass of figures had to be collected and collated regularly and that a continuous watch had to be kept for new features in the economy and particularly in the Exchequer accounts, which need a good deal of further classification and rearrangement before they can be fitted into the general picture. A third problem arose partly as a result of those just mentioned and partly because of the way in which economic statisticians obtain their information. Unlike their colleagues in, let us say, agricultural experimentation, economic statisticians have had little opportunity up to the present to collect their data according to a plan of their own design or indeed of any design that is relevant for investigations like the present one. Instead they have to take what information is available, produced, as a rule, as a by-product of some administrative process, and adapt it as best they may to the problem in hand. From a technical point of view this is a bad state of affairs, for it is a relic of the days when the sort of comprehensive statistical survey I am describing was not needed for administrative purposes and consequently was not provided for in the records collected.

New information, the better use of existing data and revisions in basic material make continuous revisions inevitable if the resulting estimates are to be in any way useful. This need for revisions came up against a common prejudice, particularly strong in the public service, that once a figure has been given it should, for prestige reasons, be allowed to stand even though a better estimate could now be made. It is to the credit of those concerned with the official national income estimates, and particularly those not mainly concerned with the technical side of the work, that no attempt was made to pretend to omniscience, and that errors were corrected as soon as they came to light even if this involved major revisions of the published series. This change of attitude was in reality a recognition that the kind of information that the national income White Papers seek to provide is radically different from the general run of published Government statistics. The essential fact is that the national income White Papers are trying all the time to provide the best possible estimates of certain particular things rather than formally accurate figures of somewhat different things which are not really relevant. That is, they attempt to measure as best they can the set of transactions that is significant for economic analysis, rather than to reach ideally precise estimates of those parts of economic activity for which data happen to be available. Moreover, the facts are complex and interrelated within time periods and over time. This kind of information differs on the one hand from the tabulation of returns which, so far as they go, should be substantially accurate, and on the other from answers to isolated questions which lose interest and do not call for revised answers.

At the outset, in the 1941 national income White Paper, all the information given was arranged in three tables: one relating to the national income and expenditure, a second to personal income and outlay, and the last to the sources and uses of capital funds arranged to show how far funds from different private sources were available for government purposes. Two kinds of extension have taken place.

The first and most important from the conceptual standpoint was the development of a completely integrated system of social accounts given for the first time in the 1947 issue. In this presentation the national income and expenditure themselves do not appear explicitly at all, but they can be derived, together with all the other national aggregates of

transactions in which people are normally interested, from the information given. These social accounts are arranged in the form of a
set of double-entry accounts for different parts of the British economy.
Producers are kept separate from consumers and the latter are divided
between public authorities in their non-commercial capacity as the
organizers of common services and persons. Separate accounts are kept
for the operating and non-operating transactions of business enterprises
and also for current as against capital transactions. The entries in the
accounts are classified, so as to distinguish radically different types of
transaction; for example, purchases of goods are kept separate from
mere transfers. Each main heading in the accounts is subdivided
wherever possible, so as to show the source of receipts or, as the case
may be, the destination of payments under that heading, so that nearly
every separate entry has an exact counterpart elsewhere in the system.
Finally, the whole circulation scheme is closed by the addition of an
account showing the transactions between the rest of the world and
the United Kingdom. The advantages in proceeding in this way are,
first, that it is possible to see how the different parts of the economy
fit together, and second, that it is possible to derive by the aggregation
of individual items all such totals as the national income, gross national
product, total available resources, and the like.

The second line of development was to add further details about
various kinds of transaction. Starting in 1942, for example, a measure,
though admittedly not a very perfect one, has been given of the distribution of income by size. Estimates are also given of the formal
incidence of the more important direct taxes on incomes of different
sizes and types. Consumers' purchases are subdivided in considerable
detail and a measure is given of the formal incidence of indirect taxes
and subsidies, so that the value of the resources going to provide different commodities can be measured. The same purchases are also corrected for price changes, so that some idea of the volume of purchases
and the level of prices can be obtained. Obviously there is almost no
limit to the additional estimates that could be made, and the practical
restriction comes through lack of material and the resources, human
and financial, that are applied to the work.

This kind of evolutionary process of improvement can obviously continue for a long while, but the opportunity exists for a rather more
radical departure. In the expanded form the social accounts provide
an admirable framework into which can be fitted almost the whole of
economic statistics. For, while they are concerned primarily with transactions measured in money terms or with similar balance-sheet items,

there would be no difficulty in principle in placing the corresponding quantities transacted or held in stock side by side with the money figures together with the average prices at which the transactions took place. But the framework could itself be used as the basis on which to collect information, it could be made a means of statistical inquiry and not simply a conceptual mould to which all kinds of diverse and non-comparable statistics must somehow be made to conform. Such an approach would be extremely difficult to bring into effective operation, but it would have great advantages. The building up of economic statistics from the records of the same set of account-keeping entities would ensure direct comparability of records of, for example, labour, output and sales in different industries, which can only be achieved by ensuring that the same producing units constitute an 'industry' in classifying each type of return. Again, an accounting approach would provide a check on the consistency of at least part of the information, would force attention on many practical difficulties arising from differences of business practice which at present go largely unnoticed, and would extend the range of information available especially in the financial field. It seems certain that a considerable saving of effort could be obtained by avoiding the same or similar questions being asked by different authorities. Finally, the very magnitude of the task would force attention on sampling methods to the ultimate gain in the efficiency with which economic statistics are collected. Such a programme may sound impossibly difficult, but when we contemplate the field covered by government policy we should not lack the courage to provide a sure factual foundation on which that policy can be built.

In this section I have said something of developments that have already been put into practice and others that are still in the early stages. As is natural in a large subject in the course of rapid development much remains to be done. I propose to conclude this section by listing a number of topics on which further information is desirable,[1] particularly in connexion with the important problem of comparing the present level of real income with the level in 1938.

First, it will be remembered that in two of the principal accounts of the national income White Paper one of the items has been obtained by difference; the inventory component of net asset (capital) formation in the business operating account and personal saving in the personal

[1] Since this was written improvements have been made in the estimation of asset formation. In particular figures are given in the latest White Paper on national income and expenditure (Cmd. 7933, April 1950) of the value of the change in inventories and inventory revaluation for 1948 and 1949 as well as for 1938.

revenue account. The only exception to this statement is that in 1938 the whole of net asset formation was independently estimated. It is obviously desirable that these gaps should be filled as soon as possible, both on account of the important checks which direct estimates of these items would provide and because of the importance of inventory formation and saving in the economic system.

Second, if direct estimates of inventory formation were made it would be possible to attack the problem of the correct valuation of inventory changes for social accounting purposes. It is generally agreed that inventory formation should be represented by the average value, in some sense, of the physical change over the period. Implicitly at the present time the measure is equal, apart from error, to the change in value as reckoned in the assessment of profits for income tax purposes.

Third, considerable reserve is needed in using, for social accounting purposes, the figures at present given for depreciation and obsolescence allowances. These provisions are mainly based on Inland Revenue allowances and therefore, in accordance with ordinary accounting convention, on original cost. As a consequence they are inadequate as a guide to the replacement cost of assets currently being used up and worn out in view of the steep rise in prices over the last decade. Allowance for this factor might conceivably reduce the money national income by as much as 5 per cent and its profit component by a corresponding absolute amount.

Fourth, as the White Paper points out, the price index of consumers' goods and services inevitably fails to make full allowance for quality changes, with the result that the price rise is to some extent understated over the war period while the corresponding volume of consumption is overestimated. It may well be that the bias on this account does not exceed 5 per cent, but this is not a negligible amount in the comparison of real incomes. The change in the 1947 White Paper from an 'ideal' price index to a current weighted aggregative, though accompanied by distinct advantages, also had the effect of reducing the apparent price rise.

Fifth, consumers' expenditure, as its name implies, measures expenditure on goods and services bought by consumers, with the exception of land and buildings, and does not measure the consumption of these commodities in the sense of the value, either at original or replacement cost, of the amount currently used up and worn out. This has an important bearing on the interpretation of the figures. In the early stages of the war when restrictions began to be imposed on the supply of durable consumers' goods, purchases fell sharply, but the services rendered by the existing stock in the hands of consumers continued and only slowly diminished as the equipment wore out. After the war the total stock, in most lines at any rate, was considerably below the 1939 level, so that for a time a much higher rate of expenditure in real terms was needed to make possible the pre-war level of services from consumers' durable equipment.

Sixth, comparison is complicated by the growth of government services during the war and especially by the growth of those concerned with economic controls. These services are usually thought of as intermediate services or services to enterprises rather than as services to final consumers, and this view implies that they are to be regarded as an element in the cost of the final goods they help to produce and distribute rather than as final goods themselves. They are, of course, part of the national income, for there is no reason to distinguish between the income earned by a clerk in an enterprise from that earned by one in the civil service. And there is no reason to suppose that they 'appear' in the profits of enterprises that 'benefit' from them, since they are rendered free so that on the assumption of competition they would not be reflected in prices. They represent an element in the excess of the social over the private cost of the final goods and services which they help to produce and distribute, and consequently, since they are not charged for, obscure the full extent of the price rise that has taken place. As a rough approximation their value should perhaps be deducted from the national income if an ordinary price index is to be used in estimating real income. The extent of the true price rise can then be measured by dividing the quantity index so obtained into the national income as ordinarily calculated.

Of course, it is not necessary to regard these services as intermediate; it can be argued that they are final services designed not to increase material production, but to provide the final service of fair play. If this line of argument is adopted, however, it must be recognized that, with given prices, the diversion of a given value of productive factors from the production of, say, chocolate, to the rationing of the smaller quantity which their absence from the chocolate factories would entail, will leave the real national income unaffected.

The last four factors all operate in the same direction in a comparison of the position since the war with the position before the war. Together they are almost certainly capable of accounting for the discrepancy between the conventional comparisons of real income based on adjusting money national income estimates for price changes and the much less optimistic picture suggested by common observation and the inspection of what information is available on levels of physical production.

USES IN PEACETIME

On pp. 86–8 I outlined the use of national income and expenditure studies in providing a quantitative basis for fiscal policy designed to maintain financial stability and to prevent financial conditions from hindering the realization of economic objectives thought of in real terms. But in the words of the 1945 national income White Paper 'there is nothing in this method which limits its application to wartime'. The principal difference is that in wartime the brunt of economic change must for practical reasons be borne by physical controls such as rationing, restriction, allocation and direction, whereas in peacetime much more could be done to achieve social ends by fiscal and financial policies. Anyone who believes in the maintenance of a social economy and the avoidance of the totalitarian direction of all aspects of economic life must be concerned at the present time with the creation of an institutional framework which will permit a social economy, with the essential features of free markets, free choice of occupations and free choice in the spending of disposable income, to function more in accordance with contemporary social ideals. In the achievement of this goal and in re-drafting the rules of the economic game in such a way that both *laissez-faire* and overall physical control are rejected as a basis for economic organization, national income and expenditure studies and their extension to the technique of national budgeting have, I believe, a great deal to offer. Let us examine this contention in some detail.

The problems in connexion with which, by comparison with the pre-war position, institutional re-drafting is generally felt to be most necessary may be arbitrarily grouped under three heads. The first of these concerns the level and stability of economic activity as a whole. Before the war not only did total activity fluctuate up and down, but its average level at least in the years between the wars left a great deal of resources unemployed. As a country we could have been economically as well as socially better off if the fluctuations had been less severe and the average level of activity had been higher. Since the war we have experienced the opposite situation. We should have been better off if we had not tried to do so many things at once and as a consequence of this found it necessary to introduce, maintain or reintroduce measures which impede the even flow of production, discourage effort and enterprise, and diminish the part played by individual choice in determining the composition of output.

The second concerns the distribution of income between rich and poor, between individuals in and out of work, and between individuals with differént family responsibilities. A considerable amount had been done by fiscal and other policies to redistribute income, but it was commonly felt that more was needed. Indeed, the principal objection to the free market system of distribution arises from the fact that with very unequal incomes the less urgent desires of the rich are satisfied before the more urgent desires of the poor. With a socially acceptable distribution of income this objection would lose its force. Of course, this problem does not exist in isolation and the effect on incentives and therefore on production of any proposed change must be taken into account.

The third set of problems may be grouped together under the heading of actions in restraint of trade whether by associations of enterprises or by trade unions. The Government itself is far more willing than heretofore to take a hand in restraining trade mainly in the interests of one form or another of physical planning.

The application of national income and expenditure studies to the first of these problems is well known and it is in this field and to a less extent in the second of those mentioned above that they have most to offer. The problem is essentially one of equilibrating effective demand with potential national production. This is a matter which must be tackled, if it is to be tackled at all, in quantitative terms; that is to say, one must be able to compare the value of potential national production in the forthcoming period with anticipated final expenditure on goods and services of all kinds. Such a comparison involves setting up some standard of the full employment of resources, since it is in terms of this standard and the current level of money values that the value of the potential national product must be calculated. The standard taken must to some extent be arbitrary, but the aim should be to choose a standard which, if achieved, would permit the maximization of production over time. The standard of zero unemployment would not achieve this aim, since it would permit no flexibility in the economy. It would also cause instability of money values and would have an adverse effect on incentives. Equally, a standard set too low in terms of the employment of resources would equally fail, since resources would be wasted which, if employed, would increase and not decrease aggregate output.

Against such a standard must be set expected final expenditure; that is, the sum of consumers' expenditure, government expenditure on goods and services, net domestic asset formation and the excess of exports over imports. If this total exceeds potential output the economy will become mainly a sellers' market and will exhibit those symptoms usually associated with the term inflation. The normal visible signs of this state of affairs may be suppressed to some extent by controls, as they have been since the war, but the condition itself will remain. In such circumstances means must be found of reducing aggregate demand by bringing about conditions in which some or all of the buyers of final goods wish to reduce their purchases. Exactly the opposite holds if aggregate demand is defective in relation to the standard; conditions must be created in which some or all of the buyers of final goods wish to increase their purchases.

Once the decision has been taken to attempt to bring about a balance by acts of conscious policy, it is necessary to have the sort of accounting picture I have described in order to assess the magnitude of the task and to ensure that the various elements in the policy are consistent and sufficient. The policies themselves may be of many different kinds. Under a regime of physical controls an inflationary situation would call for a general tightening up, as was intended in 1947 when it was decided to cut the capital expenditure programme. Another method would be to raise interest rates to a point at which capital expenditure would be sufficiently curtailed as a result of the higher cost associated with it. Yet another procedure which would operate principally on consumers' expenditure rather than asset formation would be to increase taxation while leaving government expenditure unchanged, as was done in the Budget of November 1947, thus increasing government saving and reducing the disposable income accruing to individuals. Formally, at any rate, very similar results could be obtained by operating with government expenditure, but the practical advantages of this would differ considerably according to the type of expenditure which it was proposed to vary.

A common feature of all these policies, whether physical or financial, is that they are greatly aided by, even if they do not in part depend on, a statistical programme of national budgeting based on the national (or social) accounts. Of course, the assembling of facts and figures however appropriate they may be does not necessarily indicate the right line of policy and still less does it ensure wise decisions. But it does bring out clearly the nature of the problem and, what is equally important, its size, so that steps can be taken which are not only in the right direction, but also appropriate in magnitude so that the objective is reached and is neither fallen short of nor overshot.

National budgeting is useful because it throws some light on the

question of whether the national accounts of the next period are likely
to balance in a desirable way or whether they will only be brought
into balance by the forces of inflation or unemployment. Moreover,
apart from the overall position an attempt to draw up the social
accounts for the year ahead gives some indication of how far different
parts of total demand are compatible with other factors. Thus the total
of current expenditure and asset formation may be just what is needed
to maintain a 'high' level of employment, but at the same time it
may be that the level of asset formation presupposes an impossibly high
level of saving. If this is the case steps must be taken either to increase
saving or to diminish asset formation and to readjust total demand in
the light of these changes. Again, the balance of aggregate supply and
demand may imply a disequilibrium in the balance of payments with
other countries.

But these accounting identities are not the only relationships between
the different economic variables that have to be satisfied. In addition
there are a number of relationships of an institutional or behaviouristic
and technical character of which account must be taken if the national
budget or plan is to be more than a collection of figures. Given the
level of total income, its distribution, relative prices and similar factors,
there will be a certain collection of final goods which the community
will wish to buy. In a highly active economy with little flexibility as
a result of a lack of surplus capacity, and especially one which is recovering in a period of general shortage from the ravages of war, it will be
quite easy to write down an estimated level of total demand which looks
all right in the aggregate, but which involves implicitly a demand for
certain goods in excess of what can be supplied in the period in question.
In order to deal with this sort of problem more would have to be known
about the factors which determine the overall supply of and demand
for different commodities. Thus national budgeting leads on to a study
of other relationships than those of an accounting kind. I believe that
more work on these lines ought to be undertaken because I think that
such investigations are a prerequisite to any successful economic policy
which is not based on *laissez-faire* or totalitarian control.

INTERNATIONAL CO-OPERATION

The increase in official interest during the war in national income
and expenditure studies and the development of these studies as a
consequence from the stage of academic enquiry to the status of administrative statistics led, among other things, to endeavours to improve
international comparability. Before the war the works of Colin Clark

in England and Simon Kuznets in the United States, to mention only two of the principal writers on these subjects, were read the world over and contributed to the development of an international language in matters of national income. The same may be said of the series of methodological volumes issued by the Conference on Research in Income and Wealth in the United States which was founded in 1936. This body acted as a focus for the many workers on national income problems in that country and its works became widely known outside the United States.

Meade and I contributed to the *Economic Journal* (June-September 1941) an article on national income accounting which incorporated the general ideas of his original financial survey modified in the light of our subsequent practical work for the first national income White Paper. Shortly afterwards I endeavoured to put the official estimates of the United States on a conceptual basis comparable with those of this country in the *Economic Journal* (June-September 1942) and in a paper to the Manchester Statistical Society (October 1942). These papers brought me into contact with Milton Gilbert, at that time chief of the National Income Unit of the Department of Commerce, and drew forth a comment from him which appeared in the *Economic Journal* (April 1943).

In 1944 consultations and discussions between experts on national income and related topics in the United Kingdom, the United States and Canada began. In the summer a committee was set up by the Combined Production and Resources Board under the chairmanship of Morris Copeland to investigate and compare wartime consumption levels in the three countries. This committee later issued a report already referred to, entitled *The Impact of the War on Civilian Consumption* (1945), which throws a great deal of light on constructing and comparing measures of consumers' expenditure. Shortly afterwards talks on national income problems were held in Washington which were attended by Milton Gilbert and his colleagues at the National Income Unit, by the late George Luxton of Canada and by myself. The object of these discussions was to compare the conceptual and statistical treatments employed in the three countries and to examine the problems of presenting these estimates within a common framework. The broad conclusions of these discussions were presented to the 1945 Conference on Research in Income and Wealth held in Washington in a paper by E. F. Denison which was published in *Studies in Income and Wealth*, Vol. X (1947). In the meantime many of the recommendations have been embodied in the revised estimates of national income and expenditure for the United States which appeared in a supplement to the *Survey of Current Business* for July 1947. This is a truly monumental work which all who see must admire.

The end of the war with Germany made it possible to resume contacts with countries on the continent of Europe. During the war Ed. van Cleef in the Netherlands had developed a system of social accounting (which he termed national book-keeping) and this was developed by J. B. D. Derksen and others at the Central Bureau of Statistics at The Hague. A brief account of this work is available to English readers in Occasional Paper X of the National Institute of Economic and Social Research, written by Derksen during a brief visit to this country in the autumn of 1945. This system has proved of fundamental importance in the work of the Netherlands Central Planning Office set up after the war under the direction of J. Tinbergen.

Other visitors to this country in 1945 and 1946 who were especially interested in national income problems were F. Perroux and his colleagues from France, A. van der Aa from Belgium, P. J. Bjerve and O. Aukrust from Norway, and I. Ohlsson from Sweden. In all cases the interest in national income studies sprang from the needs of government policy, and the technical discussions were conducted largely with these needs in view.

Many other countries developed national income statistics over this period and in many cases these studies started with the general layout developed in this country or the United States.

At the end of 1945 the League of Nations convened at Princeton a sub-committee of the Committee of Statistical Experts to consider problems of national income statistics. I had the honour to prepare a memorandum for this sub-committee and to act as its chairman. In the report which was circulated to governments in 1946 and was published in 1948 by the United Nations Organisation, the social accounting approach was considered in detail and endorsed. Discussion showed that there was with few exceptions close agreement among those present.

More recently several international agencies have started work in the field of national income and social accounting largely with a view to making the vast mass of statistics now available from all over the world more accessible and to improving the international comparability of the estimates. In 1948 the Section of National Income Statistics and Research of the Statistical Office of the United Nations under Derksen produced an invaluable compendium of national income statistics covering thirty-nine countries, entitled *National Income Statistics,*

1938–1947. National income work has played a large part in the research programme of the Economic Commission for Europe, as can be seen from the surveys issued annually. In 1949 the Organisation for European Economic Co-operation set up a National Accounts Research Unit with the object of assisting the provision of national accounts information in the participating countries and of improving its comparability. This last development has arisen out of the recognition of the importance of national income and expenditure studies for practical administrative purposes, this time in the international field.

It is clear from this brief description, which is by no means exhaustive, that in this subject which twelve years ago, in its practical aspects at any rate, was a veritable Tower of Babel, there has been developed a common language and on many of the most pressing problems a common point of view. It is to be hoped that in the coming decade this advance will be consolidated. With this object in view a new association, the International Association for Research in Income and Wealth, was founded in September 1947 at the time of the International Statistical Conferences in Washington. The Association is a working body whose membership is composed of scholars actively engaged in the fields of interest to the Association, which are the definition and measurement of national income and wealth, social accounting and its use in economic budgeting, international comparisons and aggregations of national income and wealth, problems of statistical methodology connected therewith, and related matters. The Association hopes to further research by bringing scholars into closer contact with one another, by the circulation of documents and bibliographical material, by the arrangement of conferences of scholars from time to time, by co-operation with other professional organizations, and by other appropriate means. Its main activities so far have taken the form of circulating quarterly world-wide bibliographies on income and wealth begun in 1948, the preparation of longer-term bibliographies and the holding of a conference in Cambridge in September 1949.

CONCLUSIONS

I hope that the conclusions of this survey of the development of national income and expenditure studies have already emerged fairly clearly. It may be useful if I group together the main lessons that seem to me important.

First, estimates of national income and expenditure and related totals have emerged from the stage of academic development to the status of essential administrative statistics for policy purposes in a large number of countries. This is very generally recognized. But those who will the end do not always will the means, and the resources devoted to the work are not always commensurate with the results anticipated.

Second, while much has been achieved much remains to be done. The thorny problems of comparisons between countries with very different institutional arrangements have only begun to be examined systematically. Again, the social accounts, as they are drawn up at present, reflect at best only private costs and benefits. For many purposes it would be useful if they could be made to reflect the social costs and benefits of different economic activities.

Third, there is a widespread recognition of the advantages of an accounting approach and an accounting form of presentation. Less generally recognized is the advantage of gaining the co-operation of the professional accountant in a field which has hitherto been the preserve of the economist and statistician.

Fourth, great possibilities are opened up by the possibility of applying the accounting approach not merely to the solution of conceptual problems and questions of presentation, but to the whole field of the collection of data. It is hard to see how statistical design can otherwise be introduced into this field.

Finally, there is need for continued and extended co-operation between all who are working in this field. Colin Clark, little more than a decade ago, sought single-handed to map out the whole economic structure of the world. This goal seems now within sight of achievement, though it is still a long way off.

H

VII

THE PROBLEM OF CO-ORDINATION IN AIRCRAFT PRODUCTION

by

E. DEVONS

THE NEED FOR FORMAL CO-ORDINATION

The problem of co-ordination was more important in the Ministry of Aircraft Production than in the other supply departments. For although M.A.P. was responsible for the production of many items, such as bombs and dinghies, supplies of which were not closely interrelated, most of the output which the Department covered was used either directly in aircraft or as spares for aircraft. For each aircraft a large number of components—engines, propellers, undercarriages, turrets, equipment, etc.—had to be made. One of the most difficult tasks in aircraft production was to ensure that the plans for the production of these components fitted in with the plans for final aircraft output and the need for spares.

This problem of co-ordination would have been easily solved if there had been an official of superhuman capacity who could have comprehended fully and realistically in his own mind the whole range of choice open to M.A.P. in deciding what to produce. Such an official would have compiled day by day perfectly co-ordinated programmes for every section of the aircraft industry. But M.A.P. never had an official of this calibre and decisions on the pattern of output had to be delegated to thousands of individuals in M.A.P. and in the firms. The task of co-ordination was to secure that each of these individuals acted in a way which fitted in with what all the others were doing.

In the early years of the war most planning action in M.A.P. was based on the assumption—an assumption implied but not usually recognized—that the necessary co-ordination would be achieved if each directorate in M.A.P. responsible for component or raw material production based its plans on the agreed aircraft programme. The aircraft programme was indeed a vital co-ordinating instrument; yet experience showed that adequate co-ordination was not secured by leaving each directorate to base its plans on what it thought was needed for the aircraft programme. Such a system resulted all too often in the oversupply and waste of some components and desperate shortage of others.

As a result of this experience a special directorate—the Directorate-General of Planning, Programmes and Statistics—was set up with one of its main functions to ensure that the plans of the individual production directorates fitted in with each other. Looking back on the experience of M.A.P. it is possible to discover why such special co-ordinating arrangements were necessary, and the limits to the degree of co-ordination that could be achieved even with such special arrangements.

While planning was left to each separate directorate with the aircraft programme as the only connecting link, it was not the duty of any of the directorates concerned to ensure that the supply of components would be adequate for any given aircraft programme or for any proposed changes in that programme. Had it been possible to formulate an aircraft programme and then instruct each directorate that it was its job to supply the components for the fulfilment of that programme, the problem would have been relatively simple. But this would have implied that airframe capacity was in every case the limiting factor in aircraft production; and that if airframe capacity was considered adequate to meet the programme, components, equipment and raw materials supplies could be made available relatively easily. This was not invariably nor even usually the case.

Final aircraft production itself depended on the volume and type of component, equipment and raw material supply that could be made available; and the principal problem in drawing up the aircraft programme was to decide which combination of aircraft would best meet the needs of the Service departments, taking into account possible expansions in components, equipment and raw material capacity and the various alternative ways in which that capacity could be used. So that any given published aircraft programme represented the completion of the process of choosing between the various alternatives open to M.A.P., not only in the use of airframe capacity, but also of components, equipment and material capacity. It could not, therefore, be regarded as the starting-point from which the individual production directorates could proceed. The decisions as to the uses to which component capacity could and should be put and the plans for further expansion had to be taken before, not after, the aircraft programme had been drawn up. It is true that such decisions were often merely implicit in the agreement to proceed on a given aircraft programme and that executive action was usually taken by the individual component production directorates only after the programme had been issued; but the assurance that such action was possible and would yield the results expected had to be given before and not after the issue of the aircraft programme.

It was often thought, and indeed maintained in argument, that this assurance could be obtained by consulting all the directorates concerned with the supply of components, equipment, materials and labour before issuing the aircraft programme. But this was only possible where the question at issue was such that the directorates could give an unambiguous yes or no in reply. For example, suppose the possibility of making ten more Spitfires a month was being considered. The directorates might be asked whether they could supply the extra engines, engine accessories, propellers, equipment, radio, raw materials, etc., for this additional production. They could give an unequivocal answer to this question only if they based it on the assumption that no other supplies were to be interfered with and that they were not to consider extensions of capacity beyond those already agreed. But it was just these assumptions that those asking the question would usually not wish to be made. They would want to know at what cost, either in terms of a sacrifice of supplies to other aircraft in the programme or in terms of extensions to capacity, the additional ten Spitfires could be produced.

As soon as the question was asked in this form it was impossible to answer yes or no, and therefore impossible to obtain the answer by asking the individual directorates. For the cost, in terms of alternative aircraft or spares to be given up or in terms of expansions of capacity, could be expressed in innumerable alternative ways. And it was necessary for someone who appreciated the alternatives in the case of each individual directorate to choose that range of combinations of choices which would be most significant. To come to the conclusion, for example, that if the Air Ministry would be prepared to see the Stirling programme cut by five aircraft a month and agree to some change in policy as to the fitment of engines to the Beaufighter, it would be possible to build ten extra Spitfires a month without any extensions of raw materials or component capacity. And it was in this form, and not the simple yes or no form, that all changes in the aircraft programme had to be considered. For it was hardly ever true that a proposed change could not be achieved at any cost in terms of sacrificed alternatives.

It was sometimes argued that discussion of the whole range of choice and selection of the most suitable one could be achieved by calling all those concerned to a meeting. But this method hardly ever worked satisfactorily. Production directors were not adept at carrying in their minds the various production possibilities that were open to them and the consequences of each on their plans. In any case such meetings were confused and inconclusive unless someone had beforehand limited the range of possible choices to the two or three which he thought the most significant and from which he considered the final choice had to be made. It was this limitation of the problem of choice to two or three courses of action which was essentially the function of the co-ordinator.

The problem of choosing between the various possible combinations of aircraft and components was complicated by the fact that components were needed for repair and squadron maintenance as well as for embodiment in complete aircraft. Constitutionally, the Service departments were responsible for deciding what supplies should be ordered to meet spares needs, even though in most cases the spares orders were placed through M.A.P. From the point of view of the provisioning sections of the Service departments these spares could be calculated unequivocally according to rules laid down for them, and the final result gave an unqualified figure of the volume required. Normally, however, these demands and those for complete aircraft could not all be met in full. But there was no regular machinery by which the conflict between these two demands could be resolved. The provisioning sections of the Service departments thought of their needs as absolute and had no means of balancing them against the needs of new aircraft. The production directorates in M.A.P. did not usually know the basis on which these spares demands were calculated and therefore could not assess the importance of meeting them as compared with the demands for new aircraft. In addition the production directorates were not concerned with the allocation between various uses of the components produced; they considered their job completed, and quite rightly, when the components supplies left the factory. And yet every issue of the aircraft and component programmes implied a resolution of this conflict between the demands for spare components and those for new aircraft. Whenever a component was in short supply it had to be decided how far the shortage could be met by cutting the supplies for spares and how far by reducing new aircraft output.

The need to have some body of officials concerned with these issues, outside the production directorates and the provisioning branches of the Services, was strengthened by distrust of the methods used by the Services in making their calculations and the ponderous machinery involved in their revision. Every change in the aircraft programme involved some revision in the plans for squadron formation and this should have resulted in turn in a revision of the demands for spare components. But the Service departments had a fairly rigid system of reviewing their demands for spares only once in every six months. Since each review took many months to complete, the results were often related to out-of-date aircraft and squadron formation plans. In revising and keeping up to date production programmes for major components, such as engines, propellers, undercarriages, etc., enormous waste and difficulties in production would have resulted if M.A.P. had taken these estimates of the Service departments as the basis for their production planning.

Further, in the later years of the war when the labour force available to M.A.P. was strictly limited, every major revision in the aircraft programme had to be followed immediately by revisions in the components programme if the required labour was to be released. In these circumstances it was impossible to wait for revised spares calculations from the Service departments. Someone in M.A.P. had to assess what should be allowed for spares so that revised components production programmes could be issued speedily. And this was a task which the production directorates were neither willing nor competent to undertake.

The function of co-ordination had to be performed continuously, not merely when an entirely new aircraft programme was under consideration. For the factors influencing the relation between aircraft and components supply were changing daily. This was not merely because the Services were continually changing their demands, but also because the prospects of fulfilment of individual aircraft, component and equipment programmes fluctuated from day to day. A continuous struggle was waged in planning between the realistic and target principles[1], and the programmes for every aircraft and component represented a compromise between the two opposing forces. The degree of realism or target was, of course, never the same in all programmes at any given time. To have planned the relationship between the various· programmes at their full face value in each case would have resulted in waste and repeated breakdowns in production. It was dangerous to leave each Director-General to allow for this factor in his own programme. For each would have insisted that all other programmes

---

[1] 'Target planning' was based on the assumption that firms would do their best only if the programmes gave them a target a little in excess of what they could really achieve. 'Realistic planning' argued that planning on such a target basis would inevitably lead to waste and lack of balance in component supplies; and that maximum output would be achieved if all programmes were based on a sober estimate of what it was really expected the firms would produce. For a full treatment of the relative merits of target and realistic planning, see my book *Planning in Practice* (Cambridge University Press, 1950), especially Chapter II.

should be 100 per cent realistic, but that he should be allowed to have any target element in his own programme which he thought necessary. This meant that some officials who had no vested interest in any individual programme except the final aircraft programme had to allow for this factor. Someone had to decide what risks should be taken in the light of possible future changes in Service demands and of the likely fulfilment of the various aircraft, component and equipment programmes.

This task was complicated by the inefficiency of the production directorates in assessing the likely fulfilment of the promises put forward by the firms. Many of the production directors learned little from production experience and continued throughout the period of the war to accept almost without question the optimistic estimates of the firms. Criticism of these estimates had, therefore, in many cases to come from somebody outside the production directorates, although that was not essentially a co-ordinating function.

There was also the risk that where the planning and the allocation of capacity were left to each directorate with the aircraft programme as the sole co-ordinating instrument, deficiencies in production would be concealed by each directorate for as long as possible. And by the time disclosure could no longer be avoided it was often too late to make the changes in the aircraft programme which would have been made if the deficiency in components supply had been revealed when it was first known to the production directorate concerned. The tendency to conceal any possible fall-down on programme was common, because such a deficiency nearly always brought a flood of criticism which never redounded to the good reputation of the responsible directorate. The production director was tempted to conceal the deficiency until the last moment in the hope that its disclosure could be avoided altogether; either through some change in the aircraft programme which would reduce the demand for the component, or because the production of some other item would fall short to an even greater extent than the one for which he was responsible. It was vital, therefore, to have some officials without such a vested interest in concealment watching the progress of the production of each component in relation to the requirements for aircraft and spares.

There was one other important reason why leaving the process of co-ordination to the individual production directorates led to waste and confusion. For every change in the aircraft programme which was put into effect, many were considered and rejected. If each production director had been aware of all the proposed changes he would have been working all the time on shifting sands. He would be tempted to take into account in his day-to-day decisions the latest proposal which was under consideration, for he would have no means of knowing which of the proposals was likely to be accepted and which rejected. It was essential, therefore, that discussion of proposals at the preliminary stage should be confined to a group of officials who, while they were not taking day-to-day decisions, could yet assess from their knowledge of the plans for components and equipment supply whether the changes were likely to be acceptable to M.A.P. They would be in a position to decide which proposals should be rejected forthwith and which should be given further consideration. In the latter cases they could also decide whether any of M.A.P.'s major proposals for changes in production capacity for components or equipment would be seriously affected by the proposed change in the aircraft programme. The co-ordinators could in this way act as a barrier preventing the many fantastic proposals for modifying the programme spreading throughout M.A.P. and causing alarm and panic.

ESTABLISHMENT OF THE PLANNING DIRECTORATE

It would be wrong to conclude that all the above arguments were in the minds of those in M.A.P. who decided to set up a Directorate of Programmes, Planning and Statistics. They were, however, the main justification for its existence and played an important part in influencing the scope of its activities once it had been established. When it was first started in 1941 the Directorate confined its activities to looking after the issue and revision of the aircraft programme and the collection of statistics indicating the actual progress of production. It soon discovered, however, that it could not exercise the function of issuing a realistic aircraft programme and calling attention when necessary to the desirability of amending that programme, unless it could be sure that component production had been planned on a scale adequate to meet aircraft and spares needs. But it could not obtain this assurance from the production directorates for some of the most important components, because there were no long-period programmes showing what was to be produced. For example, in the case of aero-engines there was merely a short-period forecast showing output only three months ahead. In the case of propellers and propeller equipment even this meagre information was not available. This was partly because the officials in the production directorates did not realize the importance of drawing programmes, and partly because they lacked the necessary information on what would be required to meet the needs for spares. They worked, therefore, on a hand-to-mouth basis. In such circumstances planning decisions were taken by default rather than by carefully and consciously considered choices from various possible courses of action.

The planning directorate felt compelled to persuade the production directorates to draw up programmes showing expected production of each type of component by each firm over a period of two years ahead. The planning directorate assumed joint responsibility with the production directorates for these programmes and they were issued as official M.A.P. plans. The first to be drawn up was for aero-engines. At that stage the central directorate was still learning the technique of programming and working out methods of allowing for spares needs without depending on the provisioning branches of the Air Ministry. But once acquired, the same technique could be applied to other components, and within a short time programmes were issued regularly for engines, power plants, radiators, carburettors and magnetos; propellers, constant-speed units and spinners; undercarriages, wheels and tyres; turrets, aircraft guns and bombs; and for certain items of radio equipment. In drawing up these programmes the Directorate had to satisfy itself both that supplies would be adequate to meet requirements and that they could be achieved within the limits of existing capacity or new capacity planned to come into operation at some time in the future.

A substantial part of the total supply of some of these components was due to come from the United States and Canada. The rate of supply expected from these sources had to be fitted in with the plans for production in the United Kingdom. As the central directorate assumed responsibility for programming home production it found it necessary to draw up comparable programmes for supplies from overseas. In consultation with the British Air Commission in Washington a programme for North American supplies was therefore drawn up. The planning directorate took on the responsibility for ensuring that this programme was revised in accordance with changing United Kingdom requirements and production and allocation expectations in the United States. It thus became the main channel of communication with the B.A.C. on programme matters.

As the planning directorate assumed important programme responsibilities it had to be closely associated with all discussions that took place on the total manpower to be allocated to M.A.P., and the effects on the aircraft programme of changes in these allocations. Eventually it took over the duty of calculating the labour needed for any given programme, and of assessing the cuts that would have to be made in the programmes if effect was to be given to the manpower allocations.

Statistics of production, employment and stocks were essential in fulfilling these planning and co-ordinating functions. A large part of the time of the directorate was spent in collecting this information and ensuring its accuracy and consistency, so that it could be used without too much hesitation as a basis for planning future production or allocating components in short supply. Regular comparison of production and programmes was also the best way of calling attention to deficiencies. To this end the Directorate compiled and circulated throughout the department regular statistical bulletins, with a commentary calling particular attention to those items where things seemed to be going wrong.

THE LIMITS OF CO-ORDINATION

The exercise of these planning and co-ordinating functions gave rise to innumerable problems. Of these the most important was the question how far the Directorate should extend its activities. All the efforts made by M.A.P. to deal with the problem of co-ordination demonstrated that planning must be a compromise between two inevitably opposing tendencies. The effective planning of any given component demanded that the official concerned should be familiar in great detail with the production problems of that section. The more he knew of the detail of these production problems the better able he was to judge what capacity would be needed for a given programme, what output could be obtained from a given capacity, and which of the requested changes in programme could be met and at what cost. But the more expert he became in the problems of this particular section the less he knew about the other sections of the industry and, therefore, the less able he was to take account of the effects on his own section of what was happening elsewhere. As a result he might be an efficient planner in the sense that he could assess fairly accurately how much labour, materials and factory space were needed to achieve a certain production of the item with which he was concerned. Yet, because he was unaware of what was happening in other sections, he might make bad mistakes in deciding what was needed from his own section and might arrange for production which would give the wrong quantities and selection of items.

On the other hand, officials who spent most of their time trying to ensure that the plans of the individual sections fitted in with each other had to know something about every section of the industry and, therefore, could not know in detail the production problems and possibilities of any particular section. As a result the plans they drew up might be perfectly co-ordinated, in the sense that if the production laid down by them for each section were achieved the right supply of components and spares would come forward for the aircraft that were being made; and yet their plans might be rendered nugatory because they were not related to production possibilities.

Every official in the central directorate was continually being faced with this dilemma. He knew that if he was to draw up a realistic programme for the component which he was looking after, he ought to know nearly as much about production possibilities as the production directorate. Yet he also knew that if he spent his time becoming a specialist in that field he would have little or no time to find out what was happening to related components or to the prospects and production plans for the aircraft to which his component was to be fitted.

Take, for example, the field of responsibility of the official in the central directorate responsible for the propeller programme. He had to assess the reliability of the estimates of production capacity put forward by the firms and the production directorate. He had to be aware of the progress of propeller production so as to give ample warning in advance of any short-fall that was likely to affect the aircraft programme or supplies for spares. He had to know what supplies could be expected from the United States; whether these would have to be modified before they could be fitted to British aircraft and, if so, at what rate that modification could be done. He had to be able to calculate at short notice whether the propeller programme could be adapted to meet some proposed change in the aircraft programme; and if this necessitated an expansion of capacity whether such an expansion was possible and, if so, at what cost. He had to know something of the progress of propeller development to ensure that the latest types were included in the production programme at the earliest date possible.

In addition to all this he had to know what was happening in the spheres for which his colleagues were responsible. He had to be aware of the likely fulfilment of the programmes for each aircraft type, so as to take account of any short-fall or excess over programme in planning propeller production. He had to be familiar with any discussions of prospective alterations in the aircraft programme, and had himself to decide whether to take the risk of allowing for these in any changes he was then making to the propeller programme. He had to watch progress in components related to his—for example, the power plant and constant-speed unit—so as to have warning as early as possible of any change which would require an alteration to propeller production. He had to allow for spares requirements, for although constitutionally the decision on this issue rested with the Service departments, experience soon showed that he could not accept their estimates without question. The resolution of conflict between spares and new aircraft requirements was largely his responsibility, and when quick changes had to be made in the programme—and this was the usual and not the exceptional case—he would have to make his own estimates of what to allow for spares. In making such estimates he had to take account of supplies that would be forthcoming from repaired components.

If he was to cover this wide range of problems, a senior official of the planning directorate could not take charge of more than one major component and one or two minor ones associated with it. And if he was to take action in line with that of his colleagues in the planning directorate, the total field covered had to be limited.

The need to limit the field of the central directorate can be seen most clearly when one considers the duties of the head of that directorate. His main function was to co-ordinate the activities of his colleagues and act as the main spokesman of the directorate. He had to draw the attention of the Chief Executive to the need for revising the aircraft programme and had to advise him on the possibility of providing supplies to meet any changes in the programmes proposed by the Service department. Sometimetimes he was given time to consult his staff, but often, particularly when various possibilities were discussed at a meeting with the Service departments, he had to give a view on the spot. This meant that he had to know nearly as much as each of his senior colleagues about component production and plans, and the possibility of modifying these plans. Also, that he had to keep his senior colleagues fully informed of the latest proposed changes in the aircraft programme so that they could decide whether these should be allowed for in their component planning, and so that they, in turn, could draw his attention to any important effects on components planning which he had overlooked. For this to be done successfully the total staff had to be small enough for him to see them all practically every day to discuss the latest developments.

Although it was necessary for these reasons to limit the field over which co-ordination was attempted, it would, of course, be a mistake to overlook the errors in planning which were bound to result from such a limitation. It was implicit in the methods used by the planning directorate that a change in the aircraft programme would be adopted if it considered that the major components for which it issued programmes could and would be made available. It was thus assumed that the plans for all the unprogrammed items would somehow or other be adapted to the change. Obviously such an assumption often proved unwarranted.

The central planning directorate was all the time torn between the desire to extend its activities to more and more components in order to secure a greater measure of co-ordination in M.A.P.'s production activities, and the fear that if it took on too much either its plans would become unrealistic or it would become so big that its own activities would need co-ordinating. The exact sphere which it could on balance cover most efficiently was not worked out from first principles, but had to be discovered by trial and error in actual practice. The field which could be covered depended on three major factors: the brainpower and co-ordinating ability of the officials concerned; the variables that had to be taken into account and the rate at which these variables changed; and the speed with which action had to be taken. The less able the officials concerned, the more numerous the variations in the factors which they had to take into account; and the greater the speed with which decisions had to be taken, the smaller the sphere of activity which they could usefully attempt to co-ordinate. The more able the officials, the more stable the variables and the longer the period which could be allowed for co-ordination before taking action, the more extensive the field over which co-ordination could usefully be attempted.

Now, these three major factors—ability of the officials, number and degree of changes in the variables, and the time allowed in which to take a decision—were, of course, continually changing throughout the war. There were some periods when the whole aircraft programme was under discussion and quick advice had to be given on the desirability of choosing one of the many different courses of action. On these occasions the need for co-ordination was at its greatest, but the task of co-ordination most difficult. The head of the planning and programmes division was so occupied attending meetings where prospective programme changes were being discussed that he had little time to see even his senior colleagues. In consequence they knew little of what was going on and he lost touch with important developments in components production. Such was the multiplicity of changes being discussed and the speed with which he had to give answers, that the most he could achieve was to take account of the effects of any proposed change on the most important component—engines—and in these circumstances co-ordination was limited to the engine-aircraft relationship. At the other extreme, when a new aircraft programme had been issued and all subsidiary programmes had been adjusted to it, there was usually a period of relative quiet when co-ordination was comparatively easy. It was on such occasions that the staff complained of lack of work and were tempted to extend their co-ordinating activities to new spheres. But they learned by experience that such periods of quiet never lasted long and that the temptation to take on more programmes had to be resisted. Indeed, one of the main features of the task of co-ordination was that it was easiest when least needed, i.e. when conditions were fairly stable, and most difficult when it was most necessary, i.e. when conditions were changing rapidly.

It was often asserted that lack of statistics set a limit to the extent of co-ordination; that if one only had complete and accurate statistics about all the variables to be taken into account, perfect planning and co-ordination would have been possible. This was a complete fallacy; for although adequate statistics were necessary, it was the limitation in the number of interrelated variables that could be comprehended by one brain that was the effective limiting factor. When decisions had to be taken quickly, which was the usual case, there was not even time to examine in detail the statistics which were in fact available; the decision had to be taken on the basis of the rough-and-ready orders of magnitude that the co-ordinators carried in their minds. Perfect co-ordination could have been achieved only by supermen.

IMPLEMENTATION OF THE PROGRAMME

There was another major factor, apart from these intellectual difficulties, which limited the sphere of co-ordination which the planning directorate could undertake. This was the enormous amount of time and energy which had to be spent by its officials in arguments and discussions as to what the correct programme should be and whether the programme once laid down should be implemented. These disputes arose because the central directorate did not always possess the power to ensure that its views were enforced. As a co-ordinating directorate it inevitably overlapped with the activities of other directorates and departments. Every function which it undertook impinged on the activities of some other directorate. In drawing up the undercarriage programme, for example, it was in theory the responsibility of the undercarriage directorate to say what could be produced and of the provisioning branches of the Service departments to say what was required. Inevitably, in trying to close any gap between these two the planning directorate had to take a view of the reliability of the estimates put forward by each side. But it had no executive power to override the view of either side. It merely acted as an advisory body to the Chief Executive in M.A.P. and could recommend to him the programme that should be issued, pointing out in what respects its proposals met neither the wishes of the Service departments nor the view of the production directorate.

For the machinery to work smoothly it was necessary that only a small number of major issues of dispute should be put to the Chief Executive, and that all others should be solved without asking for his intervention. Even when it was generally recognized that the planning directorate had the support of the Chief Executive and that he would adopt their advice if the issues were put up to him—and this was not always the case—the resolution of these conflicts absorbed an enormous amount of time and energy. On many occasions in order to secure the issue of a programme the planning directorate had to adopt the views of the production directorates or the Service departments, even though they felt these were grossly mistaken.

The influence of the planning directorate was most powerful in the engine programme, largely because it was generally recognized that the relationship between the engine and aircraft programmes was so complex that it could only be appreciated by the officials who understood the main features of both. It was least powerful in the case of radio and undercarriage equipment. In these cases the programmes issued by the planning directorate to a large extent merely reflected the views of the production directorates or the Service departments, and the planning directorate could only hope that as the course of events proved these views wrong the planning process would be improved.

The stage of dispute and argument did not finish with the issue of the programme. Only aircraft and engine contracts were automatically placed in accordance with the programme. The provisioning and finance divisions of the Service departments and of M.A.P. did not feel bound to alter their contracts to accord with revisions in other programmes. The officials of the planning directorate had therefore to spend much time persuading them so to alter their contracts. If they did not succeed, as often happened, they would then try to persuade the production directorates, and through them the firms, to arrange their production in accordance with the official programme and not in accordance with the contracts they had received.

These disputes inevitably gave rise to confusion and exaggerated the difficulties of securing co-ordination between various sections of the industry. They also absorbed much of the time of the officials of the planning directorate and limited the field over which they could extend their activities.

IMPORTANCE OF INFORMAL CONTACTS

As has been explained earlier, in drawing up and discussing revisions of programmes the planning directorate had to assess the reliability of production estimates put forward by the firms, and to be on the look out for any signs indicating that the programme would not be met. Suppose that M.A.P. was discussing with the Air Ministry the possibility of increasing the output of a particular type of aircraft and that this aircraft absorbed all the undercarriages of a particular type which were being produced. Then it was obviously important that those taking part in the discussion should know whether the firm making that particular type of undercarriage was likely to achieve its programme. Similarly, the planning directorate had to gauge the next likely moves in Air Ministry and Admiralty policy, for these had to be taken into account in any revisions of component production plans. For example, suppose that a project to expand propeller capacity to meet existing requirements was being considered in M.A.P. If it was thought likely that the Air Ministry would request a change in the aircraft programme in the near future which would increase the demand for this propeller, this would be an added reason for proceeding with the project forthwith. On the other hand, if the Air Ministry was expected to reduce its requirements for the aircraft taking this type of propeller, that would be an argument for postponing a decision on the expansion project.

To the newcomer to the problems of co-ordination it seemed easy to ensure that the planning directorate were given this necessary advance information. It merely needed an instruction to the production directors that they should provide the central directorate with the earliest warning of any sign that the programmes for which they were responsible would not be fulfilled. In fact such co-ordination by instruction never worked. The production directorates were not always themselves fully aware of what was happening at the firms. In any case such an instruction invariably aroused the suspicion in the production directorates that the planning directorate were trying to interfere in matters which did not concern them.

In order to get the information they needed the planning directorate used two main lines of attack. Firstly, they engaged in the most subtle forms of spying they could contrive. The most effective was to find some person in the production directorate who had a grievance, worm one's way into his confidence, and then get him to 'spill the beans' on what was really happening in his directorate. This activity varied in usefulness as the power and influence of the central directorate fluctuated. If it was generally known that that directorate could get things done, officials who were making no headway in trying to get action taken by their own directorates would often provide information to the central directorate and urge them to press for some action to be taken. In these cases it was, of course, always implicitly understood that the central directorate would not divulge its sources of information, for that would have jeopardized the position of the informant and he would be reluctant ever to take such a risk again. The other main line of attack was to discover officials either at M.A.P., the firms, or the Air Ministry who realized the importance of co-ordination and were not over-sensitive about the prestige of their own directorate, cultivate their acquaintance or even friendship where this was possible, and use them as the main instruments of co-ordination, especially in an emergency when quick decisions were necessary.

It was by such channels that the most efficient co-ordination was achieved and yet it would have been quite impossible to bring such a system into being by administrative arrangements. Take, for example, the problem of co-ordination between M.A.P. and the Air Ministry on the aircraft programme. It was clearly of great value to those doing the programming in M.A.P. to know the issues being debated in the Air Ministry which would affect the demand for aircraft, for they would be able to take these into account in their own work. They could also stop the Air Ministry wasting its time considering schemes for which they knew M.A.P. could not provide the aircraft. Similarly, it was of value to the Air Ministry officials responsible for planning the formation of squadrons and equipping them with aircraft to know the latest production developments in M.A.P., particularly any revisions in the aircraft programme that were being considered for production reasons. Yet it was impossible to arrange formally this interchange of advance information, although it was essential to efficient co-ordination. For each department was unwilling to admit officials of the other to its own secrets. Each feared that information so gathered might be used against it in interdepartmental argument, and wished to guard against premature action being taken by the other on schemes which were still under debate. But such interchange became possible, and did in fact take place regularly, as soon as the officials concerned in M.A.P. and the Air Ministry got to know each other well, found that they could trust each other, and as a result were prepared to divulge secrets which constitutionally they should have kept to themselves. It became common practice, for example, for the head of the planning directorate in M.A.P. to tell his contact in the Air Ministry

I

of any important proposed change in the programme being considered by M.A.P., both so that he could find out whether the Air Ministry were likely to welcome the change and also so that the Air Ministry official could take account of it in his own work. But the existence of such contacts could not be officially recognized and depended on each side feeling confident that the other would not give him away or use the advance information in any way to bring criticism on M.A.P. or on the Air Ministry.

The success or failure of the activities of the planning directorate in M.A.P. depended principally on the extent to which they were able to build up such contacts in the Service departments, in the production directorates and at the firms. They were most successful in aircraft, engines, propellers and raw materials and least successful in radio equipment. For many reasons the relations between the planning directorate and radio production directorate were formal and official, and as a consequence the central directorate attempts at radio planning were never very successful.

POSITION OF THE DIRECTORATE

Although the central directorate had to criticize the plans of the production directorates, it had itself to be above criticism. For it could only maintain its own position and ensure that its programmes and suggestions for revising these programmes were taken seriously if the advice on which they were based was accepted without fear of contradiction. For if it became generally known that the central planning directorate was being compelled to issue plans and programmes with which it did not agree its word would count for little throughout the department, and the numerous unofficial contacts on which it depended to fulfil its co-ordinating function would gradually wither away. For example, the official in charge of calculating raw material requirements was not likely to consult the planning directorate about future changes in programmes and tell them whether raw materials would be available if he discovered by experience that the changes which that directorate had in mind were regularly being turned down. The prestige of the directorate, therefore, had to be of the highest order.

The prestige of the directorate could only be maintained if it had the support of the head of the production divisions of M.A.P.—known at first as the Controller-General and later as the Chief Executive. It was not only necessary that the planning directorate should be directly responsible to the Chief Executive, but also that the Chief Executive should normally be prepared to accept its advice on programme matters. The usefulness of the planning directorate varied directly with the esteem in which it was held by the Chief Executive. At times its advice was ignored or not even sought on major issues of programme policy, and it was then unable to fulfil any of its functions efficiently. When it was generally known that its activities were being supported and its advice being taken by the Chief Executive its power was substantial.

The power of the central directorate was naturally open to abuse. To retain this power the directorate had to ensure that experience demonstrated that it gave the right advice. To achieve this it had to be certain that if the plans which it laid down for component production were fulfilled, no aircraft would be held up for lack of components. It was always tempted, therefore, to over-insure against all possible risks, for there was no special motive driving it to keep these insurances to a minimum. True, over-insurance would lead to a surplus and waste of components, but such waste was never very obvious—on the contrary, many officials regarded the presence of large stocks of components as evidence of good planning—while the existence of a single aircraft without some necessary component was always sufficient to excite heated argument and discussion.

Further, since in the last analysis an estimate of whether components would be available for any proposed aircraft programme was largely a matter of judgment, there was always the danger that the officials concerned in making such judgments would be influenced by their own views of the desirability of the objectives which the proposed change was meant to achieve. For example, if an official in the central directorate was asked whether components would be available for an increase in the programme for a particular aircraft, and he felt that such an increase would be a mistake because in his view the usefulness of the aircraft and the purposes to which it was to be put were exaggerated, it was almost inevitable that he would allow himself to be influenced by this view in making his judgment about the availability of components.

Yet another paradox in the successful operation of the co-ordinating directorate was that although it had to have substantial power and be certain that its advice would normally be taken, yet it had to be absolved from responsibility. For technically it was merely advising the Chief Executive on programme matters. Since its function was essentially co-ordinating, it was dealing all the time with matters which were the prime responsibility of other directorates or departments. As has been explained earlier, the production directorate was responsible for assessing capacity, and the provisioning branch of the Air Ministry for calculating requirements. The planning directorate could suggest to the Chief Executive that these estimates were wrong and that others should be used in drawing up the programme, but even if the Chief Executive agreed it had then to proceed to persuade the directorate primarily concerned to alter its estimates.

If it had taken over complete responsibility for ensuring that the programme really represented the production which the firms were capable of achieving, this would have had unfortunate consequences. Firstly, it would have weakened the sense of authority of the production directorates. They would have felt aggrieved because their functions were being usurped, and would also have disclaimed responsibility for the estimates of the central directorate and might, therefore, have refused to be bound by the official programme. It was essential, there-fore, that it should appear that the final estimate was theirs, even if the central directorate found it necessary to interfere and criticize. Secondly, if the central directorate had attempted to assume the major responsi-bility for assessing productive capacity it would have found it necessary to argue with the firms concerned. This would have been disastrous, for the central directorate would then have found itself dragged into dealing with the firms on detailed production issues. The discussion and solution of these would have taken so much time that the staff would have had to be enlarged or the more proper tasks of co-ordination would have been neglected. In either case the machinery for co-ordination would have broken down. This is just one more example of the general problem of co-ordination, that of finding the best balance between appreciating in detail the various aspects of one or two of the variable factors in the problem under consideration and that of assessing the significance of a large number of factors concerned but only in general terms. The co-ordinator had to be perpetually on his guard against succumbing to the temptation of becoming a specialist on one particular section, for this could only be achieved at the cost of his ignoring all other issues and so failing to fulfil his essential function as a co-ordinator.

One of the most difficult problems of co-ordination was that of securing staff. For it can be realized that to exercise their functions efficiently they had to be endowed with the most peculiar qualities. The most important capacity was that of being able to think in terms of figures. The co-ordinator had to carry in his mind in quantitative terms the various aspects of the problems with which he was concerned and be prepared to give advice on the basis of this knowledge. For he might be called in to a meeting or discussion at a moment's notice to discuss the practicability of some proposed change in programme. Given that capacity he possessed enormous power, for anyone at a meeting who could promptly present in quantitative terms the various alternatives that were open and the consequences of each could usually ensure that the course of action which he thought most advisable was adopted. Secondly, he had to realize that all problems of planning are problems in the choice between alternatives, that a decision to produce more of one product was at the same time a decision to produce less of something else. It was for this reason that those with some training in economics usually made, other things being equal, the best planners. But neither of these capacities was of any use unless the official possessed a manner, character and ability which enabled him to develop friendly relations with the production directorates and Air Ministry divisions with which he was concerned. He had to be able to criticize without irritating, to advise without appearing to interfere, and to worm his way into their secrets and confidence without appearing to spy.

Lastly, he had to realize the full limits of his capacities in relation to the task which he was attempting: that by its very nature perfect planning and co-ordination was impossible and that in the last analysis the advice he gave had to be based on judgment rather than a scientific examination of facts. Those who were best at planning and co-ordination in M.A.P. were those who felt that complete overall planning and co-ordination by one directorate was quite impossible.

VIII

THE CONTROL OF BUILDING

by

IAN BOWEN

The wartime control of the building and civil engineering industries began in October 1940. In the main it is a story of a struggle over manpower. The crucial fact for the industry during the war was that it had to sacrifice 64 per cent of its labour strength[1] to the Forces and to other industries. The necessity for control arose from this fact: that the steadily diminishing labour force had to be used to the best advantage in the gravest years of the emergency. That the method of control was successful is sufficiently proved by the volume of the work that was done on government account under very difficult working conditions by this depleted operative force.

The Government Building Programme, as it came to be called, was composed in the earlier years of the war first of the new construction for direct war purposes of airfields, camps, training establishments, defence works, storage depots and all kinds of military installations, and secondly of industrial premises, with all the necessary accompaniment of hostels and housing, roads and streets, and public utilities, to feed the Forces with munitions on an unprecedented scale. This new construction alone cost over £300 millions a year in 1940 and 1941. In addition, there was a minimum amount of maintenance cost that had to be permitted; and there were finally the unpredictable fluctuations in demand for labour to repair air-raid damage.

It is difficult to give any figures that fully illustrate the size and complexity of this programme. Altogether some £2,100 millions of work was done by the building and civil engineering industries from the beginning of 1940 to the middle of 1945, 61·5 per cent of this being for government purposes, including local authorities' expenditure on A.R.P. and air-raid damage. A more picturesque statistic was given by a Minister of Works: when speaking of the airfield programme he remarked that we had laid enough carriageway in the war to drive a

[1] This figure refers to the percentage decline in the insured male labour force between July 1939 (1,362,000) and July 1944 (496,000), when the force was reduced to its minimum.

30-feet wide road from London to Tokyo. The point is that the achievement was not just the spending of a large sterling sum; the huge factories—small new towns, they might be called—the immense runways,
the endless camps for our own and millions of allied troops, were ready
on time, and so were the floating harbours of Mulberry, the oil pipe-
lines, and the secret wireless and radar installations for the dawn of
D-Day.

Yet all this was done by an industry that lost 64 per cent of its labour
force, and for which the programme at every stage seemed to be far
beyond its capacities. It is therefore worth while inquiring on what
principles the manpower problem for this industry was solved. How
were men sent, or induced to go, to the right places at the right time?
How were the different programmes fitted in together?

PROGRAMMING FROM SEPTEMBER 1939 TO OCTOBER 1940

In the first year of the war the most striking feature about the building
and civil engineering industries was the high level of unemployment.
The number of totally unemployed males aged 16–64 in building and
public works contracting (now known as civil engineering) during the
first ten months of 1940 were as follows:

January	354,028	June	102,969
February	365,548	July	92,849
March	199,907	August	87,023
April	160,136	September	88,846
May	135,553	October	78,334

This phenomenon was caused by the closing down of new civilian
building and in particular the winding-up of the housing programme,
which had been effected in 1939 principally by means of financial
measures.

A large programme of new works could be, and was, carried out by
the departments in 1940, without much competition for labour, or even
for materials, until the third quarter of the year. The need for some
co-ordination between the departments had, of course, been recognized, and the machinery for attaining it was an interdepartmental
committee. This was called the Works and Buildings Priority Committee. As the title of the Committee suggests, its main purpose was
to secure a priority order for materials or labour if and when conflicting
claims of the departments rendered such a course necessary. The Committee was a subcommittee of the Ministerial Priority Committee, and
its successors the Production Council and the Production Executive.

The reasons why this organization proved to be inadequate for the task ahead were threefold: first, it had the weakness of any inter-departmental committee working within the British government system, wherein the departments enjoy such a large measure of autonomy. In a word, it did not have the weight or backing to secure even adequate returns or statistics from the individual departments, let alone effective action. Secondly, the actual machinery of control was far too small for the job; an efficient secretary with a fairly small staff were all the assistance that the Committee was allowed. Civil service overstaffing often occurs, but this was a case of ludicrous understaffing, and co-ordination, however wisely and well planned, was bound to fail for this reason alone. But thirdly, the co-ordination was in fact planned on entirely wrong principles. Here, as in other phases of the war effort, the priority principle was doomed to disappear. Until the principle of allocation of resources to definite purposes was found acceptable, any attempts at co-ordination were of necessity ineffective.

These were the three fundamental reasons why this organization had to be entirely revised; and the remedy adopted by the Government was to set up the Ministry of Works in October 1940. Formally, this appeared as a change of name for an old organ—the Office of Works was turned into a Ministry; but what in effect happened was the creation of a new Ministry with new staff, and the Office of Works was (during the war) a relatively unimportant section in the new Ministry.

The occasion for this change was not the real shortage of manpower, but the alleged shortage of building materials. How this 'shortage' arose affords an excellent example of bad paper planning at its worst. After the fall of France there was a drive to build defence works all over the country: pill-boxes, anti-tank ditches and emplacements, coastal defences of every kind, and home-made Home Guard pillars and blocks, began to spring up everywhere. This used a large amount of cement. Home deliveries averaged 688,000 tons a month for April to June 1940, and 792,000 tons a month in July and August. At the same time the civilian population awaited the first onslaught of the Luftwaffe with natural anxiety, and the occasion was seized, especially by the extreme Left, to agitate for the building of air-raid shelters. In this situation the Works and Buildings Priority Committee called for a statement from the departments on their needs for building materials to complete their programmes. Then occurred, in an extreme form, the phenomena known as 'rough estimating' and 'departmental caution' which were to cause anxiety to all co-ordinating bodies throughout the war. Figures were put in by the departments which had little foundation in fact; the common feature of them all was that each administrator through whose hands they passed added, sometimes substantially, to the safety margin already included.

When all these figures were totalled it appeared that the needs of the Government alone would far outstrip the total production and stock capacity of the country, as far as that could be estimated. The Government, on the strength of these figures, had to announce that an extensive shelter programme was out of the question in view of the anticipated demand of materials, and they were also led to impose a rationing scheme for cement.

The position when the Ministry of Works came into existence was thus very confused. Already it had been discovered that despite the shortage (on paper) of cement, the rationing scheme was unnecessary; apart from a few local shortages due to transport difficulties demand could easily be met. A large new call-up from the building and civil engineering and building materials industries was due. How far it was going to be safe to proceed with this depended on the labour force in the industries and the numbers needed to 'complete' the Government's building programme. But no estimates for these demands were available other than the simple additions of totals, the sum of all the departmental pipe-dreams.

Thus for the fourth quarter of 1940 the departments were asking for almost astronomical quantities of bricks and cement, and even these figures were not prepared until one month of the quarter was nearly over. On the other hand, their building plans in terms of *expenditure* were, as events afterwards showed, extreme *under*estimates, due no doubt to the difficulty of programming for the smaller items of work. What this amounted to proving was that neither millions of bricks, nor tons of cement, nor £ s. d. were very practicable units of measurement for programming ahead.

Within its limitations the Works and Buildings Priority Committee had begun the pioneering work of getting a Government Building Programme into shape. Each department had been induced to submit to the Committee a list of its works in hand, to be let before a certain date, or projected. The departments had furthermore classified their projects under three priority symbols: W.B.A., Neutral and W.B.Z. W.B.A. is a symbol still in use to-day,[1] though few who use it realize that the 'W.B.' refers to the all-but-forgotten Works and Buildings Priority Committee of 1940, and that the 'A' represented first priority at that date. In practice very few applicant departments were willing

[1] June 1950.

to relegate any substantial portion of their work to the Neutral or Z categories, with the honourable exception of the Office of Works itself, which agreed, under some pressure, to postpone many of its normal repair services to royal palaces and government buildings. The competing claims for resources of the Service and supply departments were not solved by the self-classified listing of works to be finished.

THE ALLOCATION SYSTEM

In the spring of 1941 a new system of control was worked out and put into operation. An explanation of it was given by Mr. George Hicks (Parliamentary Secretary to the Ministry of Works and Buildings) in the House of Commons in these terms:[1]

'We have, therefore, instituted a new system which is just coming into operation, whereby we first estimate the total quantity of building of which the resources of the country is capable in each given period. We measure this by value and, in accordance with the instructions of the Production Executive, we allocate it between Departments so that each Department knows what share of the building capacity of the country it will have at its disposal for a given period. . . . It is the job of the Departments to arrange within their own allocation which jobs are to be speeded up, which to be stopped, and so on. We are limiting the programme so that the amount of construction work to be undertaken will be as closely as possible related to the labour and materials available, and, as far as possible, only those works which will be effective before or by the end of the summer are being proceeded with. Works requiring a longer period for their completion or new works, are only being permitted if they are of great strategic importance.'

This statement raises a number of points on which comment at a later stage may be appropriate. Its relevance to the development of the labour allocation system is contained in the first two sentences. At March 1941, it is clear, the idea of allocating work by value rather than by a labour allocation or labour ceiling was still being entertained. One principle of the labour allocation had, however, already been adopted: to give each department a ceiling (or allocation) of work and to leave the division of this capacity between projects to the discretion of the department. This principle was basic to an orderly form of devolution. It put an end to long and feverish meetings of officials when list upon list of projects had to be gone through one by one with a view to determining their A, N or Z priority. From time to time in the war, later

[1] 370 H.C. Deb., 19th March 1941, Col. 177.

in 1941 and thereafter, similar attempts to vet detailed lists of projects at interdepartmental meetings of officials were revived, but either had to be abandoned or resulted in long, fruitless and frequently adjourned discussions.

A second point in Mr. Hicks' speech deserves attention, namely the reference to the Production Executive. It must not be thought that the ancient and proud departments of State like the Admiralty and War Office, or the new and go-getting ones like Supply and Aircraft Production, welcomed any tutelage on building plans from the newest department of all (Works). Quite clearly no one department, and certainly not the most recently formed, could be expected to lay down the law to all other departments of Whitehall, especially as some of the prohibitions or restrictions on construction cut right across the policy and plans of the staff and Ministers of nearly all the other Ministries. The prestige of the Production Executive, and at a later period of the war of the Lord President's Committee, were indispensable to the successful working of any programme. Every decision taken, after interdepartmental consultation, in the Ministry of Works had to take the form of advice to this higher authority. Because of this 'all-powerful sanction', this 'court of appeal of unquestioned authority and decisive judgment',[1] which was fully accepted both by Ministers and (perhaps more important) by their officials, the new system had a special chance of success.

It was not long before the 'value allocation' ideas of March 1941 were superseded by a thoroughgoing labour allocation system. A final push in the direction of adopting such a scheme came from the side of statistics; money expenditure from month to month—a quarterly check-up being too crude a basis of control—could not be reckoned accurately, while labour employment might be. Moreover, some five months of planning had convinced the new team of administrators that since labour was the commodity in short supply a direct allocation of that article was logically, as well as practically, the best procedure.

This idea proved to be acceptable to the Production Executive and from May 1941 a labour allocation system was in operation. The position, it was then seen, was as follows. The total building labour force in the country was thought to be of the order of 750,000 men. This estimate, which was frequently quoted in Ministers' speeches as late as the autumn of 1941, was based on knowledge of one figure only—

[1] These phrases were applied to the Lord President's Committee in a letter to *The Times* by Sir Hugh Beaver of 8th April 1947, which emphasized the point made here.

that 1,023,000 men had been insured at July 1940. This figure represented a decline of 359,000 on the figure for July 1939. No one knew how fast the call-up or the drift to other industries had affected the industry since July 1940.

It is worth observing that a technical point of great importance affected the procedure of the administration. It normally took several months to complete the count of insured workers classified by industry groups at the Ministry of Labour. No figures for July 1941 were to be expected until October. Thus, up to October 1941 all that could be known was the number insured at July of the *previous* year. Hence administrators were forced to make their own guess at wastage from the industry, and 750,000 was the net remainder at which they arrived. It is easy to be wise after the event and to point out that the actual number of men insured at July 1941 was 919,000.

Faced with the bleak prospect of a complete absence of statistics for long periods at a time, and furthermore with the fact that no existing statistical series gave any indication of the nature of employment or whereabouts of the building labour force, the Ministry of Works set up its own statistical organization. In so far as this statistical system was used to operate the labour allocation scheme it needs to be briefly described.

Statistical Controls

The labour allocation system was worked by a threefold statistical control. In principle this threefold scheme was extremely simple, and so were the statistical returns inaugurated for this purpose.

First, in order to assess the new work coming forward all projects had to be notified to the Ministry of Works on a form known as B.P.2. This asked for details of the project, its value and material requirements, and the labour that it would need during its lifetime. In practice the value figure given was of use only as the basis of a rough check on the labour estimate and because by totalling the values some useful controls could be worked out. The materials requirements were practically valueless, since they were put in as estimates only, not always being based on quantities, and because the materials supply section of the Ministry was never interested in them. Throughout the whole war materials supply went through the normal channels and there were rarely any shortages since the market steadily declined.[1] The value of

---

[1] An exception to these remarks is the case of cement. The Cement Control based its policy on a statistical forecast of demand obtained through the programming and statistical sections. Even in this case, however, the B.P.2's, as such, were ignored.

the B.P.2 was solely as a basis for estimating future *labour* demands.

Second, there was the monthly check-up on the departments' labour force. Here again the responsibility was put on the departments to make a monthly return of labour on a form called W.B.1 for each job of over £5,000 in value, and a summary return for all jobs of less than £5,000 in value. So began, in April-May 1941, a record of the monthly labour employment of the building labour force of Great Britain. The departments fulfilled their responsibilities in regard to these labour returns with varying degrees of completeness. Some departments preferred to use their own forms. Others were persistently late with their returns. The system began haltingly but gradually improved. By 1942 it was possible to circulate a figure of labour employment by departments at the end of any month by the 21st or 22nd of the following month. This did not mean, unfortunately, that all the detailed returns were in by that date, and it was some weeks before an analysis by types of work or by place of employment could be issued.

The third statistical control was the result of Defence Regulation 56 AB, whereby all building and civil engineering undertakings were compelled to register with the Ministry of Works. Under this regulation the Minister of Works was empowered to make orders requiring:

(*a*) the keeping of such records relating to the carrying on of the said activities (building and civil engineering) as may be specified by or under the order;

(*b*) the making of such returns, at such times, in such manner and containing such particulars, whether as to number, qualifications or otherwise, regarding persons employed in any of the said activities as may be so specified;

(*c*) the production of such books or other documents, and the furnishing of such information, relating to the carrying on of the said activities as may be so specified.

He used these powers to obtain a census of the industry for July 1941. The first results of this census were circulated in September 1941. Later censuses were taken for January 1942, May and November of the same year, October 1943, November 1944, May 1945 and thereafter quarterly. The series of dates throughout the war indicate that they were chosen not for statistical convenience, but as and when the administrative need of having an up-to-date figure for allocation purposes became pressing.

The moral of this is, of course, that if the Government allocates or rations something it has to have the necessary figures. To obtain those figures may involve the setting up of an expensive and elaborate machinery. As against this, the figures so obtained may be almost invaluable for many other purposes besides the immediate administrative reason for which they were mainly desired, as indeed proved to be the case for the statistics secured on the building industry.

The Administrative Machine

Development of statistics provided the tools for regulating the war-time building programme, but the use of the statistics was not left to economists or statisticians. The Minister of Works put the whole responsibility for the Building Programme on to one man, a Director-General, in whose hands lay in considerable measure the administrative as well as executive responsibility for the Ministry's affairs. (For some time there was not even a Permanent Secretary at the Ministry.) The Director-General appointed a Director of Programmes and this officer operated the scheme of control, the sanction for which, as has already been explained, was received from a Ministerial committee with Cabinet backing.

The Director of Programmes and a Statistical Officer reported direct to the Director-General, so that the chief executive was also in immediate control of planning. Parallel with these officers were a Director of Building Materials (this Directorate later divided into Directorates of Bricks, Cement and Roofing Materials), a Director of Plant and Labour Requirements, an Administrative 'Counsellor',[1] and other directorates whose functions do not concern the question of labour organization. The Director of Programmes was, in fact, the key figure in the allocation of labour. He, like the whole of the organization except the 'Counsellor' (who was a permanent civil servant), was himself a technician; the first director being a managing director of a large building firm and his successor an architect. Thus the Directors of Programmes could vet projects submitted by departments with a critical eye; they were not likely to be misled by technically inaccurate descriptions of work, and their practical knowledge gave them an immense advantage in carrying out their administrative functions.

The whole emphasis and balance of this organization was changed

[1] The Counsellor's chief functions developed into those of administrator in charge of the provisional registration of building and civil engineering firms made under Defence Regulation 56 AB, and as officer responsible for all the Ministry's contacts with the industry on questions of policy.

in the later years of the war. The organization that is here described is that which worked out the original allocation scheme; it was set up in Lord Reith's[1] period as Minister (October 1940 to February 1942) and, as far as the wartime programme was concerned, it operated more or less unchanged until D-Day. New organizations were, however, set up in connexion with air-raid damage and plans for postwar housing.

An interesting feature of the organization of the new Ministry was that it represented a substantial departure from the normal civil service framework; the theory of the seniority of the administrative grades was never completely abandoned but in practice the technical directors had to perform tasks of administration. They were organized to carry out this function under a Director (later Controller) General with the usual hierarchy of Assistant Secretaries and Principal Assistant Secretaries frequently by-passed on matters of policy. The official theory of government gradually re-asserted itself, as it was bound to do, but it is difficult to say just how far it was effective at any given date. Certainly it is not inaccurate to speak of the so-called 'technicians' acting as administrators from 1941 to 1945, for in those years they had to do so under the pressure of events. Three comments may perhaps be permitted: first, that it is difficult to swim against the tide—since the official organization could not be permanently overthrown it might have smoothed the working of the machine to accept the official theory after about two years, and re-grade the technical officers (including the chief executive himself) as administrators, and similarly for the 'technicians' (business and professional men) who were brought into the Ministry of Works in 1944 and 1945. Secondly, after the initial basic theory and techniques of control had been worked out their operation became a strictly administrative affair—but one which still needed technical advice (i.e. advice from special types of businessmen—civil or consulting engineers, or contractors or architects); again, the appointment of *some* technicians as administrators, and the grading of others as advisers might have averted some of the 'red-tape delays' of which there were some justified complaints from time to time in 1944-5. Finally, the last phase of the Ministry's work, the active planning of the

[1] Reith, 1st Baron, cr. 1940, of Stonehaven. John Charles Walsham Reith, P.C. 1940; G.C.V.O., cr. 1939; G.B.E., cr. 1934; C.B. 1945; T.D. 1947; Kt., cr. 1927; Director-General, British Broadcasting Corporation, 1927-38; Chairman, Imperial Airways, 1938-9, and first Chairman of British Overseas Airways Corporation, 1939-40; Minister of Information, 1940; Minister of Transport, 1940; first Minister of Works and Buildings, 1940-2; Director of Combined Operations Material Department, Admiralty, 1943-5.

postwar housing and building programme (there was a Director of Postwar Building Programmes at work for over three years) partly fell into confusion through the re-introduction of amateur administrators at too late a phase in the development back towards a peace-time professionally staffed administrative machinery; although this must not be taken as criticism of the individual ability of any of those concerned either as technicians or administrators, nor of the very vigorous work done on the scientific and technical side under the direction of some of the late-comers to the organization.

The Director of Programmes drew up a balance sheet of labour for each month. On the one side was the total labour estimated to be available for two to three months ahead; from it were deducted such items as the probable amount to be used on civil building for mainten- ance purposes, unemployed, men in transit between jobs, and clerical workers. The net figure represented the total operatives likely to be available for the programme. This was then subdivided between the departments. So far the planning represented paper operations only, even though the allocations were agreed one by one between the Direc- tor of Programmes (or Director-General) and the department con- cerned, or were referred for a decision to the Production Executive. It may well be asked (a) how these paper operations were transmuted into some kind of reality, and (b) on what principles the allocation as between the departments came to be fixed or was fixed at the start.

Translation of allocation into reality was by way of the Ministry of Labour machine. A building labour division was set up in the Ministry of Labour, and this division had to work in daily contact with the programming division of the Ministry of Works. The Ministry of Labour represented operational tactics, while the Ministry of Works represented headquarters strategical planning. If, after a few months, by which time the statistical checks were in working order, the Ministry of Works dis- covered that any department was employing a considerably larger amount of labour than it had been allocated, instructions were given through the Ministry of Labour to the local employment exchanges that requests for labour from contractors working for that department should not take precedence over the requests of any other department. This began by being, and always remained, the most effective of the administrative measures that could be found to keep each department within its allocation limits.

Many difficulties arose from the nature of the labour supply machin- ery and of the organization of the building industry, but before some of these are described the original basis of the actual allocations allotted to departments ought to be mentioned. This was, perhaps unheroically, fixed as roughly equal to the actual labour which each department was employing at the time when the allocation system began. This was, in fact, the only practicable course. Grave as was the future outlook for an extensive building programme, there would have been little sense in, and enormous political and administrative opposition aroused by, cutting down the level of employment already enjoyed by the departments. The best that could be hoped was that the wilder fancies of the building planners would be pruned as time went on, so that projects became completed more rapidly, and so that dates of completion could be given to Ministers with some fair chance of their being realized. As things were, when the allocation system began none of the major projects started in 1939 or 1940, and still in course of construction, seemed certain of finishing before the end of 1941. Nor was immediate success attained on this particular point. It was at least another two years before constant pressure, and querying from the highest level, induced departments to put in realistic forecasts of the dates when projects would be completed.

THE TECHNIQUE OF LABOUR CONTROL

Three steps were taken, before the Ministry of Works came into existence, to control the labour supply of the building and civil engineering industry. The first was the drawing up of the Schedule of Reserved Occupations, which prevented certain age-groups and types of craftsmen in the industry from being called up; secondly, there was the Control of Employment Order of 4th April 1940, which forbade the advertising of vacancies by building and civil engineering undertakings; and thirdly, there was the Restriction on Engagement Order of June 1940, which gave the employment exchanges a monopoly right to fill vacancies for these (and other) industries. The Restriction on Engagement Order remained the keystone of the control of labour supply for building and civil engineering throughout the war. The fact that all labour had to be engaged through the exchanges meant, in the case of building and civil engineering, that it came under the hand of the Ministry of Labour at fairly frequent intervals, since jobs in building and civil engineering are less continuous and have a more rapid turnover of labour than factory jobs.

The situation as seen by the new planners in the autumn of 1940, before the allocation system had been worked out, was somewhat paradoxical. The object of the new Ministry of Works was specifically to secure that a balanced production programme should be laid down for

K

the industry, so that its labour and material resources could be used to the full and to the best advantage. There was unemployment still in parts of the country, yet there were labour demands unsatisfied elsewhere. The total volume of building and civil engineering work in hand did not seem to be perhaps much over half the volume in 1937; but no one knew for certain whether or not this was true, in the absence of any even partially complete statistics. The efficiency of labour was already believed to have fallen; one guess which had some currency at that period was that an average of 50 bricks laid per hour before the war had declined perhaps to 30 by 1940. There was a dispute as to the optimum number of hours that could be worked weekly in the industry; 'experience' was said by some employers to 'show' that 54 hours per week was an optimum; but whose experience this was, and over what period, was not made clear.

In view of all these doubtful points, even the basis on which a future building programme could be worked out seemed to be uncertain. By the summer of 1941 it had become clear that the Schedule of Reserved Occupations, amended though it was to include building labourers, had left the industry badly out of balance. There was a shortage of at least 50,000 labourers. Moreover, the decline in the total labour force, overestimated as it was, alarmed the Government. In July 1941, as a result of an even more alarming decline in the number of men in coal-mining, a registration of all men who had since 1935 done six months' work in the mines was made by Statutory Order. It was natural that a similar idea should be discussed in connexion with the building industry; and the possibility of individually registering each man who had been in building, or at least each one who was now in the industry, so as to put a 'tab' on each of the individuals needed for the programme, was entertained very seriously, and indeed the idea was always simmering in the background until 1945. The strongest objections to such a plan were the administrative inconvenience of dealing direct with some three-quarters of a million operatives by means of written returns and the floating nature of the labour force in the industry. An industry such as building and civil engineering has almost continual entries and exits occurring even in wartime.[1]

A less drastic, but equally thorough control, was established through the medium of the employing firms. This was sound, since the administrative control of labour in the industry is after all organized, at any

---

[1] Thus, from mid-1942 to mid-1943 it was estimated, on the basis of a sample, that 137,000 men left the industry for other industries, but that, over the same period, 99,000 men *entered* the industry *from* other industries.

given moment, most easily through the firm. The *raison d'être* of the firm
is as an organizational nucleus. Registration of firms in July 1941 was
accomplished at the same time as the issue of an Essential Works Order.[1]

This Order not only compelled all building and civil engineering
firms to register with the Ministry of Works and to make returns there-
to; it also became the basis of the scheduling of particular sites. Labour
was tied to these sites, and could neither be dismissed nor resign without
the agreement of the National Service Officer of the district. Scheduling
of contracts under this Order was the second new weapon of administrative control.

The only loophole left was that contractors, once they had engaged
men, could move them from contract to contract without reference to
the employment exchange, and in this way labour was found for a
certain amount of low-priority work. This was stopped by the Restriction on Transfer Order of 18th December 1941, which became effective
on 12th January of the following year. These Orders were the instruments through which the allocation system was operated in practice.

At first some of the departments did not fully grasp the nature of the
allocation scheme. They were inclined to say that the 'allocation system
had broken down' if in any month they found that they had not
employed the whole of the labour allocated to them individually.
Gradually they learned three things: first, that to make sure of employing all the allocated labour their own contract departments must make
sure that the exchanges were notified ahead of impending demands for
labour; secondly, that to let too many contracts either singly or jointly
in a given region might mean that special delays in labour supply would
occur; and thirdly, that the Ministry of Labour machine for
filling vacancies might be slow, but it was very sure. Departments
with less than their allocation of labour found that the position
might not be restored in a month; it was almost certain to be made
good in two or, at the worst, three months; that is, if the contracts had
been let and if there was no special bunching of contracts into one small
area. Areas of specially difficult labour supply were handled as 'super-
priority' regions and a special procedure was adopted for them, including the banning of all new works in the regions concerned (except
those needed for immediate strategical purposes), a ban which always
had the effect of throwing up some labour for the exchanges to place,
after a few weeks had gone by.

[1] Registration was used as a means of grouping some of the smaller contractors,
and great efforts were made to see that these groups were employed for sub-contract
work on government jobs.

Under the Essential Works Order the Minister of Labour took powers to direct labour to specific jobs. This power was used extensively for some parts of the programme, but it was a weapon of last resort rather than the mainstay of the movement of labour. For one special purpose it was specially valuable: to restore the balance of the building labour force. Under the powers of direction craftsmen could be 'designated' to do unskilled work, still receiving craftsmen's wages. But for the general filling of vacancies the labour exchanges' monopoly of placings was the main instrument of labour control. Even 'directed' men tended to desert sites that were remote and with bad welfare conditions. The provision of travelling allowances and canteens and, later in the war, of holidays with pay under an industrial agreement, did more than 'direction' to keep the more difficult sites adequately manned.

Once the allocations had been laid down changes in them usually involved decisions at the Cabinet committee level. The steady decline in the labour force entailed that any large new Government building scheme almost always resulted in the cutting down, or slowing down, of some other part of the programme that had already been sanctioned. The history of the allocation scheme therefore became closely bound up with the changing fortunes and aspect of the war.

Fluctuations in Programmes and Plans

The Government Building Programme, as it was planned in 1941, excluded all work done on air-raid damage repairs. For this special arrangements were made through a Director of Air-raid Damage Repairs and Salvage. Much of the employment was carried out through the local authorities, the public utility companies, and the Ministry of Home Security, and the planning of the repairs programme was handled through the offices of the Regional Commissioners. Owing to this extreme decentralization and to the emergency nature of the work, adequate statistical controls could not very well be imposed. There may or may not have been some waste of manpower. Very high wages were paid in the spring of 1941 to anyone who could lend a hand with the clearing up of bomb damage. Juveniles earned particularly high wages, a fact on which London magistrates commented at a later date. The labour market was still sufficiently fluid for these methods to work adequately. Special administrative action had to be taken from time to time when a particular town had been exposed to a sudden severe blitz. Hostels for building workers were often a first priority before anything could be done to clear away the rubble to restore the city or town to a working basis. All this, however, came outside the main building programme, the pool of 'maintenance-cum-air-raid-damage' labour being left as a residue, the main task of Government being to see that this residue did not decline below a minimum.

This residue was estimated to amount to some 363,000 men in August 1941 and to 284,000 men in August 1942. In the winter of 1942–3, when there seemed to be a danger of the residue sinking dangerously below the minimum necessary for maintenance, even at a very low level, of existing buildings, and as a reserve for air-raid emergencies, steps were taken to ensure that in each locality a minimum 'garrison' of labour was left free from other claims. This 'garrison' notion was not administratively very practical in the absence at that date of local committees for watching the situation, but sufficient pressure was brought through the employment exchanges, and otherwise, to ensure that at least some labour was left for these minimum purposes. This was one of the main purposes of the Restriction on Transfer Order already mentioned.

In August 1941 the total on 'Government work' using the term in the programming sense, was 520,000, inclusive of 55,000 on maintenance of buildings and installations. The Ministry of Supply programme was on the decline. It was correctly anticipated that, within a year, the numbers employed thereon might be reduced by some 40,000 men as the Royal Ordnance Factories were completed, but this was not to be accomplished unless the Production Executive cancelled projects for new R.O.F.'s being commenced. This was done in August 1941. The Admiralty programme seemed likely to decline rather slowly. There were always a certain number of new projects being fed into its programme, just about sufficient to keep some 30,000 men employed. The building of War Office camps and depots seemed to have reached its peak, and a gradual saving of some 5,000 men was anticipated. As against this, there were the huge new schemes for the Air Ministry and the Ministry of Aircraft Production. Each of these departments wanted an increase of at least 50,000 men at the earliest possible date. The problem, therefore, was whether to cut the other allocations still further or to reduce the 'residue' available for achieving maintenance level and for the ever-recurrent danger of renewed heavy raids on London and other cities.

In the event the solution reached was that the Air Ministry's labour force was to be increased through 1941 and 1942 as well as that of the Ministry of Aircraft Production. At its peak the Air Ministry's labour force reached 119,400 in November 1942, the M.A.P. peak coming a few months earlier with 52,800 men in August of that year.

The pressure for more labour from the Air Ministry, which had to build airfields for the U.S. air forces as well as for our own, was accompanied by a similar demand from the War Office. The programme known under the code name Bolero[1] amounted in all to some £100 millions of work, or enough to keep 170,000 men employed for ten months. The original target date laid down by the Cabinet to meet the wishes of the Combined Staffs was 31st March 1943. The programme was in fact completed by April 1943. The War Office and Air Ministry programmes had to be carried out through the worst possible building months of the year from the point of view of weather, and it was only by vigorous action by the building directorates of these Ministries, and by their contractors and workmen, that the programmes were finished in so short a time. The peak of War Office employment was in January 1943, when nearly two-thirds of their building labour was employed on U.S. camps.

The airfields and camps completed, the R.O.F. and other supply programmes still running down, and even the M.A.P. demands for labour well past their peak, made the summer of 1943 seem like a breathing space for the building and civil engineering industries and for those who guided its programmes. It was agreed that 70,000 men should be called up from these industries in the next 12 months, which, together with wastage, would reduce the numbers in the industry from 592,000 in June 1943 to 496,000 in June 1944. The beginning of this reduction was already in full swing when the plan for Mulberry was launched.

There were many aspects of this great project, and its success was due to the War Office first and foremost, to the Ministry of Supply, and to the contractors who carried it out. A less publicized, but vitally important, link in the chain was the planning and organization of labour supply, which was the responsibility of the Ministry of Works. A labour force of about 30,000 men had to be found within the space of a few weeks. Much more had to be done than the simple paper allocation of this figure. By this date the Director of Building Programmes had established links with the regions through a Chief Allocation Officer at headquarters and regional allocation officers in each of twelve regional offices. Through this organization it was possible to keep track of the realization in practice of any allocation of labour, and to turn the tap on or off before any department's labour force was far out of gear with the general plan. This machinery was now strengthened and used for helping the Ministry of Labour to find recruits for the pre-

[1] Bolero was the code name for the movement of American troops to the United Kingdom.

invasion plan. The lists of departmental jobs in the regions proved to be invaluable. The less important of them were closed down or 'milked' of labour; the men sent to work in London or other centres of work were provided with accommodation, travelling allowances, and every inducement to stay. Even so, in those difficult times there was inevitably a turnover and wastage of labour. This had to be made good by yet more draftees and directed operatives. The job was done, and over 25,000 men were transferred within 16 weeks.

At the beginning of June 1944 came D-Day, and the long wartime labours of the building labour force, now reduced to the over-forties to a very considerable extent, seemed at an end. Then the first flying-bomb arrived. London was just about to enter its last and greatest trial. For the first time in the history of the war air-raid damage repair assumed the importance of a major operation, and the whole task of finding labour had to be planned and programmed as a matter of first priority.

THE BUILDING PROGRAMME: JUNE 1944-JULY 1945

The labour employed on 'London house repairs'[1] amounted to 32,000 at the end of June 1944. By the end of November this figure had been increased to 118,000, a build-up of 86,000 in five months at an average of 17,200 per month. This was an achievement comparable with the 'Phoenix'[2] build-up of a year before. Needless to say, it was not sufficient to satisfy everybody. There was grumbling, criticism and impatience. Without some public impatience, however, the sense of urgency which stimulated the drafting of labour into London might have been missing.

The number of men working in London was increased still further in the following months. A 'target' for repairs of houses was set in September 1944 by the Government, which planned that 719,000 houses should be repaired by the end of March 1945. This figure was in fact accomplished. At the end of the period an average of 40,000 houses per week was being repaired.

The labour force on the emergency programme of air-raid damage was increased from 21,000 to 142,000 between 15th June 1944 and 16th March 1945. The number of men drafted into London under official schemes over the same period numbered 54,500; the remainder of the

[1] Which meant, in the jargon of the time, the repair of war damage to houses under schemes operated by the ninety-three local authorities of the London area exclusive of military labour or prisoners of war. (See *Monthly Digest of Statistics*, No. 1, January 1946, page 50, Table 64.)

[2] 'Phoenix' was the name for the concrete caissons which formed the main breakwater in connexion with Mulberry harbour.

increase came from two other sources: the transfer of men from other kinds of work; and the arrival, under private arrangement or voluntarily, of men from the provinces. The provision of accommodation for the inflow of labour meant repeating, under more perilous and disorganized conditions, the task of 1943 and 1944. The Ministry of Health requisitioned lodgings and the Ministry of Works provided beds in hostels for nearly 40,000 of the provincial workmen. This was accomplished in a period when some 200,000 persons, rendered homeless by the damage, had also to be found shelter by means of compulsory billeting and requisition.

It ought perhaps to be pointed out that the figures for 'houses repaired' were much easier to accomplish at the beginning than at the end of a repair programme. Obviously, the more lightly damaged houses could be done first. The target, some unkind critics suggested, could never have been reached had the V2 campaign not been intensified, thus providing the opportunity of a steady volume of relatively easy (quick-scoring) results in 'numbers of houses receiving first-aid repairs'. This is all quite true. It diminishes, but does not explain away, the merit of having finished a programme on time.

To meet the new emergency, a special co-ordinating committee was set up under the chairmanship of Sir Malcolm Trustram Eve, and this committee, working together with the appropriate sections of the Ministry of Works, guided the plan for bringing men and materials into London, and for sharing resources out among the different London boroughs according to their need. The whole organization was improvised, the existing departmental machine being adapted to fit in with the new co-ordinating committee, which came to be known as the London Repairs Executive. The scheme was flexible and effective.

At the same time as this crisis was being met and overcome there arose more and more strongly a demand for improved civilian housing. In retrospect, that demand, urged so loudly a year before the war was over, seems to have been strangely ill-timed. The labour on 'war housing' had fallen to 5,000 by the end of July 1944 and remained obstinately at that level until January 1945. By then some beginnings of the temporary housing programme were discernible, and also of the preparation of sites for the essential permanent house-building programme. The labour force on new housing had been increased to 26,000 by June of 1945. This was the limited extent to which, in view of the air-raid damage crisis, the clamour for reconstruction could be met.

The demand for new housing had begun as early as mid-summer of 1943, and had been met for the time being by the Government's plan to build 3,000 'cottages' for agricultural workers; the demand for reconstruction plans in general went back further still, to the Parliamentary and Press discussions of 1941. But before these early developments can be discussed it may be as well to complete the story of the building programme during the war.

The upshot of the pressure on the programme in 1944 was that labour planned to be used on the Government Building Programme proper had to be diverted on to London air-raid damage repair. The change in the programme meant a substantial reduction in the labour force for the programme at the end of September and a serious cut by the end of December 1944. It was hoped, on the other hand, that by strenuous efforts the Ministry of Labour might be able to bring the labour force of the industry up to 487,000 by the end of 1944.

The demands of the Government departments, even so, exceeded the anticipated supply by 60,000 for September, and by 83,000 if programmed ahead as far as December. The Minister of Production, appealed to for a decision on what allocations of labour should be made, came to the conclusion that allocations of any kind would be unrealistic. Lists of departmental works in progress in the London area and all those not of operational or first-aid urgency were stopped. In the provinces only the most urgent new works were allowed to begin, and the 'B.P.2' approval machinery operated as a sieve.

The allocation system was not, as might perhaps have been expected, wound up, now that the wheel had come full circle. Priorities were again the basis of the programme. In the first six months of 1945 housing became a more and more urgent first priority. The labour force was now seen to be steadily increasing, instead of decreasing. The actual numbers in the industry at the end of December 1944 proved to be 521,000, instead of the 487,000 that had been feared five months earlier.

Nevertheless, it was difficult to fill the allocations. In the war years the essential position had been that the total demand for labour far exceeded the supply. This was true of current, short-term and effective demands at the labour exchange; and it was true, secondly, of the long-term total demands of the departments, on the basis of the total of all their desires and intentions. In this context both a short-term and a long-term allocation plan were logical. But at the end of the war the problem was no longer merely one of sorting out the competing claims for labour of many conflicting purposes. This problem still remained and an allocation system continued to be operated; but there were further complications to be considered.

First, there was the special difficulty created by the intense demand for labour in 'Southern England', which meant in effect London and 'Bomb Alley', the area from Dover to London. On previous occasions in the history of the allocation system, one or other area of the country had proved to be of special difficulty, and some plan outside the over-all allocation plan had had to be devised. In the middle of 1941 the Swindon-Salisbury area had had so many building projects in hand that a ban was placed for some months on the commencement of new works of over £5,000 therein; later the Orkneys and Hebrides gave rise to special difficulties. Later still, the demands for labour in East Anglia, to complete the large aerodrome programme, meant that a 'super-priority' system had to be superimposed on the normal alloca-tion scheme. But the flying-bomb and V2 damage created an area bottleneck far worse than those previously experienced.

The London Repairs Executive adapted the allocation system to their special purposes. Each local authority was made responsible for the whole of the repairs to be carried out in its area. The labour in each local authority area was regarded as a pool which could be switched over to whichever building firm seemed to have the greatest need, as the damage occurred. London was divided into four zones, and the 'zonal' office was responsible for similarly pooling labour as between borough and borough, while finally the Executive Committee itself watched the relative progress of each of the separate zones.

Towards the end of the repair programme London was divided into First and Second Priority Areas, the former big areas with a large amount of first-aid repairs still to be carried out, the latter those in which all, or nearly all, damaged houses had been repaired up to an emergency standard. Materials as well as labour were allocated through the same machinery to the individual boroughs.

While the 'allocation system', in its wider sense, was thus modified, there arose a second major difficulty in the carrying out of the pro-gramme. This was that sufficient contracts for new housing had not been let to absorb the labour allocated for that purpose. There were many reasons why the contracts could not have been running in time to mop up the increasing labour of the industry, right up to the end of 1945; the point here is that this new difficulty made the allocation system, for the time being at any rate, slightly out of place. It was only after a period of considerable changeover of demand (for schools, further repairs, offices, factories and many other buildings) for a peacetime economy that the old problem of too great a demand for a limited labour force arose in a form suited for the labour allocation technique.

In the interregnum between war and peace—the year 1945—allocation of labour to new housing did not mean that labour immediately went to new housing. The contracts could not absorb the labour except by a steady build-up. This was, in the circumstances of 1944–5, unavoidable.

Finally, a third major difference between the conditions of 1945 and those of the earlier years was that the shortage of materials, first seriously felt during the flying-bomb period, began to assert a mastery that it was to retain for some years to come. Plans had to be laid in the first half of 1945 to meet the demand for materials in 1946 and 1947. On the basis of the intention to build 300,000 houses in two years from the end of the war, it appeared that the production of many materials would need to be accelerated by the building of factories and the drafting of labour into the building materials industries. These problems had not, of course, been present in the war years, when the value of building work done in each year was declining; timber and steel had had to be rationed, but for other materials the difficulty had usually been one of local shortages, up to the time of the flying-bomb attack.

The situation at the end of the war was thus not one for which the allocation system alone was wholly appropriate. The increase in the supply of building labour was about to begin. This had been planned with some care and considerable political skill as far back as 1943. The important points were to draft the newcomers entering, or returning to, the industry on to the most important work, and particularly on to new housing and industrial facilities; and to secure an adequate flow of materials. While allocation might still play its part, the stopping of non-essential work, or any other method of channelling labour in the right directions, became of even greater importance. The mobilizing of a decreasing labour force to carry out a large programme had been the special context to which the allocation system was relevant. To find work and materials for a growing labour force demanded a readjusted programming technique.

IX

THE ALLOCATION OF TIMBER

by

P. FORD

The methods used in the allocation of raw materials in a controlled economy must depend on how severely supply is limited, the organization of the industries concerned, and the range and variety of the demands to be satisfied. There is no one method suitable for all materials, but a review of one critical case will throw into relief the nature of the problems, the extent to which they were solved and which of them were unsolved.

CHARACTER OF SUPPLY AND DEMAND

First, in pre-war years we spent more money on timber and plywood imports than on any other raw material; the pre-war average import of softwood, hardwood and pit-wood was $9\frac{1}{2}$ million tons as compared with the next highest, $7\frac{1}{4}$ million tons of iron ore, pig iron, scrap, steel ingots and semi-finished steel. Timber is in any case a bulky material, making great demands on shipping space and, in addition, the loss early in the war of the normal sources of softwood supply from Russia and the Baltic meant purchase from trans-Atlantic sources, involving a longer haul and even railing large amounts right across Canada for shipment from the eastern seaboard. It was thus a headache to the transport authorities, and for this reason alone was likely to be eyed critically when shipping cuts became necessary. This $9\frac{1}{2}$ million tons was in 1942 reduced to $1\frac{1}{10}$ million tons, and in 1943 to $1\frac{3}{4}$ million tons, a cut without parallel amongst the bulky raw materials. The initiative and energy of the restrictive Controls in developing alternative sources of supply to make good such deficiencies is worth remembering. In this case, the expansion of small-scale commercial home production and of State home production to supplement it, with the aid of Canadians and the girls of the Women's Timber Corps; the search for balsa for Mosquitoes and for large supplies of aircraft spruce; these were amongst the brighter sides of the history of war production. The increase of home production—from only half a million to $3\frac{3}{4}$ million tons in 1943—was considerably greater than in the case of any of the other bulky materials. But all these efforts still left the total supplies only 4½ to 5½ million tons, and it was the severity of this reduction which dominated allocation procedure and practice.

The second determinant was the structure of the trade. Compared with highly organized industries like iron and steel, the timber trade was a very competitive one. According to Leak and Maizel's study of the Census of Production returns[1], while the three largest business units in the chemical trades employed 48 per cent, and in iron and steel 39 per cent of the total numbers in their industries, the timber trades show one of the lowest degrees of concentration, the proportion being only 10 per cent. Thirdly, the scope and variety of the demand for wood presented special rationing problems. Its use was not concentrated in a relatively small number of industrial enterprises grouped in a limited industrial region, but occurred in every town and village. The individual householder used it both as raw material for house repair and the garden shed, and in the form of finished products like furniture, matches, spade handles and prams. It was used industrially not only for constructional work, but for the wooden parts of machinery, vats, rollers and drums, as well as for mining, packing, railway sleepers and telegraph poles. Timber has the further peculiarity that it is capable of immediate use in its imported state for constructional work and of further conversion into a manufactured product. Some logs can be boiled, peeled and turned into plywood for the hulls of speed boats, radio cases and furniture. Finally, timber is the prime emergency material for jobs that have to be done quickly, yet with adequate strength. Throughout the war, the stock was always liable to be raided for large emergency requirements, whether for air-raid precautions, emergency bridging, millions of shelter bunks, shuttering for Mulberry, or for millions of yards of chestnut paling for invasion purposes. Some towns in the danger areas even demanded wood for emergency stocks of coffins. The claims of these urgencies were thus often pressed strongly against the long-term requirements for offensive action.

ADMINISTRATIVE CONSEQUENCES

The wide dispersal of demand between uses, consumers and areas explains both the division of the whole country into a number of licensing areas and the decision to base control on a licence to individual consumers for specific jobs and contracts. Where a raw material passes through the hands of a limited number of merchants and importers to

[1] H. Leak and A. Maizels, 'The Structure of British Industry', *Journal of the Royal Statistical Society*, Vol. CVIII, 1945, Pts. I–II, p. 142.

a relatively few manufacturing plants concentrated in a given industrial region, it is often possible to control use by a combination of directions to merchants as to the classes of work for which materials may be released, and of general prohibition by Order of its use for specific types of production. But in this case the jobs were widespread and varied, and even a modest percentage of excess consumption on the minimum necessary would make a respectable overall total. The number of licences reached 500,000 to 700,000 per annum, and a decentralized organization to deal with them was needed to ensure speed and scrutiny by licensing officers acquainted with the technical needs of the area. In addition, it was possible, through central instructions to area officers, to guide the licensing policy as between trades and classes of work more effectively and speedily than by the more formal alternative method of Order under the Defence Regulations.

This issue of licences was only the first stage of control. For the licensing officers were quickly off the mark in perceiving that the quotation of a war contract number or a letter urging priority gave them no indication of the size or term of the contract. They thus arrived empirically at the point so clearly brought out in the official narrative on munitions production in 1914–18, that 'priorities' were inadequate and that only a system of allocations was workable. Faced with the necessity of restricting consumption, Timber Control was thus obliged at the outset to determine priorities itself, a matter in which it felt it should receive authoritative guidance from departments. Within a few weeks of the outbreak of war it had already refused to issue timber for houses not yet commenced or which had not passed a certain stage of completion. For this reason, before the close of 1939, the allocation system was commenced for softwood required for works and buildings and, in January 1940, extended to all purposes other than works and buildings; as supplies became shorter and war demands greater, at later dates it was made to include hardwoods and plywood. Each department was given a softwood, hardwood and plywood account against which it wrote timber certificates (or timber cheques, as they were later called internally) in favour of the contractors or other claimants on their account. The differences from an ordinary banking account were that the banker (Timber Control) had the right not to honour in full, or even at all, any cheque deemed excessive for the job in hand or issued for an inappropriate purpose; and that at the end of each rationing period all unspent balances were returned to the pool for re-allocation.

Once an allocation system had been started there was no help for it but to extend it over the whole field; it could not be limited to the department's main contractors. Not only were subcontractors involved, but also the demands of bodies whose relationship to a Ministry might be statutory and administrative only, and not a contractual one. Thus the Ministry of Health had to collect and present the requirements of local authorities, hospitals, etc., the Ministry of Transport those of railways, canals and road undertakings, while the Ministry of Fuel and Power sponsored mines and gas and electricity undertakings. There is no doubt that the system not only was inescapable, but did guide supplies in accordance with war priorities.

But this supersession of the free market forced on to departments a great deal of work normally performed automatically by the price system. Some of the problems which arose in consequence were successfully handled, but others were never solved. When in a free market a department places a contract for a store, it does not have to reflect that the article it orders is but the end of a chain of productive processes; the relation of its contract to the preceding and adjacent processes is looked after by the price system, which secures the necessary adjustments. Why should a department suspect that its order for base paper for sensitizing, previously imported, would mean a demand for a particular type of wood for rollers? Or that its order for thousands of a particular store involved large quantities of wood for packing cases, ordinarily assumed to be part of the delivered contract? As the pattern of production changed from peace to war and timber supplies were reduced, it became necessary for departments to be made aware of the remoter effects of their own policies, for sometimes the timber content of the immediate store or component which the department agreed to cover with a cheque was the least of the material (timber) consequences of their order. Timber Control wanted guidance as to what was an essential demand and what could be postponed, and naturally pressed departments to take responsibility for and accept as a charge on their timber accounts the requirements of more and more services. The departments, on the other hand, at first preferred to limit their liabilities to demands of which they had direct knowledge, i.e. those of their own contractors, or of bodies with whom they were in a supervisory relationship; e.g. the Ministry of Transport looked after the requirements of transport agencies of various kinds. Much work had to be done to ensure that all the innumerable, essential users of timber had and could find speedily a department from whom they could secure their timber cheque. As our economy reached its maximum war production, so that all that remained of civilian consumption could be regarded as essential,

Timber Control itself looked after the general needs of basic industries which served war industries in general but were themselves remote from any direct contract, and also took care of a wide variety of civilian needs which were not, like prams and furniture, part of a departmental programme.

The second result of the supersession of the price system was that the adjustment of the demand to supply could take place only through the collection of detailed statistics of timber uses. Departments were thus plunged into a sea of trouble in collecting quantitative requirements from contractors, local authorities, public utilities, industries. There was little information of value about timber consumption in the Census of Production, and the timber trade was so competitive (in the sense that it was in the hands of many firms, none of them dominant) that it also had relied upon normal movements of the market and had little organized information of its own. The consuming trades were nearly all in the same position. No one had ever found it necessary to have the information, so that both the departments and the Control had to commence their work in the dark. The first couple of ration periods were thus largely ones in which the departments were getting a clearer notion of their quantitative problems. Only in the case of works and buildings had the practice of breaking down a contract into material quantities been a normal procedure, and this had to be extended to thousands of stores and components of every kind. Form-filling and the creation of a statistical bureaucracy all along the line were thus unavoidable. The consumer had to supply a copy of his licence to the merchant holding national stock before the merchant could supply the wood. The Control's Area Officer needed a copy to enable him to know how far stocks of various timbers and specifications in his area had been pledged, and Control Headquarters also had to know the total amounts of each main variety for which its stocks had been made liable. The timber cheque was needed to ensure that the amount released was debited to the proper departmental account. It seemed adding insult to injury to ask, as did one or two branches of consuming departments responsible for large volumes and ranges of miscellaneous stores, that contractors must fill in an application form for a timber cheque! But the knowledge of the timber content of some component often lay with the contractor or even subcontractor and not with the department, and we never completely succeeded in persuading departments to eliminate this extra move. Many efforts were made to reduce and simplify the procedure, but the minimum of form-filling for speed and effective work always proved substantial. Thus the shortage of timber and the replacement of the price system meant unavoidably the expensive use of another scarce factor, manpower.

Thirdly, economies in the use of timber had to be obtained not simply through rises in price, as in a free market, but by quantitative restrictions which sometimes ignored price differentials. Economies were enforced through the voluntary action of departments working a tight allocation and through the vigorous pressure of Timber Control Economy Officers, who scrutinized every licence. It is in this field that the Control did some of its most striking work. The use of wood for some purposes was stopped altogether, as in the case of house building in the early months of the war; in June 1940 the release of hardwood for domestic furniture was stopped completely for many months. For other purposes the amount released was reduced. Thus the import of matches and wood for them was reduced by three-quarters, while reducing the height of ladies' shoe heels and making them of home-grown instead of imported wood saved thousands of tons of shipping. Slimming the thickness of coffins gave an economy of half a million cubic feet per annum. Much of the economy was achieved by down-grading; that is, the use of inferior qualities and specifications of wood. The relaxation of Post Office requirements for telegraph poles, the revision of thousands of War Office stores, the substitution of hardwood and concrete for sleepers, of home-grown for imported wood, of ply-wood for solid timber for packing, are samples of measures which required continuous discussion in terms of technical qualities and availabilities, instead of in money. Large numbers of these substitutes, e.g. of hardwood for softwood, involved a sharp increase of cost and the free use of a materials variation clause in contracts.

Did this system of allocation mean that some department was rela tively over-supplied, so that its less urgent needs were satisfied before the more urgent needs of another? Was it possible to keep the marginal efficiency of timber for war purposes equal in all uses? In a broad way, within each department's individual allocation, one may say yes. As between departments it is not so certain. It was not easy to be sure that the large bulk allocation made to departments did not enable some of them to go further down their list of priorities than others were able to do. Reliance had to be placed upon the scrutiny of the detailed requirements they submitted, based on Timber Control's technical information and its knowledge of the details of the licences and timber cheques of all departments; on the power, in fact, of making well-informed, invidious comparisons. One had to keep an eye on a department's use of its power of *virement* between its 'sub-votes' and compare

L

its estimates at the beginning of each ration period with its performance at the end of it. But obviously, no refined marginal calculus of urgencies and efficiencies was possible; and no one could claim more than that the system sorted the urgencies into categories and satisfied the more before the less important of them. Nevertheless, a good deal of evidence could be brought to suggest that the balancing was more precise and that the range within which mis-allocations were made was narrower than some critics suggest. The fact that production for the Services was in the end related to an operational date meant that in the relevant sector the vital supplies had to be available, whether in the primary or in a substitute material.

LESSONS

A general appraisal of the system would be out of place here; its merits have already been hinted at. But it is well, in great emergencies of this kind, not to make the same mistake twice, not to repeat the errors of the first world war in the second, nor those of the second in any future emergency. That this is perhaps easier for the vanquished, filled with bitter reflections, than for the victor, who may forget how far the success was jeopardized and made more costly than it need have been, is a reason for concentrating on the lessons of admonition to be derived from the experience. One must begin with the obvious; the way to avoid some of the asperities of the rationing system is to begin with a good timber stock. But, in fact, stocks were lower at the outbreak of war than they had been for some time. This question had been raised even before the outbreak of hostilities and some had urged the purchase of an additional stock of such an important material, certain to make large demands on our shipping space. For its restricted use must mean additional calls on manpower, acceptance by departments of reduced specifications they regretted, and real austerities for the civilian population. That this was not done was deplorable, and for the failure to grasp the economic realities of the situation Ministers of the day must accept their constitutional responsibility.

Secondly, through most of the war, when the level of imports was being settled insufficient appreciation was shown of the significance of the minimum stock. The stock required to run a given annual level of consumption varies from trade to trade. The industry may be concentrated into a small geographical area or the basic raw material may be convertible with fair ease into any of a whole range of secondary materials or products. But timber consumption is dispersed, so that widespread stocks each containing a range of specifications have to be kept. There was thus a minimum for each effective stock and a very large minimum number of stocks. It was not easy to give a figure which could be proved statistically, but that the figures submitted were realities was clearly shown when by decree they were allowed to fall to near, or even below, the level which the practitioners of the trade suggested. For there occurred exactly what had been forecast—long delays in obtaining the required specifications, cross journeys using up scarce transport, and waste because for urgent jobs long lengths had to be released and used where shorter lengths were required. It is, of course, the danger to which statistical tables giving comparative stock figures are subject, when read without an understanding of the real substance they try to describe. There may be very good technical reasons why a stock of four to five months' consumption for one material is, in relation to its function, smaller than a three months' stock for another material. Timber in the course of transit and piling (movement from landing to merchant's yard ready for issue), which took as much as six weeks at one stage, while it was physically in·the country from a shipping point ·of view was not, in fact, available for consumption. It was thus illusory to include it in the stock required to keep departments' contractors supplied without serious delays and real waste.

Thirdly, there were some difficulties in the substitution of one material for another, and it is not clear that we always had the right answer or possessed the right machinery for securing it. Some of them were unavoidable. Owing to shipping and production difficulties, the occupation of sources of supply by the enemy, or the entry into the war on the allied side of a supplier which thereby became a rival consumer for its own war needs, the relative supplies of the different materials expanded and contracted at varying rates. The range and direction of substitution also had to change, but often it seemed impossible to keep up with the facts. It takes time for a consuming department to change its designs and specifications to satisfy its technical officers and to bring those changes to the contract stage. Sometimes the time lag was such that (as occasionally between softwoods and hardwoods, or solid wood and plywood, or even timber and steel for casing) by the time the substitution had been carried through by the consuming departments, the relative supply position had been reversed, and the substitution taking place was, in fact, a substitution of a less for a more scarce material. Again, if one control took a less rigorous view of its economy functions it might grant material for a use another control had deemed inessential. In so far as the control with less exacting standards depended on imports, its demands for shipping to meet its programmes would be based on the lower level of economy, and since it may be presumed that the substitution was of a material technologically or in price inferior to the primary material, in such cases the result was an incorrect one. *Ad hoc* and spasmodic inter-control meetings, and good work by the technical officers of controls and departments, did much, but were not sufficient. Perhaps the establishment of a small, well-qualified scientific and technological economy group, closely linked with the controls and with a position sufficient to get its views consideration, would have been able to give guidance as to the right answers within this range of interchangeability. The general economy organization actually set up in one department did not have, or claim to have, the level of scientific competence or technical prestige to enable it to perform the function which is here suggested. Without being dogmatic, it looks as if an experiment of this sort would have been worth while.

Fourthly, austerities of the magnitude which had to be inflicted both on industrial users and individual consumers required public acquiescence if they were to work smoothly. In face of the acute shortage, the wide variety of pressing demands could be handled only by the combination of a clear conception of priorities, with a determination to implement them with firmness as well as flexibility. For security reasons, it was impossible for Controls to make plain their grounds for the restrictions they imposed, by giving the public the statistical information which would have justified them. It is by their works that controls are judged and these must not only be reasonably consistent with one another and with the spirit of the understood priorities, but be obviously so. It is criticism based on fears of privileged treatment and on unfavourable comparisons of releases for purposes not consistent with declared priorities that is so damaging. It is a snare and a delusion to imagine that acceptance can be won by 'appeasement releases' on political grounds or on spurious as distinct from genuine grounds of public morale, when they are not justified by the supply position. This only leads to further demands until the capacity to supply the real priorities is undermined. The dash of Puritanism with which the Timber Control adhered to the distinction between essential and inessential needs, and for which it was occasionally twitted, was justified by its results, in the co-operation its officers received in the grim and troublesome business of substitution, reduction of stocks, and down-grading.

Many interesting problems must be omitted from a brief survey, but it would be wrong to conclude without referring to the personnel of the 'Raw Materials bureaucracy'. Whether or not the separate organization of the Raw Materials Controls, each with a parallel branch of the Ministry, was more appropriate than some more unified arrangement, whether the controllers should have been drawn from the trades they controlled, as in this war, or from the businessmen from other trades, as in some cases in the last war, are matters which will be discussed for some time. But the country owes an acknowledgment to the combination of civil servants and trade representatives who had before the war been preparing the organization and sketching out the control orders of the early months, so that we began with good machinery and some grip on the opening problems. Similarly, no one who reviews the work of substitution or reads the long price schedules in control orders can have any doubt of the extent to which the work of control rested on the wealth of knowledge and experience of the controlled trades and industries. From a study of this experience we could, no doubt, gather hints of how a state should man its economic administration.

X

THE WORK OF A DEPARTMENTAL PRIORITY OFFICER

by

RICHARD PARES

In the allocation and use of scarce resources, responsibility could not be sharply divided between the interdepartmental authorities on the one hand and the departments on the other. The former could not be content with allocating blocks of material or labour to departments without asking how they would be used or whether they could be used at all; the latter had themselves to allocate what they had received between one departmental use and another. But although the line could not be clearly drawn it was there. The function of the departments was not so much to take a hand in the allocation as to use what was allocated. Failure to do so dislocated departmental programmes and kept resources idle. It also brought its own Nemesis when the allocations were next considered, for the interdepartmental authorities cut down the allocations to departments which had not used what they had received.

The duties of the departmental priority officers arose out of this responsibility for presenting programmes and getting them executed. The work could only be done well by considering the use of all scarce resources together—labour, materials and (where it was a limiting factor) fuel. This was the more difficult, and the more necessary, because materials, labour and fuel were controlled by three different authorities—the Ministry of Production, the Ministry of Labour and National Service, and the Ministry of Fuel and Power.[1] These three authorities were not generally in touch with each other on questions of allocation, and had different policies and prepossessions. Thus the Ministry of Production might bear especially hard on the carpet and linoleum industries because jute was scarce, the Ministry of Labour on the woollen industry because the Yorkshire munitions factories needed manning, and the Ministry of Fuel and Power on the pottery industry

---

[1] It was even more complicated than that: materials produced from coal, e.g. naphthalene, were allocated by the Ministry of Fuel and Power and many minor materials by the Ministry of Supply's Controls.

because it used a great deal of solid fuel. Somebody had to see that the demands of these industries for materials, labour and fuel made sense. Probably no authority could conveniently have been set up for allocating all resources, but each authority might have known a little more than it did about what the others were doing; in particular, it was felt that the Ministry of Labour might have taken more interest in the allocation of materials. In default of such co-ordination the departments' priority officers, or other representatives, had to go the rounds of the authorities presenting them with the same arguments and trying to arrive at consistent results.

This could not be done precisely. Materials and solid fuel could be allocated; gas and electricity were not, nor was labour, in general, until a late stage of the war. A munitions department which desired to man-up a particular factory could put in a demand for a supply of labour which should correspond to the material to be handled. This could not be done with the same precision for the non-munitions industries, whose output was shared between service and civilian production. For these industries there could not be a precise allocation of labour— only general tendencies of labour supply and withdrawal, with which it was difficult to match precise allocations of material. Even when labour was allocated to each of these industries, in the later years of the war, this was little more than a notional or paper transaction.

Nevertheless, the inconvenience or waste arising from this lack of precision should not be over-rated. It was not very difficult (subject to strategical surprises) to keep labour, materials and fuel in one's head at the same time, and to arrive at a rough and ready correlation for any important industry: for example, anybody could tell that it was useless to ask for a large allocation of paper for the production of books, if one had reason to think that the book printers or bookbinders were so short of labour that it could not be used. Anything more precise than this would probably have been an unnecessary piece of perfection, especially as movements of labour between industries did not always follow the lines of the Ministry of Labour's policy for labour supply.

Where waste and inconvenience were caused it was more often because general labour supply policy was traversed by peculiar considerations of location. Here it does appear, at first sight, that there should have been more careful co-ordination of departmental plans from the first. There were certain occasions when the use of available materials, and the supply of necessaries to the Services and civilians, were seriously curtailed by the placing of war work in the centres of highly localized civilian industries—to say nothing of the interference of one kind of war work with another. The most conspicuous instance was the heavy load of aircraft work which was put into the cotton-spinning districts of Lancashire. In the later stages of the war all the departments pulling together could not get labour back into the cotton industry, because of the counter-attraction of better-paid engineering work; and consequently the Ministry of Production could never allocate nearly enough cotton yarn for all departmental and civilian needs. There were other crises of the same kind, tiresome but less serious, as at Leicester, where all the munitions departments, apparently without consulting each other, had simultaneously had the same idea or taken the same hint, and planned new engineering production whose demands for labour could not have been fully met without heavily curtailing the main body of the hosiery industry and the output of certain kinds of shoes. It seems that more consideration should be given to this matter in planning production for any future war.

Yet it would be very difficult to make the basic assumptions of such a plan in advance. Wars—especially long wars—develop unexpected strategic requirements which are certain to upset such a plan. Moreover, the possibility and the necessity of such a plan depend partly on the assumption that an irreducible minimum of output can be determined for the non-munitions industries. Now this is not true. The Service demand for the output of such industries will vary unpredictably—witness the immense increase of the Service demand for cardboard boxes (luckily the cardboard box industry is one of the least localized in the country). The irreducible minimum of civilian needs depends, likewise, on the state of the war. Victories make shortages more tolerable, and defeats strengthen the need and the resolution to tolerate them. If anybody had tried at the beginning of the war to make a plan for the location of war industries on any hypothesis as to the irreducible needs of the civilians of Great Britain, he would almost certainly have placed them higher than he need have done, as the Board of Trade did when it determined the first year's clothing ration and the concentration level of industries in 1941. The war was not lost by reason of the subsequent and largely unintentional reductions. It therefore seems that the interests of the country were better served by treating the civilian as a cushion which could be further compressed without a great deal of careful planning, than they would have been by staking everything on satisfying his wants on a certain scale. This somewhat weakens the argument for greater definiteness in planning the location of war industry; yet it remains true that the interests of war industry itself require it, and that there is everything to be said for avoiding such extreme inconveniences as the overloading with war work of the one great cotton-spinning district of the country.

The problems described above were common to all departments which used labour, materials and fuel, or had programmes under which these resources were used by private industry. What departmental official was to be responsible for considering them together, was a matter of departmental organization. The great munitions departments— Admiralty, Ministry of Supply, Ministry of Aircraft Production—gave their priority officers comparatively restricted functions, primarily in estimating, demanding and perhaps sub-allocating the raw materials required for their production programmes. Being direct employers of labour they had their own labour departments which were not under their priority officers. The work of co-ordinating the requirements of labour, materials and fuel, and of dealing with the location of industry, was naturally controlled by very high officials in the secretariats. In the Board of Trade, which represented, taken all round, the largest civilian interest in the product of industry, the principal priority officer was responsible for this co-ordination. This arrangement probably would not have suited a munitions department, but it did provide the necessary unity of outlook which might otherwise have been lacking in a department which employed no labour directly and had no financial responsibility for production.

The problems of civilian departments will be treated in special detail below, not only because the writer had personal experience of them, but also because, besides illustrating the role of civilian economy in wartime, they may throw a special light on the allocation of resources in peacetime within a society whose industry is still largely conducted by private enterprise.

PROGRAMMING OF PRODUCTION

The first duty of the civilian departments was similar to that of the munitions departments, namely determining and presenting production programmes. Naturally, the programmes were not made up in quite the same way as those of the munitions departments. The latter had their ends determined for them by extraneous authorities and considerations, and did not have to assess to the same degree the importance of the respective ends for themselves. The priority officers of two munitions departments were working to execute plans determined by their customers, the Services (the Admiralty alone, after the summer of 1940, was both a Service department and a supply department). These plans were, in their turn, related to a strategic scheme or schemes. The munitions departments might have to point out to their customers that not all their plans could be realized at once because of the scarcity of resources, and perhaps to indicate which could be realized and which could not. But the priority officers of civilian departments were in a more indeterminate position even in wartime—still more so when they began to plan for a peacetime economy. The few landmarks were mainly political. Anybody could tell, for example, that if supplies of a new plasticizer were limited, it had better be used for increasing the production of rubber substitute for children's shoes before it was used for putting on the market a new kind of waterproof, for children's shoes had a value in morale and politics that even children's waterproofs had not. Anybody could tell that the official who allowed or obliged the manufacturers of grain-milling machinery to export their entire output, so that the British flour mills broke down, would be incurring a political risk, but that he would not be incurring any risk if he did the same thing to scent-making machinery. But beyond these elementary political facts, officials, and even Ministers if they had had time to determine such questions as these, were necessarily at sea until experience and increasing statistical knowledge taught them what was urgent and what was not. (Ministers may, of course, have been equally at sea in choosing between strategic possibilities which could not all be realized for reasons of supply; but at least they had expert advisers in this field.)

The nearest approach to a strategic scheme was in the clothing programme. In this (and later in the utility furniture scheme) there was a definite commitment in the shape of certain coupons which had to be honoured. But the clothing commitment was a short one—generally for a period of six months—and the furniture commitment could be varied by postponing the validity of certain classes of coupons. Thus the relation of the Board of Trade to its customers was wholly different from that of the munitions departments. Nor were the commitments precise. The original understanding was to supply so much clothing, not to supply so many boots, so many shirts, etc. In time, however, the programmes became more precise as the Board of Trade became better able to forecast consumers' purchases and learned more about the shortages of particular articles through its 'consumer need' services. (These services would remain a necessary instrument of administration in any future crisis which involved prolonged or intense shortages of consumer goods in the home market; but their findings would still have to be controlled by a highly empirical and largely political judgment as to the importance of the shortages disclosed.) In this way the clothing programme became subdivided into clothing and household linen, underwear and outerwear, and so forth. It goes without saying that in times of shortage the proportions of these could not be varied at will. Thus, in spite of some help which the Cotton Control was able to give, the cotton-spinning industry, as concentrated in 1941, never managed to produce as much hosiery yarn as was wanted and sometimes produced more towelling than was absolutely necessary; all that the Board of Trade could do was to make a virtue of necessity and reduce the coupon value of towels with an air of deliberate benevolence, hoping that this would placate some of those who were suffering from shortage of underwear.

Where the same department was responsible for satisfying the home and export requirements, yet another element of uncertainty and responsibility, that of fixing the proportion between the two, was introduced into the business of determining allocations. Nor was it even quite clear whose responsibility this was, at the official level. In the most important cases, such as cotton and steel, it was the Board of Trade that proposed an allocation between home and export trade or between one kind of export trade and another, and the Ministry of Production or its predecessors that disposed. (For example, it was the Production Executive, not the Board of Trade, that took the important decision to allow no more jute, flax or cotton for 'currency exports' at the beginning of 1942.) This relation was complicated by the fact that if a department responsible for protecting the interests of a particular class of consumers (such as the Colonial Office or the Dominions Office) did not like the Board of Trade's proposals it could appeal to the allocating authority. This was pre-eminently a political question and one which Ministers had frequently to be asked to handle. But they and their advisers were embarrassed by the lack of measurable, still more of commensurable, standards, and it was always a toss-up how a particular Minister or meeting of Ministers would react to the argument that 'a riot in Whitehall was worth two in the Bush'.

Although the civilian departments were thus embarrassed by the indeterminateness of the principles by which their system of priorities was supposed to be guided, there was one problem which—partly for that very reason—they did not have to take so seriously as the munitions departments. This was the problem of balanced production. It was quite useless to produce aircraft without clocks, machine-guns and bomb-sights; equally useless to produce clocks, machine-guns and bomb-sights without the rest of the aircraft. It was inconvenient, but much less disastrous, to produce boots without suits or even coats without trousers. Each shortage could be treated by itself. It might react on other shortages; for example, those who could not spend their coupons on stockings might buy shoes they did not really need, or those who could not buy torch-batteries would use cycle-lamps instead of torches, thereby accentuating the shortage of batteries for cyclists. But it could not render the production of something else quite useless. In theory the production of civilian goods could be rendered useless by lack of containers and packing materials; but the number of times that the output of goods other than food was proved to have been curtailed for this reason could be counted on the fingers of one hand. Without much conscious contrivance of civil servants the industries concerned made their own arrangements to avoid it. Not until the Board of Trade took over, almost at the end of the war, the responsibility for cookers, wash-boilers and other components of the housing programme, did it find itself really up against the problem of obtaining balanced production of the parts of a whole. Assembling a cooker from parts made by many different manufacturers involved, on a smaller scale, the same kind of programme and the same kind of progressing as assembling a Lancaster aircraft; and the task of keeping production of cookers, etc. for the temporary housing programme in step with that of the houses themselves was comparable to that of adjusting the output of munitions to a strategic plan. But this was the first time that the Board of Trade had had to face such problems: Ministers soon decided that such a purely regulative department ought not to deal with them, and the responsibility was transferred to the Ministry of Supply.

On the other hand, the civilian departments had their own difficulties, which resulted from the fact that they were not customers for the goods which were produced according to their programmes. A department which employs its own labour to work up the materials which have been allocated to it, or at least pays for the product, presumably need not worry so much over the thought that the manufacturers may not think it worth their while, or patriotic, to execute the programme at all. This, however, was one of the great, though intermittent, troubles of the Board of Trade. It was sometimes accentuated by the existence of large Service demands for the output of the civilian industries. These orders were, perhaps, more regular than the civilian demands for the same goods. They could, at least, be obtained with less trouble. Sometimes they were more profitable, at other times they seem to have been less so, and then it was more likely that the Service orders would go unexecuted. Service contract prices and manufacturers' profit margins were not always successfully related to each other, and it could not be foreseen whether, for example, the clothing industry would find it better worth while, at any given moment, to make uniforms or utility clothing. Whether this business was more profitable or not, the supply departments had machinery for seeing that it was punctually performed. Lastly, the prepossessions of the workpeople (sometimes encouraged by officials of the Ministry of Labour) often interfered with the execution of civilian programmes. Government propaganda was mainly concentrated on armaments production and created the impression that it was less patriotic to produce, say, saucepans than munitions. The labour supply inspectors reinforced this impression by directing workers away from saucepan production more often than they pruned redundancies in the munitions labour force. Small wonder, therefore, that in a factory where both saucepans and munitions were made the workers crowded to the munitions side of the house and the steel duly allocated for saucepans was left partly unused.

This reluctance of manufacturers and workpeople to produce for the civilian market, even when such production was authorized and urgently needed, could be partly overcome by propaganda designed to reassure them as to the importance of the work. It was harder for the civilian departments to overcome the disadvantages they suffered from the want of the power to place definite orders, and of a staff of progress officers to go round and keep manufacturers up to the mark. In the engineering industry a major project, such as an urgently needed power station or a big piece of oil-drilling machinery, could be pushed on against the competition of munitions by special measures, with the consent of the Central Priority Committee[1]. But it was much less easy to supervise, for example, the execution of the utility clothing programme by the cotton industry. In fact, for long periods together the Board of Trade's allocations of cotton yarn for home and export trade were insufficiently used. First it was the home allocation that was not taken up, but with the help of the Cotton Control the producers were finally spurred on to execute at least the utility clothing programme. Then the export trade, which had, of all claimants upon the output of this industry, the least definite organization for placing and progressing orders, fell behind in its turn, and provided the clearest instance of the weakness of the private customer in the face of organized programmes for purchase and production. Certain export customers fared better than others. The Dominions High Commissioners' offices developed some machinery for progressing, and the West African trade,

---

[1] The Central Priority Committee considered and reported to the Minister of Production upon applications by Departments for the award of priority to the production of munitions and other war stores.

which is largely in the hands of a great export company, did not come off too badly. At the other end of the scale, East Africa, where the import business is conducted mainly by small Indian bazaar merchants, never managed to use its allocations in full either in Great Britain or in the U.S.A. (Incidentally, the discrepancy between programmes and actual exports of cotton textiles was at least as great in the U.S.A. as here, which seems to show that the 'set-aside' system was no more effective than the British allocation system; but it should also be remembered that for the American exporters most of the markets which had to be supplied in this emergency were new and temporary.)

Against all these difficulties, however, the civilian departments had certain guarantees for the general execution of their programmes: the shortages, and the seller's market. Although the manufacturer was sometimes induced, by one consideration or another, to postpone civilian production to Service demands, it did not often happen that the civilian programme exceeded what he thought he could sell. (Where it did, as in torch-batteries, this was generally because public outcry caused a department to protect itself by raising its programme too high, and to under-rate such considerations as the seasonal character of the demand or the short shelf-life of the product.) The Board of Trade also had some hold over the manufacturer by reason of the fact that he desired to keep his name before the buyers and the public against the return of peacetime trading at home or abroad. This applied more to some things than to others—e.g. more to the manufacturer's pre-war brands than to utility or wartime models, and more to export markets which had prospects of permanent importance than to those which we were only supplying in an emergency. For instance, many manufacturers expressed great reluctance to accept orders for relief supplies to European countries with which they did not habitually trade. Unfortunately, the Government had, for one reason or another, to give a place in its programmes to many things for which the manufacturers saw no future after the war. These things were the hardest of all to get made.

The extreme case, perhaps, was that of the wooden-soled shoes. The manufacturers never believed that these would sell, even at reduced coupon values. Indeed, the only justification for sticking to the programme was the fear of an extreme shortage of leather which would make the public only too glad to buy anything; this fear was well grounded, although in the end the shortage was avoided. The logical thing would have been for a government department to order the goods and pay for them. The Board of Trade had no financial or purchasing machinery for this purpose. The Ministry of Supply would not undertake it. It was one thing to place orders for uniforms which were related to a definite programme for the strength of the Forces, or for bomb-sights which were related to a programme for producing a given number of aeroplanes, or even for cookers and wash-boilers which were related to a programme for producing a given number of temporary houses in a given time. In all these instances, if the programme to which the Government was committeed was carried out, the components were sure to be wanted. But the Ministry of Supply shrank, even in the last stages of the war, from entering into the market as a buyer of a highly speculative article in order to re-sell it to the general public. For the wooden-soled shoes the Ministry would only place a definite order on account of European relief, which was not a means of getting the shoes on to the home market.

In this kind of way the production programmes of civilian departments had a certain unreality about them, except where they were directly tied to a ration, which was only true of articles rationed by the Ministry of Food. Compared with the programmes of other departments they were not, in the full sense of the term, programmes at all, but estimates. This was not always understood by the critics or the spokesmen of these departments. The former complained of shortages as if nothing else were the matter but that the programmes were too small, and the latter justified themselves as though by making the programme all the necessary measures had been taken.

So far we have considered the execution of departmental programmes as a whole. Further questions arose over the execution of these programmes by a particular manufacturer, and also over the supply of finished or half-finished goods to a particular user.

DISTRIBUTION OF MATERIALS

The scale of production in a particular firm was more closely controlled by the allocation of material than by that of anything else. It is true that shortage of fuel or labour might interfere with production, too, but these were less calculable factors. Fuel cuts, when first applied, more often brought about fuel economies than reduction of output. In many industries each establishment had a 'permitted labour force' or an 'approved labour force', but the inflow of residual labour on the one hand, and the spontaneous drift to war work on the other, rendered these figures unreal as a basis of calculation. On the other hand, allocation of material was itself not a perfect guide or control to a producer's industrial activity. Most producers started with stocks of

material, raw or half-finished, and others, intentionally or not, accumulated stocks during the war by overestimating the materials they would
need for government contracts. The various raw material Controls
tried, of course, to discover these stocks, with increasing success. But
there were still, in certain industries, widows' cruses of material and
half-finished goods quite late in the war. Some of these were never
formally notified at all, and their existence was only traced by the
unexpected deficits of production which were experienced when they
finally gave out. This and other imperfections in the system of controlling industrial activity by the allocation of materials led to more
positive measures for legally limiting output by quantity or (more often)
by value.

The organization for distributing materials among manufacturers and
the principles on which they were distributed varied much. Generally
this was done by the Ministry of Supply's Raw Materials Controls,
but the user departments themselves issued steel, subject to supervision
by the Iron and Steel Control. Presumably the munitions departments
related their issues of steel to the individual manufacturer's programme
of work to be done for them. The Board of Trade had also to face the
problem—a still more important problem in peacetime—of issuing steel
to manufacturers whose programmes were not determined by Government orders. There were various ways of doing this.

The programme of the manufacturer might be determined by
licences to supply to the home market (known as machinery licences)
or licences to export, and the issue of steel and other metals might be
related to these licences. At the height of the war all machinery licences
and most export licences were licences to supply a particular customer.
This was necessary so long as capacity in the engineering industries
had to be reserved for war production by restricting all other uses of it
to the bare minimum; it was also necessary so long as the export customer had to be scrutinized in case he should be an enemy or an agent
for the enemy. Neither of these things furnished a precedent for postwar policy. It became rather doubtful whether the administrator in
charge of the licensing system could claim to know enough about the
merits of individual customers for machinery to justify him in continuing a system of individual licences in peacetime. A system of bulk
licences was therefore developed which merely limited the total supply
to the home or export market without specifying the customers. The
issue of steel continued to be correlated with the programme so licensed.
If on grounds of location, or for any other reason, an individual customer was to have priority over others, this could only be signified by

an exhortation to the manufacturer, and it is doubtful how much it would mean in practice.[1]

The chief point of this system was to control the ratio between home and export business. It would also be used to apportion exports between one market and another, should that be necessary. But it implies a seller's market; failing this, a manufacturer who chose to say that he had no export orders would have a very strong case against a department which threw his workpeople out of employment by refusing him additional licences and material to supply the home market.

None of this applies to the smaller metal manufacturers, or to the manufacturers of cotton, paper, jute, leather and the like. The production programmes of firms in these industries were generally dealt with in bulk. They were controlled not merely by allocations of material, but often, as well, by a system of licensing production—prohibiting that of certain articles, limiting that of others. The departments had to work out some principles for allocating materials and regulating activity as between one firm and another in these industries. The most popular, because the least controversial, principle was to grant to each firm, for civilian business, the same percentage of its pre-war user. A strong Control, such as the Cotton Control, which was trying to implement a definite programme such as the utility clothing programme, would be able to depart from this principle of equity all round; but a weak Control or department would adhere to it as the most obvious guarantee of its impartiality. There are certain objections to it. For one thing, it is not easy to reconcile (except at the height of a seller's market) with a well-defined policy as to the direction of exports. For another, it ignores the location of the manufacturing establishments. It might perhaps have been expected that considerations of location would have been provided for, once for all, by the concentration of industry, which closed establishments for preference in the 'difficult' labour areas and kept them open in the less congested. This was not so: only certain industries were concentrated and in most of those which were concentration was complete by the spring of 1942, whereas the worst instances of local congestion of industry only began to come to light in the middle of 1942. Thereafter the adherence by Controls and departments to the principle of equity all round caused some inconvenience to the Ministry of Labour; it did not make enough allowance for districts of exceptional congestion in wartime or for development areas in peacetime. This inconvenience could have been avoided by

[1] The author of this article left the civil service in December 1945 and cannot describe administrative developments since that date.

M

continual use of the regional machinery set up by the Ministry of Production; that is, by subjecting the production programmes of important industrial establishments to regional approval to be given in the light of the local supply and demand for labour. But there was a danger that this might have overloaded the regional machinery, and some headquarters administrators were inclined to consider submission to the regions as a piece of unnecessary red tape. Moreover, the headquarters administrator was exposed to 'the industry' whose national representatives were strongly interested in holding their organizations together by avoiding every kind of discrimination. It is therefore not surprising that consultation of the regions and, indeed, deference to the principle of differentiating according to location, were rather half-hearted in certain departments.

The same objections, and perhaps others besides, could be made to the practice of handing over allocations of material to export groups or other trade associations to be distributed by them among their members. This saved much labour, especially clerical labour, in government departments, and the groups and associations which took on this work rendered a public service with great devotion and often at great expense. But—without any conscious unfairness—there were difficulties about the performance of these expensive services for non-members; the departments sometimes found it awkward to have divested themselves of the power of control; and, above all, there was some danger that a corporative state would grow up, as it were, 'in a fit of absence of mind'.

The principles and technique of determining and using allocations, and of distributing materials to the firms within an industry, were not completely worked out in the war. The need for obtaining full cooperation from industries governed by competitive (even if imperfectly competitive) private enterprise sometimes caused the Government to falter in the execution of its policies. But the greatest cause for hesitation was the consciousness of imperfect knowledge. Although the statistical services available to the Government as a whole were much extended and improved in the war, and although a beginning was made with the exploration of consumers' needs, the civil servant was still governing largely by hearsay when he dealt with the factors which make for the rise and fall of production, and was still completing his education when the war ended. If he is to continue in peacetime to play the same kind of part, more definite arrangements will have to be made as to the incorporation of businessmen in the administrative service, consultations between the Government and organized industry, and the enlargement of the professional administrator's experience of industrial life.

XI

THE CONCENTRATION OF PRODUCTION POLICY

by

G. C. ALLEN

The concentration of production policy made an important contribution to the task of transferring resources from peacetime to wartime purposes and of ensuring that the available manpower and productive capacity of the nation were fully used. It carried forward governmental intervention from the stage in which it was confined to the imposition of general restrictions on the sales or the material-supplies of the civilian trades to a stage in which it penetrated into the fields of industrial organization and location. The policy, like many others that were followed between 1939 and 1945, depended for its success on close co-operation between government departments on the one hand and manufacturers and workers on the other, and, by reason of its novelty, it called forth new administrative devices for its execution.

Concentration of production may be regarded as the logical consequence of the restrictions on production that resulted from the Limitation of Supplies Orders and from various raw material controls. The Limitation of Supplies (Miscellaneous) Order, which came into force in June 1940, prohibited manufacturers and merchants in a wide range of consumption goods industries (e.g. hosiery, pottery, floor coverings, leather goods, cutlery) from supplying the home market with more than a stated proportion of the amount of goods supplied by them in a basic period. The objects of the Order were the release of manpower and other resources for war production or export and the conservation of stocks. The restrictions placed by the Ministry of Supply on the delivery of textile and other raw materials to the producers were designed to serve the same purpose in the group of industries to which they were applied, as well as to save shipping space. These measures were obviously incomplete, for to reduce the production of every firm in an industry by a uniform proportion was to ignore both the diverse capacities of firms for occupying their plants with government orders and also the contrast that existed at the time between areas in which labour was already scarce and those where it was still plentiful. Over a large section of industry the restrictions naturally led to a condition in which many firms were working well below the capacity of their plants and, therefore, uneconomically. This was most clearly seen in such trades as hosiery, where firms responded to the restrictions by putting their existing labour force on short time; but everywhere production far below capacity meant a heavy waste of resources. When the limitation on supply and on raw material allocations was intensified in the early months of 1941, the necessity for supplementing the policy of restriction became even more obvious, especially as by then a widespread shortage of manpower had begun to appear. Further, the increase in war production and the destruction of factories in air raids gave rise to an unsatisfied demand for space for production and storage. Much of this space, it was realized, would have to be found by the civilian industries of which the production had been curtailed, and it was not easy for those industries to make suitable space available as long as all their plants were in operation. At the same time the Government was concerned with checking the rise in prices. It was obviously undesirable that the diminished volume of civilian goods should be put on the market at prices which had been raised to cover costs inflated by uneconomical methods of working.

By the spring of 1941, therefore, conditions were favourable for the introduction of a measure for supplementing the general restrictions on civilian production and for ensuring that the resources no longer required in that production should be released for essential work. The principles underlying the new policy were set out in a White Paper (Concentration of Production: Explanatory Memorandum, Cmd. 6258) presented to Parliament by the President of the Board of Trade in March 1941. The main object of the policy, as indicated in paragraph 3 of the White Paper, was to concentrate the reduced production of each of the restricted industries on a proportion of the factories, so that every factory in operation might work to full capacity. The remaining factories would then become available for war production or for the storage of essential materials.

THE PROCESS OF CONCENTRATION

The industries selected for concentration were those in which it was believed a substantial amount of surplus capacity had been created by the restrictions, and the process by which concentration was to be achieved was that of self-selection on the part of the firms themselves, subject to conditions and sanctions imposed by the Government. This process, which was sketched in paragraphs 6–9 of the White Paper, requires detailed description. The Government definitely rejected methods which involved the formulation of 'schemes' for whole industries by representative bodies, and the policy thus presented from the outset a marked contrast to pre-war rationalization. The Government also decided against the official selection of 'runners' and 'closers'. Instead, they looked to individual firms, acting in small groups, to initiate the required changes in organization in the light of information, and under stimulus and encouragement, provided by the responsible department. The Government, accordingly, was to decide the degree of concentration appropriate to each industry and to determine the conditions which a satisfactory concentration arrangement in it should satisfy; but the actual arrangement in every case, including the choice of the 'runner' and the 'closer', was to be worked out by individual firms who would put up proposals to the Government. Normally, an individual firm was to arrange to transfer a sufficient amount of production from other firms to enable its establishment to 'run full'; or a firm with several establishments was to arrange to close one or more of them so that the surviving establishment might fulfil that requirement. A satisfactory arrangement, in addition to bringing about the complete closing down of the establishment from which production was to be transferred, also had to provide for the maintenance intact of the closed firm's plant (unless the premises should afterwards be requisitioned) and compensation for the 'closer'. When a concentration proposal which satisfied the conditions laid down for the industry was accepted by the Board of Trade, the continuing firm was officially recognized as a 'nucleus' firm and, as such, it was able to enjoy certain benefits. These included safeguards for its labour and raw material supplies, a qualified promise of protection against the requisitioning of its premises and, where possible, the offer of government orders. Promises were also given that closed firms would be assisted to re-start after the war, for the Government repeatedly emphasized that concentration was to be regarded as a wartime expedient and not as equivalent to rationalization of the pre-war character. The withholding of these benefits from firms which were unwilling to participate in concentration arrangements constituted the main sanction behind the policy.

The firms in each industry were given a stated period in which to put forward 'voluntary' concentration proposals. If at the end of that period it was found that some firms had not become parties to arrangements, then the Government regarded itself as free to impose concentration. In a few industries where there was a significant number of non-participants, the Government did in fact nominate 'nucleus' firms and 'closers' and required them to come to arrangements with one another within a short period. Failure to act might mean the invocation of the full sanctions against the reluctant firms.

At the outset it seemed probable that the provision of compensation for the closed firms would prove to be the most intractable problem of concentration, and pre-war experience of industrial reorganization certainly justified those fears. The system of individual arrangements, however, provided in fact a neat solution of this problem, for under it compensation could be left to mutual agreement between the parties. Normally, the 'nucleus' firm contracted to produce part of its output on behalf of its closed partner, which continued to sell through its usual marketing organization the supplies allotted to it. Certain safeguards were adopted to ensure that prices were not swollen by any compensation payments passing between 'nucleus' and closed firms. It was laid down, for instance, that, in general, compensation payments were to be regarded as a charge against profits and that they could not be put forward as a cost when price increases were claimed under the Government's price control system. Thus the proprietors of a closed firm were able to share with those of the 'nucleus' firm any profits that might be earned, but the possibility of loading prices with excessive compensation payments was ruled out. Satisfactory financial arrangements between concentrated firms were apparently reached with surprisingly little difficulty, and the swift execution of the policy was never delayed or endangered by trouble from this quarter.

The choice of the method of self-selection for effecting concentration is not to be explained solely because it offered an easy solution of the compensation problem. It was justified in the White Paper on the ground that it ensured 'the greatest possible degree of flexibility and variety in the devices that may be applied in each trade'. There was force in this argument. In many of the finished consumption goods trades, where the nature and scope of each producer's output varied widely, and where marked contrasts were to be found within the same trade between the firms who were able to change over to war production and those who were not, self-selection was probably the only practicable method. But experience showed that there were other industries which could best be covered by a general scheme drawn up for the producers as a whole, and in several large and important industries this method of concentration, although it had been rejected in the White Paper, was in fact adopted. In such trades as cotton spinning, concentration arrangements by which each 'nucleus' firm produced part of its output for a closed partner would, indeed, have been slow and difficult to work out and, in the circumstances of the time, would have created a cumbersome and artificial organization in the industry. Where industry-wide schemes were introduced it was usually necessary to provide compensation for 'closers' by establishing a pool into which all 'nucleus' firms paid levies and from which the 'closers' drew sums sufficient to provide for the care and maintenance of their plants. At first the compensation paid was limited to that purpose; but later schemes provided, in addition, for a share in profits. Compensation schemes of this sort called for government supervision, and they had to be presented for official approval, since it was necessary to ensure that such schemes did not result in either the evasion of taxation or the enhancement of prices. The difficulties that arose over them showed the wisdom of the Government's reliance on the method of self-selection wherever it was practicable.

It is necessary here to refer to a further source of difficulty. In many industries the number of very small firms was considerable. Often the labour force of these firms was immobile; the premises were usually valueless to the Factory and Storage Control; and the economies to be realized by concentration were frequently very small. Further, the Government was anxious to defend its policy from the charge that it was calculated to destroy the small producer. At the same time it was considered unjust to withhold from small firms the benefits that participants in concentration arrangements were to enjoy. Hence it was decided that while small firms were to be permitted to participate if they chose, no compulsion or pressure was to be exercised on them. If, of course, they decided to remain aloof, their abour and premises were unprotected; but as their labour and premises were largely unsuitable for war work this risk was generally inconsiderable. A small firm, in most industries, was defined as one which normally employed fewer than twenty workers.

The Board of Trade was the department mainly responsible for the administration of the policy, although the Ministry of Food acted as the responsible department in the food and drink trades and the Ministry of Works and Buildings in the brick-making industry. Many other departments, however, were affected and had to be consulted over each concentration arrangement that was proposed. For instance, the Ministry of Labour was closely interested in number and type of workers to be released and in the location of the firms designated as 'nucleus'. Industries were informed that they were required to transfer production to areas where labour was relatively plentiful and that agreement might be refused to arrangements which did not satisfy this condition. 'Nucleus' firms had to be prepared to release their more mobile workers for the Forces or for munition trades and to replace them by other workers from the closed factories. In the early stages of each concentration arrangement, firms were therefore obliged to consult the Divisional Controllers of the Ministry of Labour. After a proposal had been formulated the labour force of the participants had to be examined in detail, and the selection of the workers who were to be employed in the 'nucleus' firm and those who were to be transferred elsewhere was undertaken in close consultation with the Divisional Controllers. In some industries local panels representative of Government, the trade unions and the employers were set up to help in this task.

The Factory and Storage Control in the Board of Trade had responsibilities, similar to those of the Ministry of Labour, in respect of premises released by concentration, and its agreement was required before any arrangement could be concluded. The supply departments also were consulted, since the choice of 'nucleus' firms was dependent in some degree on their actual or potential importance as government contractors. Further, those departments were committed to a policy of discriminating against non-participants in the bestowal of orders as well as in the allocation of materials. Thus close co-operation among several departments was required both in judging the content of every concentration proposal and also in the subsequent execution of policy.

Scope

Concentration was applied at the outset to the majority of industries covered by the Limitation of Supplies (Miscellaneous) Order and to a few large industries subject to raw material control (e.g. cotton spinning and weaving, woollen and worsted, boots and shoes). During 1941 and 1942 its scope was extended, and ultimately some seventy branches of industry were covered by the policy as administered by the Board of Trade, apart from the food industries and the brick-making industry. The process of concentration had been largely completed by the spring of 1942 in the industries originally selected, but it continued for some time longer in industries which were later brought within the scope of the policy, and some schemes of reconcentration had to be introduced to deal with industries that suffered a further contraction after an initial concentration. By July 1943, when little remained to be done except in the clothing industry, some 6,200 nucleus certificates had been issued by the Board of Trade, and these provided for the closing of about 3,500 establishments.

Since concentration was designed mainly to save scarce resources, its success (so it might be supposed) could be measured by the quantity of labour and factory space released as a direct consequence of the policy. In fact, however, it is difficult to furnish accurate statistical evidence of this kind. The Board of Trade estimated that by July 1943 257,000 workers and 70 million square feet of gross factory space had been released by concentration. These, however, are figures of releases provided for in the several schemes, and as many acts of policy other than concentration were occurring contemporaneously it is impossible to determine precisely the contribution made by any one of them. This is especially so because, while in many cases concentration followed the contraction of an industry's output, in other cases it coincided with it.[1] Moreover, the policy was responsible not merely for net releases of workers, but also for changes in the composition of the labour force of the firms affected. So, even in industries where the net release was small, concentration often helped to bring about a transference of mobile workers to munitions production and to their replacement by older or part-time workers. Again, additional resources were made available for the war by means of the geographical shift in civilian production that concentration sometimes caused. These effects of the policy are hardly susceptible to measurement, since they involve qualitative as well as quantitative changes in the distribution of resources. A full assessment of the results of the policy thus requires a detailed study of its operation, and this will be attempted after the machinery for the execution of the policy has been viewed.

Administrative Machinery

Interdepartmental co-operation in the administration of the policy was matched by the co-operation between the firms affected and the Government. Indeed, the Government saw this to be a necessary condi-

---

[1] It should be noted that while concentration was originally thought of as an operation that followed, both logically and in time, the various restrictions on output, in practice concentration and contraction sometimes occurred simultaneously and were administered as a single act of policy. Further, after 1941, when the Government began to introduce 'utility' and 'quasi-utility' schemes which prescribed the types of goods to be manufactured, concentration, contraction and a quasi-utility scheme were occasionally introduced and operated together. What, in fact, happened was that the department responsible for concentration, having in mind the main purpose of its policy (viz. the realization of economies in the use of resources), was sometimes able, in the course of working out a concentration scheme, to associate with it other means for saving space or labour in the trade affected. Thus the activities of the officials concerned with concentration often strayed beyond their own special field when circumstances revealed the advantage of doing so.

tion of success when it first formulated its policy. For, while the Government enunciated general principles, laid down the broad conditions with which approved concentration arrangements were to conform, and devised sanctions, the application of the principles and their working out in detail were left largely to the industrialists themselves. This applied both to the individual concentration arrangements and to the industry-wide schemes. No other division of responsibility, indeed, had the slightest chance of success, for only men who were themselves engaged in the operation of the industries could devise the particular arrangements that both were reasonably equitable between the parties and also achieved, without serious dislocation, the transference of production contemplated. The information available about the industries in the government departments was, except in a few instances, quite inadequate to have enabled civil servants to select the 'runners' and 'closers', and even if this had been done the task of settling terms and compensation in a multitude of intricate cases would have led to intolerable delays. The reasons for the willingness of the business community to co-operate will be discussed presently.

The method of self-selection also enabled the Government to overcome (or rather to side-step) the formidable task of defining the several industries. There were, it is true, a few occasions when it was necessary to take somewhat arbitrary decisions on whether certain firms on the periphery of a trade should be subjected to any pressure to bring about their participation, but in general the system of individual arrangements avoided the need for raising the question of definition. It is significant that the industry-wide schemes were applied to trades where definition was relatively easy. Here the body of manufacturers concerned had little difficulty in reaching agreements that were generally acceptable about the treatment of peripheral firms.

A second feature of the policy was the flexibility with which it was administered. Since the White Paper had contented itself with a very general statement of aims and means, those charged with the administration of the policy were left with a wide discretion. This was possible largely because the policy could be carried out without the granting of new powers. The sanctions which could be invoked were already available to the Government, and the concentration policy thus relied on the use of existing powers for a new purpose. Flexibility in administration was greatly assisted by the close association of the businessmen who formed part of the Board's Industrial and Export Council with the departmental officials. A committee of that Council was set up to examine the various problems that were thrown up from time to time;

but the most valuable work was done by the business members in their individual capacity. To each of them a number of industries was allotted, and they undertook the task of explaining the policy to the firms and of advising them on ways of carrying through the reorganization that was necessary. This procedure certainly helped to win the confidence of manufacturers, since they felt that the policy was being applied by persons who were familiar with their problems and sympathetic with their difficulties.

The business members were, of course, assisted by civil servants who themselves took an active part in the discussions of particular schemes, besides being responsible for ensuring that the broad principles of policy were adhered to. They had to interpret, in the context of every industry, the somewhat elusive concept of 'running full', the condition which every 'nucleus' firm was supposed to satisfy, and they had to provide themselves with statistical information (the lack of which seriously hampered their work at the outset) by instituting *ad hoc* inquiries and censuses. It was customary for them, whenever a new industry was brought within the scope of the policy, to spend some time in visiting factories and in acquiring basic information about the trade. In the course of their work their knowledge of the industries with which they were concerned became fairly substantial.

The staff of the Concentration of Production Department, even in the latter part of 1941 when the volume of work was at its maximum, was quite small. This was because the method of administering the policy made possible the decentralizing of many decisions and threw much responsibility on bodies and persons outside the Department. Even in industries where individual concentration arrangements were the rule, the trade associations gave much help in acting as channels of communication to their members, in advising on compensation arrangements, and in discussing the multitudinous consequential problems as they arose. Where industry-wide schemes were adopted, the trade associations, or *ad hoc* committees of manufacturers, often worked out the detailed proposals in consultation with the officials. In some industries (notably those subject to raw material controls) the Ministry of Supply Controllers played an important part in the selection of the 'nucleus' firms. This was so, for instance, in the cotton spinning and weaving industries, where 'nucleus' firms were chosen on the advice of the Cotton Controller, who worked in close association with the regional representatives of the Ministry of Labour and the Control of Factory and Storage Premises. In these industries, which were covered by a central compensation pool, the Cotton Board was responsible for formulating the detailed proposals and for administering the payments to and from the fund.

It can be claimed that the policy was successful in freeing a larger quantity of suitable resources for the war, and in obtaining this result with less dislocation in the industries affected than would otherwise have occurred. In the absence of the policy the Ministry of Labour would have had a harder task in obtaining from those industries the manpower needed for the Forces and for munitions, the prices of many civilian goods would have risen more than they did because unit-costs would have been higher, and the financial position of the restricted industries would have deteriorated more seriously. The policy was carried out with a comparatively small expenditure in administrative manpower, and on the whole it proceeded smoothly and rapidly.

Whether concentration succeeded equally well in its secondary aim of keeping industries in better condition for redevelopment than would otherwise have been possible is, except in regard to their financial condition, open to argument, and on this the experience of the several industries points in different directions. Closed firms were certainly able, through their 'nucleus' partners, to maintain their access to the market and to preserve their selling organization, and funds accrued to them under the compensation arrangements for the care and maintenance of their plants. But once a firm has ceased production it inevitably finds greater difficulty in rebuilding its business than one which has been kept running, however low its level of activity may have been. The reconstitution of the labour force of the closed firms has in some trades proved to be very difficult. It must be remembered, however, that for many firms the alternative to closure under a concentration scheme was not continued operation at a low level of activity, but closure by an act of requisition or by the withdrawal of key workers. The absence of a concentration policy would certainly have caused greater hardships to the individual firms on whom the lot fell than those which, in the event, they had to endure, and the transference of civilian production would have taken place piecemeal and usually in circumstances of considerable confusion. Concentration may be said to have organized this transference and to have introduced conditions in which it was possible to give weight to all the factors that were relevant to the major task of mobilizing resources for war, viz. the types and location of manpower and space required for the war industries, the need for continuing certain kinds of civilian production, and the importance of the firms concerned as government contractors.

FACTORS MAKING FOR SUCCESS

The smoothness and speed with which the policy was, in general, carried out can be largely attributed to the administrative methods that were followed. These have already been described; but, if any aspect of them is selected for emphasis, it should certainly be the well-judged division of function between government departments on the one hand and the manufacturers who were the object of the policy on the other. Since the co-operation of businessmen was a condition of the policy's success, a division of function that was acceptable to them, while it left unimpaired the Government's authority to determine objectives, was obviously of supreme importance. Many of the decisions that were taken inevitably led to hardship and disappointment for individuals, and it may seem surprising that, in any circumstances, the ready co-operation of business in such a policy could be secured. A patriotic recognition of the overriding needs of the war does not afford the whole explanation. Doubtless many industrialists thought that failure on their part to co-operate would have left the framing of the schemes to civil servants, and this, they believed, would have produced less equitable and satisfactory results than those reached under the influence of men with an intimate knowledge of the trades affected. It may well be, moreover, that some manufacturers had an exaggerated conception of the force of the sanctions which the Government would in fact have invoked against non-participants.

The achievements of concentration were by no means uniform throughout industry. The policy, judged both by the smoothness with which it was carried out and by the quantity of resources which it released, was most successful in substantial trades located in a few main centres and composed of a considerable number of medium-sized establishments engaged in the manufacture of broadly similar types of goods. For example, it achieved noteworthy success in hosiery, pottery, leather goods, cotton spinning and weaving, and jute. It encountered the most serious obstacles in trades in which production was conducted in a few large establishments (as in rubber manufacture) or where the units of production were scattered geographically (as in paper manufacture). In these cases it was difficult to arrange for the complete closing of plants, and although production might be transferred, concentration did not yield substantial economies in overhead charges or make available whole factories. Its application, moreover, was narrowly limited in industries in which there were large numbers of small firms (e.g. toys, fancy goods). Here the space and labour made available were often unsuitable for war uses. There were also striking contrasts between the various concentrated industries in the ratio of net space made available to gross space released. Where the machines in a closed works were comparatively small they could be stored in a section of the premises, and nearly the whole of the gross factory space could thus be put to other uses (e.g. in boot and shoe factories and weaving sheds). But where the plant consisted largely of massive units of equipment it was seldom worth while to take these down, and consequently only a small amount of net usable space was made available in the closed factory (e.g. in rayon spinning).

It might have been expected that concentration would have been easier to bring about smoothly and quickly when it coincided with the process of contraction than when it followed that process. In the former case it was indeed possible to review the labour force as a whole before it was dispersed and to organize its subsequent distribution in the most economical fashion. When concentration occurred some time after a steep contraction, the labour force of a factory that was a suitable candidate for nucleus status might already have been drawn into other employments, and difficulties were sometimes encountered in rebuilding it, especially when the closed partner was situated in a distant place. On the other hand, some of the most successful concentrations (notably hosiery, pottery and leather goods) were in industries in which contraction had preceded concentration, and it is probable that experience by the manufacturers of the damaging effects of contraction on their businesses made them readier to co-operate in the concentration policy than they would otherwise have been. Moreover, the difficulties in connection with the labour supply that have been referred to hardly arose in industries such as hosiery where, in spite of the contraction of trade before March 1941, the workers had not been dispersed but were being employed on short time. When these circumstances were present they provided a more forcible demonstration of the need for concentration than any abstract argument could have done.

It is debatable whether concentration should have been applied to the most 'inessential' industries which afterwards had to be closed down completely or subjected to a drastic reconcentration. The Government, in issuing nucleus certificates, had given a qualified promise to safeguard the labour and factories of the firms to which they were issued. When, as happened in a few instances, the over-riding claims of the war required that these safeguards should be withdrawn, the firms naturally felt aggrieved, and this may sometimes have led to delays in taking steps which the demands of war required. It is, however, easy to be wise after the event, and the circumstances which occasionally brought concentration schemes to an end could seldom be foreseen. Such circumstances were not confined to inessential trades, for some important industries (e.g. floor coverings) were affected because of a steep reduction in supplies of materials. Further, these misfortunes were at times bound to attend the application of the principle, enunciated in the initial stages of the policy, that all firms in the contracted industries should be given an opportunity of sharing in such advantages as the Government had to offer to participants in concentration.

It is clear that in some respects the primary purpose of concentration (viz. the freeing of resources for the war) was likely to clash with the secondary purpose (viz. the preservation of the structure of the several trades so that they could resume their activities after the war). Thus the maintenance of a selling organization by firms that had ceased production—a practice which was encouraged in many industries—meant some waste of resources, although this was probably small, since the firms as a rule merely retained a skeleton staff. Of greater importance in this connexion was the provision that the plants of closed firms should be kept intact (unless the factories should be requisitioned), as the application of compensation payments to the care and maintenance of such plants meant that the savings in indirect labour were not always as great as had been hoped. This provision, however, was an integral part of the policy, and its omission would have jeopardized the postwar prospects of the closed firms and would have greatly increased their reluctance to participate. There were, however, a few industries where the costs of maintenance were very high (e.g. rayon spinning), and it may be that some alternative method of obtaining the required resources from these industries would have been preferable to concentration. These shortcomings could scarcely be avoided in view of the speed with which the policy had to be pursued, and concentration was not, of course, pushed through to a logical conclusion when strong practical reasons against doing so emerged in the course of administration.

The speed with which it was necessary to apply the policy was also responsible for such failures in interdepartmental co-ordination as occurred. It was obviously necessary, if full advantage was to be reaped from the policy, that the machinery for surveying and directing the labour force should be ready to operate as soon as the closure of a factory took effect, or indeed before the workers began to drift away in anticipation of closure. Close co-ordination both at headquarters and in the regions was therefore essential, and at the outset this was sometimes lacking. Furthermore, experience showed the importance of a precise and detailed knowledge of the composition of the labour force in every concentrated industry. In a few concentration schemes there was a loss of labour, because some workers who were not subject to direction, or who in some way escaped direction, passed out of employment altogether when their firms were closed and so were not available to build up the labour force of the nucleus firms. A completely successful concentration policy thus depended upon the existence of a tight control of labour of all ages.

The 'lessons of war' are not always useful in peacetime, and wartime analogies are often misleading. Nevertheless, the experience gained in the administration of the wartime concentration policy is not without relevance to the general issue of State intervention in industry. One of the main administrative problems that has to be solved in that connexion concerns the distinction which must be made between the types of decision that can most usefully be taken by the central authority and those that should be left to individuals in the trades affected. It may be claimed that in the concentration policy a reasonably efficient compromise was reached. Here, as we have seen, the Government set out the objectives of policy, laid down the conditions that had to be satisfied and established sanctions; but the firms and industries to which the policy was applied were given the task of working out the arrangements in detail. This division of function has much to commend it. The industrial structure is so complex and the differences between firms even in the same industry are so wide as to make reliance upon any single prescription for industrial reorganization or control very unwise, and flexibility in administration is therefore of first importance.

It must be recognized, however, that such a division of function can only be successful if certain conditions are satisfied. In the first place, much depends on the measure of success achieved in enlisting the support of the manufacturers in the industries affected. In peacetime this support is more difficult to obtain than in war, for the claims of patriotism are then ambiguous and the sanctions that can be invoked are usually less powerful. So there is need for the Government to seek the means of obtaining willing co-operation. If this is to be given, the businessmen must have confidence both in the good sense of the Ministers and officials with whom they have to deal and also in the determination of the Government in the pursuit of its objectives. The concentration policy showed clearly the necessity for a combination of firmness in regard to principle with a willingness of departments to compromise over detail, and such failures as occurred can be attributed largely either to attempts to apply the policy to industries where conditions were unfavourable for its success, or to a failure to insist on conformity with the main principles of the policy in cases where strong and un-justified resistance was encountered.

Obviously, the fulfilment of these conditions makes heavy demands on those responsible for administration. They need knowledge and judgment in discriminating between what must be insisted upon and what may be the subject of compromise. They must, therefore, be sensi-tive to the industrial atmosphere and capable of estimating what is likely to work in any particular situation. As already pointed out, the association of leading businessmen with the officials in the execution of the concentration policy greatly strengthened the capacity of the re-sponsible department in these respects; but it is not easy to enlist the services of such men in peacetime. Concentration further demonstrated the need for a substantial and up-to-date body of statistical information as a prerequisite of a policy of this kind, and it suggested that some technical knowledge of the industries would greatly benefit the officials who have to handle their affairs. During the war day-to-day contacts with manufacturers gave civil servants a keener sense of industrial realities than they previously possessed, and businessmen a glimpse of the wider implications of policy. This mutual understanding of each other's problems is a condition of success in most acts of governmental intervention in industry. Without it the official is liable to disregard (or to doubt the reality of) the intricacies of industry that so often com-plicate the task of applying a measure of economic policy, and he may then be inclined to content himself with a rigid adherence to bureau-cratic procedure; while the businessman comes to view governmental intervention as inevitably arbitrary and ill-informed and is tempted to use all his ingenuity in finding means for evading what the State intends.

N

XII

RATIONING

by

W. B. REDDAWAY

THE NEED FOR RATIONING

A total war effort implies, almost by definition, shortages of consumers' goods. In this country there is the special problem of shipping,
which may drastically reduce the flow of imports with no chance of
wholly replacing them from home production. But it is now generally
realized that this is by no means the only factor cutting down supplies.
Labour, factory space, internal transport, domestically produced materials and fuel—indeed, resources of all kinds—must be diverted to the
war effort, leaving only enough on civilian work to produce the 'essential minimum' needed to maintain the population's strength and
morale. If this is not done then the war effort is not total.

Theoretically, it might be possible to reduce demand so much by
taxation and savings campaigns that the fall in supplies did not lead
to 'shortages' in the popular sense of queues and 'no beer' notices,
or even to excessive prices and profiteering. There are, however, many
powerful and well-known reasons for thinking this unlikely to be
achieved in practice: many family incomes will have increased with
overtime and the greater employment of women; taxation must not be
made so drastic as to kill all incentive or create intolerable hard cases;
heavy taxation may lead many to live on their savings rather than
reduce consumption further; even where consumption in general would
be cut sufficiently, key items like petrol, fats or sugar would not; and
so on. For the purpose of this chapter I shall simply assume that
shortages cannot be avoided by fiscal devices, whilst stressing the desirability of using the latter as far as possible to moderate the tide of excess
demand against which the distributor of supplies must battle. I shall
also assume, without arguing the merits of the case, that prices of nearly
all goods are to be controlled, so that queues and shop shortages will
not be avoided by the classic method of the free market.

These premises lead almost inevitably to the subject of rationing and
kindred devices. If supplies of important goods are not enough to satisfy

all would-be purchasers, then the administrators must provide some system to secure orderly distribution and a certain degree of equity.

The second of these objectives is deliberately couched in modest terms. Perfect equity will clearly be unattainable, since individual needs vary in ways which are too complex for the administrative machine to measure and follow exactly. The real test of a rationing scheme so far as equity is concerned is that it should produce a more acceptable pattern of distribution than would emerge from the alternative 'system' of queues, favoured customers, shop-crawling, and the like. Clearly our standards in this respect can be fairly low: for most goods, a system of rough justice imposed by an impartial rationing authority is likely to give better results than a general scramble, and by securing *orderly* distribution it should also have the merit of cutting out the unpleasant and time-wasting process of scrambling. One may perhaps add that distribution under rationing will nearly always be more equitable than in peacetime, even if the administration is too heavy-handed for fine adjustments.

SPECIFIC AND GROUP RATIONS

The rationing system which might seem to follow most logically from the analysis of *general* scarcity of productive resources and consequent general excess of demand is a limit to each person's *total* purchases taken over a wide field, with the maximum of freedom of choice within that field. Historically, however, rationing was evolved from the opposite end, with separate schemes for particular commodities and no right of interchange. Such a system would, of course, be entirely appropriate if there were acute shortages of particular key items without any *general* excess of demand; the United States in 1947 was still rationing sugar to ensure everyone a fair share of the inexpansible supply of that highly prized foodstuff, even though traders were already worrying about excessive stocks of many other goods. But this is not the typical war-time position, and rationing was, in fact, introduced in the first world war at a time of general shortage. A 'specific' basis was adopted then because that seemed the easiest way to make rationing work quickly and the easiest system to explain to the public, rather than because it was thought desirable for everyone to have precisely the same amount of *each* rationed food as his neighbour, with other things left to the free market. The success of that heroic pioneering venture caused the 1918 system to be regarded between the wars as almost synonymous with rationing, both by academic writers and by the committee which considered the preparations needed for rationing food if another war should come. 'Group' rationing on a points basis, especially as applied to non-consumables like clothes, received little or no serious attention, and its problems had to be worked out as the war progressed against a background of 'specific' rations which were already in operation for many items.

Nobody would now deny the necessity for group rations on a points basis. It is not merely, or even mainly, that specific rations limit freedom of choice; in the last resort consumers to whom the standard menu is unacceptable can probably find a fellow rebel with whom to exchange bacon for mutton or tea for sweets. The real difficulty is that only a limited part of the field can be covered on such a basis, even if we are prepared to have a whole library of different ration books. The available amounts of almost anything but the staple items would only yield a minute ration, even if this is fixed for a period longer than the traditional week; a ration of overcoats or sheets would, for example, be out of the question, since even in peacetime the average number purchased is less than one per person per annum. The administrative effort needed to set up a whole series of rationing schemes for the secondary commodities would be fantastic, and the results of sharing them equally in the face of widely differing tastes and needs would be far from ideal.

Granted, however, that points rationing is essential, two questions remain: For what commodities (if any) should we have specific rations? and, How many group schemes should there be, and what should they cover? These subjects are far too wide for proper treatment here. If it should ever again be deemed necessary to set up a committee to consider the rationing preparations needed for another war, it should undoubtedly be given the widest terms of reference. In drawing on the experience of the recent war, moreover, it would be well advised to remember that our actions were much influenced by the initial preconception in favour of separate, specific rations; changing horses in mid-stream is notoriously dangerous, and once the public, the trade and the administrative staff had grown accustomed to certain arrangements the most powerful arguments would have been needed to justify a change of principle.

It is almost inevitable that an economist's instinct should be in favour of a small number of group rations covering as wide a field as is practicable. The advantages of consumers' freedom of choice are an essential part of his stock in trade, and he is not much impressed by the bogy of disputes about the rival claims on the family ration of father's tobacco,

mother's cosmetics or Johnny's sweets, because precisely the same problem arises with the family's money income in peacetime. He is, on the
other hand, much impressed by the disadvantages of an unorganized
market in which supply is chronically below the level of demand, and
is well aware that many commodities can only be covered by rationing
if the principle is accepted of having very broad groups, preferably
including some major item(s) in general demand; variations in individual needs which would make a narrowly based scheme indefensible
can be tolerated in a wider one, where they will to some extent even
out and where the remaining inequity can be regarded as preferable
to the alternative of a general scramble. Indeed, if it were not for the
insuperable administrative difficulties of making it work properly his
sympathy would probably be with the advocates of the single 'expenditure ration' or something on similar lines; he will almost certainly
consider that the onus of proof is on anybody who wants to establish
a specific ration for some commodity, or to exclude it from rationing
altogether—though he will be perfectly prepared to agree that a good
case can be made out in particular instances.

To take the other extreme, specific rations for the essential foodstuffs
make possible an exact balancing of supply and demand, and a certainty of correct distribution to meet the ration, which cannot be
guaranteed under points schemes, especially with perishable goods.
The advantage of this is not only that it makes life much easier for
the administrator and the trader; it also insures the housewife against
the fate of many in America who found it difficult to use their points
for a Sunday joint, and did not consider that the ration was fully
honoured by an offer of butter instead. We may prefer to dine à la carte
on the points system when we are genuinely free to select from the
whole list, but the certainty of reasonable table d'hôte meals on specific
rations may be preferable to a 'free choice' from a menu on which all
the meat dishes may be 'off' simultaneously.

Clearly these questions call for a very careful balancing of conflicting
arguments. The general public's initial attitude was probably in favour
of the 'simplicity' of specific rations and against mixing up dissimilar
items; but people have learnt to manage the complexities of points and
coupon values, just as they have learnt that in times of shortage the
ration book is their ally rather than their enemy. This change in the
general outlook is sufficient in itself to call for a reconsideration of
fundamental principles, and so is the experience which has been gained
in administering a points ration covering goods which are subject to
quite different influences on the supply side. If there should ever be a

'next time' things would be possible which were rightly rejected as out of the question in the recent war.

THE REQUIREMENTS FOR A SUCCESSFUL RATIONING SCHEME

There are really two logically separable tests which a proposal to introduce a rationing scheme must pass: it must be reasonably equitable as between different consumers, and it must be administratively workable. As so often happens, the two overlap a good deal in practice, since a greater amount of administrative action will nearly always improve the equity of the scheme by introducing more special arrangements for hard cases. But it is useful to think of the two sets of difficulties separately, because they raise some quite distinct issues. Perhaps a better division would be between the problems on the *demand* side associated with consumers and those on the *supply* side associated with the control of production and distribution and the honouring of the ration.

Two examples from the field of clothes rationing will show how a proposal may pass one test easily but fail at the other. Thus, from the consumer's angle there would have been no objection to the inclusion of headgear in the ration, and the general argument in favour of a broadly based ration would have supported it; but the methods of its production happened to raise acute problems of control and coupon collection for the administrator, as explained on p. 195 below.[1] On the other hand, the machinery for controlling the production and distribution of cloth and clothing could easily have been extended to cover blankets, sheets and other household textiles; indeed, it would probably have been easier to devise a comprehensive system, but their inclusion would have raised acute 'consumer' difficulties (e.g. new households) which could hardly be added to the inevitable problems involved in launching a novel rationing scheme which had to be prepared in secret.[2]

Little will be said here about the consumer problems. The administrator's great objective is, of course, to arrange the system so that, in the main, it will be considered sufficiently equitable if all people are given the same number of coupons—or at least that the special cases shall be restricted to a small number of clearly defined and easily

---

[1] The same was true of the fur trade, but in that case the difficulties had to be faced so as to avoid the inequity of demanding coupons for cloth coats whilst leaving fur coats off the ration for those who could afford them. Hats are not a substitute for rationed clothing.

[2] Later, when the machine was running smoothly, these could be covered by special arrangements.

identifiable classes, such as 'children under five', to whom a differential ration can be issued without great difficulty. The thing to be avoided if at all possible is a great number of individual applications for special treatment—and it must always be remembered that if even 1 per cent of the population apply in a year that means nearly 10,000 applications *per week*. If a few clear general rules can be adopted, as with the issue of coupons to people who have been bombed, then a flood of this kind may be manageable, and, of course, it is worth while undertaking a fair amount of administrative work to deal with the fringe of hard cases if the alternative would be the breakdown of an important rationing system. But if the great bulk of the supply has to be authorized by individual special issues, then the scheme will only be worth while in exceptional cases (e.g. petrol).

The issue of special supplements can to some extent be reduced by a suitable arrangement of the ration itself. Thus a broadly based ration covering a number of diverse commodities will lead to a considerable levelling out of individual requirements, and will also provide more scope for individuals whose needs are on balance above the average to make the best possible adjustments. There will be less pressure for concessions to particular classes under such circumstances, and it will be much easier for the administrator to argue that, over the whole field of the ration, the needs of that class are not really sufficiently exceptional to justify special treatment. He has, as we saw above, no reason to be ashamed about accepting a rather low standard of equity in order to make a rationing scheme work, and on the whole the public will accept this view, too.

Apart from this a 'points' system gives some scope for fixing the points values of particular articles so as to make an *equal* number of coupons give an *equitable* amount of purchasing power. The clearest case of this was the lower pointing of children's clothes, which enabled the ration to be launched without any special arrangements for them to have more coupons; 'infants'' clothes were pointed still lower, so that children under about four automatically got an even bigger number of garments to offset their rapid growth, etc. Something can be done by exempting items which are only wanted by people whose needs are likely to be exceptional (e.g. blacksmiths' leather aprons), but this policy can only be applied with great caution if the freedom from coupons might attract a flood of other purchasers; thus it was found unsatisfactory to exempt industrial overalls, but a special low pointing was fixed for them.

Even with all these devices, however, there will almost certainly have to be some supplements if supplies (and so the ration) are reduced to the minimum level postulated by a total war effort.[1] Experience with clothes rationing suggests that the wise course is to have a few major classes of supplement, to correspond with very broad assessments of differential needs, and not to attempt anything over-refined. Thus in the first year a fairly elaborate set of 'industrial supplements' was evolved, with different rates for different occupations. Unfortunately, the relative amount of strain on clothing experienced by people in the various occupations was not only extremely difficult to assess, but also seemed to differ greatly from factory to factory, so that in some cases the wrong man clearly got the higher award. These anomalies led to the adoption in later years of a 'flat ten' for all manual workers, coupled with the issue of small pools of coupons to the really heavy industries, to be administered by works committees. This system cost far less administrative effort, since it involved no attempt to discriminate from Whitehall between one man and another, except at the boundary where the dividing line was drawn; nevertheless, it seemed to give considerably greater satisfaction, despite the obviously varying needs of the people who all received ten coupons. In the matter of discrimination errors of omission were forgiven as inevitable, where errors of commission created a sense of real grievance.

THE MECHANICS OF A RATIONING SYSTEM

The 'mechanics' of a rationing system may be said to fall into two broad parts: the work of actually printing and issuing the coupons to the various classes of consumers (the 'issue' side), and the work of ensuring that they are properly honoured (the 'supply' side).

I do not intend to say more than a few words about the issue side. It is indeed a most formidable task to devise suitable ration books, get 50 million of them printed and distributed, ensure that everybody gets

[1] Supplements will be particularly necessary if there are no unrationed items (e.g. potatoes, bread and restaurant meals) which can serve as a safety valve. Differential food rations for 'heavy' workers were not given on a large scale until bread was rationed, whereas the comprehensive nature of clothes rationing made them necessary from the outset. It is not possible to discuss here the rival merits of a comprehensive scheme, with differential rations, as against a narrower one which relies on unrationed items to serve as balancers. The former system is theoretically capable of being more equitable, since the unrationed items (notably restaurant meals) can be bought by people without any real claim to a supplement even if special allowances are given to industrial canteens; there is also the difficulty that some people with good claims may not be able to get the unrationed items. But the differential rations cannot be fixed with perfect equity, and the need for administrative simplicity (which may tell in either direction) must be carefully considered in each case.

one and virtually nobody gets two, maintain security regulations at all points, and so on. Such a subject well deserves a full account, but a large part of the field has been most admirably covered elsewhere by the man who was mainly responsible for reducing this gigantic operation to a common-place incident which the public took for granted.[1] I should, however, like to stress two points.

Firstly, it takes a staggeringly long time for any decision about a ration book to get itself incorporated in the books which the public actually possess. To have an additional document printed and distributed separately absorbs a great deal of scarce man-power, and should clearly be avoided if at all possible. Without this, however, there may be a time-lag of anything up to a year before the new decision can even be incorporated in the next draft for the printers, and after that there is a further long wait whilst the documents are printed and distributed —so much so that the preliminary note asking for suggestions for one clothes ration book was circulated before any coupons in the previous one had actually become valid. The designer of a book must look two years ahead and try to cover all possible developments.

The moral of this point is, of course, that any book which is issued must contain as many different sorts of spare coupons as are at all likely to be wanted. The difficulty of providing for all contingencies without a gross extravagance in paper is, however, frightful—as witness the rather unsatisfactory devices which had to be adopted for bread units, despite all the Ministry of Food's forethought and experience.

The second point is in a sense an extension of the first. Most rationing schemes need to be introduced without any advance warning, so as to avoid forestalling. This raises a whole host of problems, since it implies a lack of trade consultation, but for our immediate purpose the important corollary is that the necessary coupons must be got into consumers' hands without any indication of their function. Even if there were no objection on the score of delay to waiting whilst (say) clothing coupons were printed and distributed, the inevitable forestalling would forbid it. Hence the need for spare coupons in any book which is distributed, to take account of possible uses for quite unrelated schemes. Clothes rationing could not have started so successfully without the fortunate accident that the margarine coupons in the food book had not been used; we should not rely on such accidental good fortune again.

---

[1] *The Market Square, The Story of the Food Ration Book, 1940-44,* by 'Impresario' (printed for official use by the Ministry of Food).

The Supply Side

The satisfactory running of a rationing system on the 'supply' side calls for the solution of a great many problems, which may be grouped under the following headings:

(a) Clear rules must be laid down about the exact scope of the rationing scheme and the number of coupons (or other documents) which are required for each transaction.

(b) There must be a satisfactory system for getting the goods to the places where they will be needed to meet the coupons.

(c) There must be a workable system for enforcing the rules laid down.

(d) The supply of rationed goods and the demand for them must be kept in balance.

Little will be said here about (a). With a widely based points scheme it is a lengthy and difficult job, and whatever one's intentions may be the pointing schedule which finally emerges has a habit of also being lengthy, because it is so difficult to combine clarity and fairness. The clothing scheme provided a good example of the way in which an apparently simple initial list had to be elaborated, partly so as to strike a better balance between different garments, and partly so as to clarify the doubtful cases. The number of borderline problems which arose was legion, particularly in women's clothes, because one garment 'shades off' into another—the jacket grows into the short coat and then into the long (over)coat by almost imperceptible stages. The only general principles are to class together, if at all possible, the garments which are hard to distinguish at the boundary, and if that is quite unacceptable to lay down some definite criterion (e.g. a length of twenty-eight inches) as the borderline between one class and the other, choosing a figure which will produce as few 'near-misses' as possible.

As regards (b) there are only two fundamentally different principles which can be followed. The first is based on *registration* by the public with particular shops; the latter collect the counterfoils out of their registered customers' books, and present them to some authority in support of a claim to a buying permit or other document authorizing a corresponding flow of supplies. The second is based on the *passing back* to the suppliers of coupons which the retailer has cut out from his customers' books; this means that he gets a claim to the replacement of whatever goods he has sold and so in effect continuously adjusts supplies to the level of sales in the recent past.

These two processes are familiar to everyone from the customers' end, but they deserve rather more careful analysis. The great merit of registration is that by tying the customer to a specific shop it makes for accurate and economical distribution; the administrators know exactly how much of each rationed article must reach each shop in each period, and arrangements can be made to guarantee that this will happen under any but the most abnormal circumstances. With perishable foods this is a matter of very real importance, and with bulky articles (e.g. coal) it is also possible to plan the deliveries so as to secure a valuable economy of transport.

The most obvious disadvantages of registration are that the consumer does not like being tied to one shop, particularly if he travels at all; and that the actual procedure of registration is troublesome and has to be repeated by everybody from time to time to keep the records up to date, as well as by the people who move house. Apart from this, however, registration is a technique which has a very limited application, being practically confined to "specific" rationing schemes with a narrow coverage. It is clear enough that the system would have been impossible with clothes rationing, for relatively few shops sell all the various goods, ranging from shoes to suits and knitting wool; if people had had to be tied to one shop they would have been bound to choose the department store type, leaving the specialists with no trade at all. But in fact this difficulty crops up in far less obvious cases, the fundamental point being that registration will only work properly when each trader who handles *any* of the goods handles *all* of them. It would not work if the bacon and meat rations were merged, unless the grocers all started butchery departments and the butchers all sold bacon.

The great advantage of the passing-back system is its flexibility. The coupons can be carried about and used anywhere, and there is no need for records to be kept up to date after each removal; the chemist with a small trade in babies' rusks does not have to choose between giving it up or stocking a full range of 'points' foods to attract registrations. The coupons become, in effect, a sort of second currency so far as these transactions are concerned, and they can flow along the regular channels of trade without upsetting them.[1]

---

[1] There is, however, one important qualification. The passing-back system makes no provision for any trader to increase his stock: he has no (coupon) profits to plough back into the business, no power to borrow or raise fresh coupon capital. Under registration a trader who secures more customers automatically gets more supplies. With passing-back a trader might be able to turn over his stock more rapidly, but there is a limit to this, and only deliberate action by the rationing authority can give him the coupons to increase his stock. The point is particularly relevant where districts are increasing their population or a new trader wants to begin business.

It would, of course, be possible to apply the passing-back technique to all rationing schemes, whether 'specific' or 'points'; indeed, it does apply to tea and petrol, which are specific rations, and the cutting out of coupons is used as a supplement to registration when travellers are issued with emergency cards or soldiers are temporarily on leave. Whether it would be desirable to do so, if preparations were to be made for a completely fresh start, is another matter which should be very carefully considered *ab initio*. There are arguments on both sides, as can be seen from the discussion above; we may add that the 'certainty' of registration has its advantages for the consumer as well as for the administrator, and it speeds up shopping (and saves paper) by allowing coupons to be marked off (on both sides) instead of being cut out. Of course, if the decision were to abolish specific rations, then the question of registration would almost lapse, though a modified form of registration for particular items within a group ration would be possible and might be desirable for perishables.

Enforcement

The successful enforcement of a rationing system and the avoidance of a black market is not primarily a matter of test shopping, flying squads and the like, but rather of devising a rationing system which will be relatively easy to enforce, and which will, indeed, to a large extent 'enforce itself'. The ease with which this can be done varies very greatly from commodity to commodity, and it is these differences which make the test of 'administrative practicability' so important in deciding whether a particular commodity should be covered by rationing.

The general principles of enforcement can be seen by taking the easy case of a ration covering only non-perishable foodstuffs which are all imported by the Ministry of Food in a state which requires no further processing or even cutting up; the original points scheme, covering tinned goods only, comes near to providing the perfect illustration.

Under these circumstances 'automatic' enforcement by passing back coupons can be applied throughout the whole chain. If the retailer sells without taking coupons he will not get his stocks replaced unless he can persuade the wholesaler to break the law, too; similarly, the latter can only do so at the expense of his own stocks, and so on right back to the Ministry of Food. There may be minor offences, especially if some trader starts with large stocks, and there is always the danger of forgery or stolen goods; but so long as there is effective control of the ultimate source of supply the system can largely run itself. There is in principle no need even to know how many retailers or wholesalers handle the goods, or who they are; the coupons are issued to the public, flow through a network of channels in exchange for goods, and end up in the safe hands of the Ministry of Food.

The picture is much the same if registration is used. The retailer will get a buying permit or other document entitling him to the supplies needed to honour the rations of his registered customers. If he sold goods to other people, or gave some customers excessive amounts, he would be unable to serve the rest with their rations (except by depleting his stock) and they would complain to the Food Office. He is therefore bound in his own interest to observe the law, apart from minor deviations, and the same is true at the earlier stages of distribution. In essence the system of automatic enforcement is similar, and we can concentrate on the more general case of passing back.

There are really three vital conditions to be fulfilled if automatic enforcement is to work, and we can see how they are met in the above simple cases before considering the complications.

Firstly, *there must be effective control over the whole supply of goods at some point to which the coupons will all flow and at which they can be effectively withdrawn.* In the simple case this is secured through the Ministry's monopoly of importation and consequent initial ownership of the whole supply. One of the major reasons why rationing was more successful in Britain than in some other countries was the fact that our food was so largely imported, so that there was a reliable system ready to hand for withdrawing the bulk of the coupons when their work was done.

Secondly, *the rule must be laid down that beyond this point anybody who sells any rationed goods must secure a stated number of coupons (or some equivalent document), whoever the purchaser may be.* This is the general principle of control by coupon. It creates serious problems when you are rationing something.which is needed by 'businesses' as well as by individuals, since every purchaser whom you wish to receive supplies must somehow be given an appropriate number of coupons or their equivalent. These problems would be most formidable with things like household brooms, which must be bought occasionally for use in almost every shop, office, factory, church or other building. A ration based on purchases in a past year would be inappropriate, since it would be zero for many buildings and would give a ration to many others where a further purchase would be unnecessary. Individual applications for each purchase would savour of bureaucracy run mad, and the desperate expedient of 'bill-signing'[1] lays the scheme wide open to all kinds of fraud. This constitutes one powerful administrative reason against rationing such articles.

Thirdly, *the rules about the number of coupons to be surrendered must ensure that, to a reasonable approximation, every honest trader will just obtain replacement of his stock – neither more nor less.* In our simple case it was tacitly assumed that the number of coupons would be prescribed 'per tin', and that each trader would therefore give the same number of coupons when he bought as he took when he sold. Complications would arise if the goods were so perishable that some wastage was inevitable—the retailer would get no coupons to replace the stuff that went bad—or if the coupons were fixed 'per pound' and the goods lost weight (as happens with many vegetables). The ideal is to be able to tie the coupon rating to some unchanging characteristic of the goods so that it can metaphorically pass along the chain with them; any attempt to make the number of coupons required proportional to the *value* of the goods is bound to create difficulties, unless by 'value' we mean a sort of 'list price' which is known to everybody and is an 'unchanging characteristic' in the above sense.

The first great problem which arises in any but the simplest cases is how to secure 'effective control' where this is not automatically secured through government ownership. The objective will be to define a sort of 'ring fence' round all the sources of supply, and make any firm within the fence not only demand coupons for any rationed goods supplied to an outsider, but also surrender them periodically for cancellation and keep such records as will enable a check to be imposed on the correctness of the number collected and surrendered. In practice it is bound to be difficult to impose this check, so that it is a prime requisite of a satisfactory scheme that it should be possible to compile a register of firms who are within the fence, that they should not be too numerous, and that they should be reputable and able to keep proper records.[2] A tremendous lot depends on the accuracy and honesty of these 'registered persons': the outside checks cannot be really comprehensive, and the coupons which they are supposed to surrender will

[1] A term derived from the early days of clothes rationing, when officers and various other people were allowed to make purchases by signing a declaration on the back of the bill, which the retailer could then pass back as a coupon equivalent. (It would, theoretically, be possible to send an inspector to a sample of cases to check that the business purchaser really did need a broom.)

[2] In general these records will have to distinguish sales to unregistered people from export sales, sales to the Government and sales to other registered firms, for which coupons are not required.

always have a black market value, even if they arrive in the form of 'coupon cheques' instead of physical coupons.

This problem may be illustrated by reference to clothes rationing. There are many thousands of small firms which buy cloth and make it up into garments; they are constantly changing, many keep little in the way of records, many also act as retailers of ready-made garments, and altogether they would be most unsuitable to act as registered persons. Consequently it was decided that the ring fence should be placed farther back to enclose only the producers of cloth, together with the producers of other types of rationed goods, such as boots and shoes, knitwear and hand-knitting yarn.

This decision very greatly reduced the number of firms who were registered as 'ultimate recipients' of coupons, from whom they had then to be collected by the Board of Trade, and it also greatly improved their average standard as record-keepers, etc. It had the inevitable corollary, however, that the coupon value of each made-up garment must be fixed so as approximately to balance the coupons fixed for the amount(s) of cloth(s) needed to make it. Some of the consequences of this are discussed below; for the moment we merely note that if the coupon is to be used as an automatic controller of the maker-up, as well as of the retailer and wholesaler, then this is the *only* principle of pointing which can be adopted for made-up garments. In effect it made the yardage of cloth into an 'unchanging characteristic' to which the coupon rating could be tied, despite the fact that the cloth might be transformed into a dress or a shirt or even the lining of a suit between its crossing of the ring fence and its arrival on the customer's back.

The difficulty of including headgear in the ration will now be apparent. Some types are mainly made in large factories which could quite properly be included on the register, like the shoe manufacturers; but others, notably women's 'fashion' types, are made from all kinds of substances by all kinds of people, including retailers. These small producers could not be automatically controlled through giving coupons for their materials, as the dressmakers were, because they largely use unrationed material. Doubtless it would have been *possible* to devise some system which would work after a fashion, but the gain did not seem to be worth the administrative effort involved.[1]

Finally, it is worth noting some of the reasons why an automatic

[1] The experience of bread rationing (under which the bakers did not have to pass back coupons to get their materials, but were supposed to hand them in to the Ministry of Food) provides an excellent illustration of the paramount need for a suitable class of 'ultimate recipients'.

passing-back system will not work if each coupon is made equivalent to a certain *value* of goods, since that system has some obvious attractions (equity, avoidance of elaborate pointing schedules, discouragement of 'trading up', etc.). The fundamental trouble is, of course, that value is not an 'unchanging characteristic' as the goods pass down the chain, even if these undergo no physical process. It may sound easy to prescribe that the coupons should only be worth a certain percentage of their face value for wholesaler-retailer transactions, and a smaller one for manufacturer-wholesaler, etc. If all the goods under the ration had roughly the same mark-up and always followed a stereotyped course, with each firm only fulfilling one function, this might work, though it has the unfortunate consequence that any trader who adds *less* than the assumed margin to the price he pays will not recover enough coupons to maintain his stock. But mark-ups vary from article to article and for almost every article there are all sorts of alternative courses, using different numbers of intermediaries who may combine various functions, and in many cases ending up with a different retail price.[1] It would be impossible to classify all the possible transactions and lay down a schedule of percentages to apply to the face value of the coupon which would even roughly balance the coupons taken by the various traders with those needed to buy an equivalent amount of goods.

The position becomes even worse, of course, if the goods may undergo some processing outside the registered field. Clearly there would have to be some system for making the coupons worth an even lower percentage of their face value when they were used for buying, say, cloth for making-up, but unfortunately the value of a finished garment does not bear anything like a constant ratio to that of the cloth used for it. Once again we should be faced with the dilemma that the virtuous firm whose selling prices included *less* than the assumed addition to the cost of the cloth (e.g. because it makes simple garments instead of luxury models) would not be able to replace its stock of cloth. Furthermore, the rules would imply that a wholesaler of cloth would have to demand a greater 'value' of coupons when selling to the dressmaker than he does when selling to the draper for the counter trade—and presumably an intermediate rate if the draper also has a workroom for making up some of the cloth. There is clearly nothing which will 'automatically' make him do this, even if he had the necessary information; moreover, his own coupon position is almost certain to be unbalanced, because the 'percentage of face value' laid down for cloth merchants buying

---

[1] Thus, the maximum retail price for a utility vest is lower if the retailer buys direct from the maker than it is if a wholesaler has handled it.

from producers cannot be right both for the ones supplying retailers and for those supplying dressmakers. To have attempted to apply a system of value pointing to the clothes ration would, in fact, have made it impossible to meet either the second or the third of the conditions mentioned above as essential to an 'automatic' system of enforcement.

SOME PROBLEMS OF POINTING

The fourth problem which must be tackled is the balancing of supply and demand under a ration. I shall say virtually nothing about the problems of the overall balance, which must be maintained by equating the coupon value of the goods coming forward per month and the rate of coupon release, with stocks serving as a shock absorber. It is, of course, vital that this balance should be preserved, and too great a reliance on distributors' stocks creates very serious dangers; if the retailer cannot turn his coupons back into goods the system of distribution becomes uncertain, and he has much less incentive to *demand* coupons from his customers, so that 'automatic enforcement' is weakened. It may be possible to maintain the balance by keeping supplies, in total, at a desired level, but if the level of supply changes, then the effective number of coupons issued per period (or the length of the period) should be suitably varied; it is possible to restore the balance by altering the number of coupons required for all items, either upwards or downwards, but this only makes for unnecessary complications.

Given that there is an overall balance between supply and demand, it is tempting to say that the balance for individual items can and should be maintained by varying the pointings, so that everyone may genuinely have a free choice in using his coupons. The extent to which this is true, however, varies a great deal according to the nature of the goods rationed. With the food points scheme there was little objection to making such changes every period, except the general one that every change had to be duly advertised and made life more complicated for both traders and consumers. With clothing, on the other hand, changes were much less frequent, and it is instructive to examine some of the fundamental reasons for this difference.

Firstly, of course, the system of control described above will only work if the pointing for made-up garments is kept in line with that for the cloth from which they are made. This virtually precludes the use of pointing changes over this part of the field as a means of bringing supply and demand for particular garments into line, except as an exceptional and temporary measure, which will probably involve a complicated procedure for 'reimbursing' traders who have lost coupon

o

capital. The maintenance of equilibrium for the various made-up garments must depend primarily on adjustments in supplies, which will
largely be 'automatically' made by the trade if suitable cloths are
available in adequate quantities. With the food points scheme, on the
other hand, there is no 'processing' by unregistered traders, so that
relative pointings are not tied in this way.

Secondly, changes in relative pointings would affect different classes
of consumers differently and might well cause complaints about unfairness. It is tempting to argue that under rationing 'we all start equal',
so that these objections on the score of equity should not apply to
increased coupon values as a means of securing equilibrium, in the way
that they do to higher *prices*. With food points this might be broadly
true, but with clothing it certainly cannot be taken for granted, because
of the great variations in the needs of particular classes for particular
items. Thus it would be technically possible to fix any pointing one
liked for boots and shoes, but to meet a shortage by doubling the pointing would be to court a shoal of applications for special supplements
from people whose work is particularly hard on their footwear. It would
be useless to reply that the higher pointing of shoes had been balanced
by a reduced pointing for, say, underwear, so that the ration was unchanged: many people would not have the average budget and would
undoubtedly suffer from the change. Their position after the change
might still be no worse than that of many others, but this would be
hard to demonstrate. 'An old pointing is a good pointing', and sleeping
dogs should be allowed to lie.

Thirdly, the coupon periods have to be much longer in the case of
clothing than under the points scheme, because it is bought at less
frequent intervals. There are objections to raising coupon values within
a period to meet a shortage, since it appears to penalize those who have
obeyed the official injunction not to buy before they need; if one must
wait until the end of the period, then it may well be possible to avoid
the need for a change by doing something on the supply side, or the
trade may have switched its production without any official action.

These arguments do not, of course, mean that pointing changes
should never be made. No list can ever be perfect, and some changes
will be needed on technical grounds to secure greater clarity, or a
better 'fit' between the cloth and the garment, or a fairer relationship
between one garment and another. Changes may also be made to secure
greater equity between consumers—e.g. the special low pointing of
industrial overalls (made possible by a corresponding reduction for the
utility cloth used) and the reduced pointings for certain cheap utility

cloths and garments made from them. The latter of these examples was also partly based on the need to keep supply and demand in line for these articles, but it was a long-period, 'once for all' change, and the same was true of the increase of footwear pointings in 1943. Such changes are justifiable, even if they are undesirable on equity grounds, if it is certain that a serious disequilibrium would otherwise persist; if necessary, the equity objections must then be met by revising the rules about supplements.

XIII

WARTIME CONTROL OF FOOD AND AGRICULTURAL PRICES

by

E. F. NASH

Wartime food control was called forth by the prospect of physical shortage and inflation. Its purpose was to feed the population adequately and with the greatest economy of resources. The extent to which this general aim was achieved is, however, beyond our present scope. The measures of price control with which we shall be concerned had the purpose of regulating the cost of the food supply (in so far as it was home produced) and of its distribution; in conjunction with rationing and the control of supplies they were designed to mitigate or prevent the inequities likely to be caused by shortages and rising prices, and to control the cumulative growth of inflation. They were, of course, powerless to prevent inflation altogether. But with the assistance of similar controls over other consumable goods they substantially modified its symptoms. Many of the characteristic features of the classical type of uncontrolled inflation were avoided. What took its place was a 'suppressed' inflation, marked by a general excess of demand over supply, an increase of savings partly due to the absence of worthwhile outlets for spending, and a multiplication of rules and regulations designed to limit the free use of money, and resulting in the partial abrogation of its familiar function as a universal measure of value.

We shall confine this discussion in the main to the two major issues of food price policy which arose during the war. These were concerned respectively with the control of agricultural prices, and with retail food prices and food subsidies. It is convenient to begin, however, with a brief general review of the wartime changes in food price levels, food expenditure and consumers' incomes.

GENERAL SURVEY

The main facts are summarized below in Table I, which is based on figures derived from the White Paper on national income and expenditure for 1949 (Cmd. 7933). Before the war the British public spent on food an average of about 10s. 8d. per head per week, out of an average income amounting, after payment of direct taxes, to about 37s. a head. During the war the cost of food rose and the quantity and quality fell; in 1946 the weekly food expenditure of civilians averaged about 14s. 6d. a head, but the food bought is estimated only to have been worth 10s. 2d. at the prices of 1938. This implies that prices had risen on the average by 42 per cent and that the food supply per head had fallen by 4 per cent. On the other hand, the average income had risen to over £3 per head per week after payment of direct taxes. The proportion of income used to buy food had therefore fallen from 29 per cent in 1938 to 23 per cent in 1946.

Table I. *National Income, Food Expenditure and Food Costs*
(from Cmd. 7933)

	1938	1946	1947	1948	1949
1. *Personal Disposable Income* (after direct taxation):					
(i) £ mn.	4,521	7,592	7,953	8,517	8,829
(ii) % of 1938	100	168	176	188	195
2. *Personal Expenditure on Food:* (c)					
(i) £ mn.	1,305	1,777	2,048	2,221	2,381
(ii) % of 1938	100	136	157	170	182
3. *Percentage of Income spent on Food*	29·0	23·4	25·8	26·1	27·0
4. *Expenditure on Food at 1938 retail prices:*					
(i) £ mn.	1,305	1,248(a)	1,321(a)	1,338	(b)
(ii) % of 1938	100	96	101	103	(b)
5. *Expenditure on Food after adjustment for Taxes and Subsidies:*					
(i) £ mn.	1,267	1,993	2,317	2,577	2,748
(ii) % of 1938	100	157	183	203	217
6. *Approximate Index of Food Prices* (2 ÷ 4)	100	142	155	166	(b)

(a) From Cmd. 7649.

(b) Not available.

(c) The population to which these figures relate is the population fed from civilian sources, which is estimated to have amounted to 47.1 million persons in 1938 and 1946, and to 48.6 million and 49.2 million in 1947 and 1948 respectively.

In terms of aggregates, the increase in personal incomes after deducting direct taxation was £3,071 millions a year, while the increase in expenditure on food was only £472 millions. It is obvious that the public would have been prepared to use a far larger proportion of its additional income in buying food if it had not been prevented from doing so. The proportion of income spent on food usually varies inversely with the general standard of living and with the degree of inequality in the distribution of incomes; thus the fall in consumption standards during the war, and the less unequal distribution of income brought about by wartime taxation, are both changes which by themselves would be expected to raise the proportion. That in actual fact the proportion fell is therefore in one sense a measure of the efficacy of rationing, price control and the other restraints by which expenditure was checked. If the proportion had merely remained the same as before the war the public would have spent on food in 1946 about 3s. 6d. more per head per week than it actually did, equivalent in the aggregate to the large additional sum of £425 millions or so a year.

The control of prices and supplies by the Government rested in part simply on the issue of orders and regulations, which involved no other cost beyond that of paper, office space and the salaries of the officials needed to work them out and apply them. But as the war proceeded these measures were supplemented by a large direct expenditure on the part of the Government in the form of subsidies. Certain subsidies on foodstuffs were already paid before the war (though their purpose at that time was to keep producers' prices up rather than to keep retail prices down), but in 1938 the Government collected £38 millions more in customs and excise taxes on food than it paid out in subsidies. In 1946, however, according to the White Paper, the proceeds of taxes on food fell short of the cost of subsidies by £216 millions. The total wartime increase in the annual cost of the food supply therefore exceeded the increase in consumers' expenditure on food by £254 millions, and amounted altogether to £726 millions. This is an increase of about 57 per cent over the total pre-war cost, but it was incurred for a smaller aggregate supply. The drop in the aggregate supply shown by Table I (line 4) is 4 per cent, and on the basis of this figure the cost *per unit* of the food supply must have increased roughly in the relation 157 : 96; that is, by 64 per cent. In fact this is an underestimate, since it makes no allowance for deterioration in quality.

The total cost of the food supply is made up of payments for imports and for home produce as purchased from the farms, and of charges incurred for transport, storage, processing and distribution. No detailed analysis of these costs is possible, but since the first two items and the total are known, the aggregate amount of the third can be estimated by difference, as in Table II. This table shows that the aggregate costs of home-produced food more than doubled, those of imports rose by over 50 per cent, while the total costs of processing and distribution increased

Table II. *Chief Items in the Cost of Food, 1938 and 1946*[1]

(£ millions)

	1938	1946		1938	1946
1. Retained imports of food	358	569(a)	6. Expenditure of consumers, caterers and Service depts., less value of consumption in farm households (d)		
2. Home food production:					
(i) Farms (b)	247	572(c)			
(ii) Fisheries	17	40		1,305	1,817
3. Estimated decrease(+) or increase (−) in stocks	− 5	37	7. Deduct production on non-agricultural holdings	− 9	−15
4. Deduction for wheat and oil-seed by-products	−13	−14		1,296	1,802
			8. Exports of food	18	31
	604	1,204			
5. Apparent costs of processing and distribution	671	833	9. Subsidies	12	270(e)
			10. Deduct Customs and Excise duties	−51	−66
	1,275	2,037		1,275	2,037

[1] From unpublished material kindly supplied by the Statistics and Intelligence Division of the Ministry of Food and by the Ministry of Agriculture and Fisheries.

Notes

(a) Includes bulk payments (£10 mn.) to other governments in respect of food.

(b) Excludes non-food output and consumption in farm households. Acreage payments and subsidies on fertilizers and feeding-stuffs are included, but direct subsidies to agriculture (e.g. drainage and ploughing-up grants, hill sheep and cattle subsidies, etc.) are excluded. These totalled £9 mn. in 1945–6 and £10 mn. in 1946–7.

(c) 1946–7.

(d) Includes non-personal expenditure on food (e.g. by public institutions). Not comparable with line 2 of Table I, which relates to personal expenditure exclusive of service consumption but including that of farm households.

(e) Excludes costs of National and School Milk Schemes and of the Vitamins Scheme (which are treated as transfer payments and therefore included in consumers' expenditure) and also certain items in the Ministry of Food's expenditure not properly attributable to the national cost of food. These items, of which the largest is the Ministry's administrative expenses, totalled £12·5 mn. in 1945–6 and £13·8 mn. in 1946–7.

by only about one-quarter. These changes are, of course, the combined result of changes in quantities and in prices or costs per unit. The volume of retained imports of the articles covered in the table declined between 1938 and 1946 by about one-quarter, so that since the total value increased by 59 per cent the average price level of imports had approximately doubled. The value at pre-war prices of the home agricultural output in 1946–7 is stated to have been about 6 per cent higher than before the war,[1] so that here the average increase in cost per unit must have been over 100 per cent. Home landings of fish in 1946 were about 10 per cent below the 1938 quantities, indicating in this case an average increase in cost of about 160 per cent.

In regard to processing and distribution, the absence of any measure of the quantitative change in output makes it impossible to do more than guess at the change in the cost per unit. It is in respect of these items that changes in the quality of the goods sold to consumers and in the amount of services, e.g. delivery, rendered with them are of greatest importance. Wartime changes in quality were in general downward; delivery and other services were necessarily restricted, and the output of many food manufacturing trades was curtailed by shortages of materials and manpower. But it is impossible to make statistical allowance for these changes, and the estimates already quoted in Table I largely ignore them and must therefore understate the wartime decline in supplies and the increase in prices and costs. It seems likely, however, that the total increase per unit in the cost of these services was considerably less than in the other items covered by the table. If we assume that the total food manufacturing and distributive output had fallen by 25–30 per cent, proportions which accord with the decline in the manpower employed, the rise in the cost per unit would be 65–77 per cent.

The changes reviewed above obviously do not represent the fulfilment of a deliberate policy. The plans for food control drawn up before the war made it possible for the principal foods to be brought under control soon after the outbreak of war with comparatively little difficulty, but the main issues of policy encountered during the war, whether concerned with agricultural prices or with retail prices and the cost of living, had not been solved or even fully foreseen before the war began. The measures adopted to deal with them were less the execution of plans laid in advance than a response to the strains and pressures generated by the war itself. They must be considered therefore in relation to the circumstances in which they arose.

[1] United Nations, Economic Commission for Europe, *Survey of the Economic Situation and Prospects of Europe*, Geneva, 1948, p. 11, Table 8.

The First Nine Months of the War

The outbreak of war occurred during the period of recovery from a world agricultural depression of unprecedented severity, as a result of which an active policy of State aid to farming had been developed during the thirties. The claims of the farmers to government assistance on a considerably larger scale were not without influential support even in peacetime, but two decisive obstacles stood in their way: the heavy cost which they would have imposed either on consumers or taxpayers, and the possibility of serious disturbance to the country's international economic relations. It should perhaps have been foreseen that these claims would be pressed with vigour as soon as war broke out. But pre-war official discussions had not recognized any need for an immediate general increase in agricultural prices in the event of war. The preparations made for the imposition of control on the outbreak of hostilities assumed that prices both of produce and of requisites would be stabilized in the first instance at about their pre-war levels, and that the machinery of control would be used to regulate and delay their inevitable increase.

These expectations, however, soon proved to be wrong. In the first place, import costs rose much more rapidly than had been expected, and increases in the prices of imported feeding-stuffs, in the absence of any arrangement to stabilize them by subsidy—a measure discussed, but rejected, before the outbreak of war—made it necessary to raise the prices of livestock products several times during the first few months. Secondly, the outbreak of war at once gave the farmers' claims for improved rewards a much more favourable hearing. It soon became evident that in spite of the comprehensive apparatus of control which it had created on the outbreak of war, the Government would not in fact offer any firm resistance to a general increase in the agricultural price level.

The difficulties of establishing a satisfactory price policy for agricultural products were complicated by the division of functions between government departments. Agricultural policy and the wartime production programme were, of course, the special concern of the agricultural departments. These departments were the parents of the various schemes of assistance to agriculture brought into operation during the thirties, and were regarded by farmers—in the words of a former permanent secretary of the Ministry of Agriculture—as 'their advocate in all their relations with the State, and the medium for all their difficulties and troubles'.[1] The Minister of Agriculture at the outbreak of war was himself a former president of the National Farmers' Union. But the wartime functions of these departments did not include the control of agricultural prices. With the exception of the prices of wool and flax (which were controlled by the Ministry of Supply), control of the prices both of food and of agricultural products was formally the responsibility of the newly created Ministry of Food. For commodities other than food the Board of Trade and Ministry of Supply were the price-controlling departments. Except in so far as the Treasury exercised an overriding authority, no single department was responsible for price policy in all fields.

In the event the pre-war plans for price control were largely ignored, and no serious attempt was made to hold agricultural prices at the levels ruling on the outbreak of war. Thus the prices of fat stock, of which, with the establishment of the meat and livestock control scheme in January 1940, the Ministry of Food became the sole buyer, were fixed, after negotiations with the farmers' representatives, at levels designed not merely to reimburse farmers for the higher costs of imported feeding-stuffs, but to include a substantial element of 'incentive' (as it was called) or increased profit. This decision caused the Ministry of Food to incur a loss on the sale of home-killed meat. Retail prices could not be raised enough to cover the higher prices granted to producers without public protest and a real risk that consumers' demand – not yet appreciably influenced by higher earnings – would be insufficient to absorb the supplies coming forward. This loss considerably exceeded the pre-war fat cattle subsidy, which was henceforward merged in the price paid to the producer; and it was allowed to grow, with the many subsequent increases in producers' prices, for more than nine years. It was not until the spring of 1949 that retail meat prices were raised above the levels at which they were fixed in 1940.

The prices of fat stock had been discussed without direct reference to those of other products. But the costs of milk production had also increased, and milk was a commodity of the first importance which could not be treated less favourably than fat cattle. The fat stock price decisions therefore made it impossible to resist similar claims by the milk producers. The increase in milk prices also necessitated a subsidy, though it was (for the time being) withdrawn in the summer of 1940 when the introduction of the National Milk Scheme removed the main objection to a rise in the ordinary retail price.

In these two cases the machinery of control was used to raise the

[1] Sir Francis Floud, *The Ministry of Agriculture and Fisheries*, 1927, preface.

producers' price, but there were other commodities for which, in the sudden scarcity produced by the outbreak of war, a sharp increase in prices could only have been prevented by prompt control. Home-grown oats and barley fell into this category; no control was at first imposed on their prices and by January 1940 they had risen to more than two and a half times the level of August 1939. Price control of home-grown oats could no longer be delayed, but it could not be effected at a lower level than 11s. a cwt.—considerably below the open market price, but 47 per cent above the pre-war average. The price of imported oats, which the Ministry of Food had proposed to sell at 7s. 9d. a cwt., had suddenly to be raised to the same level owing to the impossibility of enforcing different prices for products so nearly indistinguishable. Even so it was not until the summer of 1940 that a maximum price was instituted for home-grown feeding barley, while malting barley prices were left free until July 1942.

These and other changes were responsible for an increase in the general agricultural price level, which was estimated to amount in May 1940 to 29 per cent compared with the years 1936-7 to 1938-9. In spite of the controls, prices had risen during the first few months of the war faster than in the closing months of 1914, when no controls had existed. Moreover, the increase was of an irregular and haphazard nature. The greatest advances had occurred in the prices of commodities such as oats and barley, where control was too long delayed, and eggs, where its technical difficulties had not yet been seriously tackled; on the other hand, many products of greater intrinsic importance had fared relatively badly—milk, for instance, had no more than kept pace with the general increase, and wheat and potatoes had fallen behind. A general overhaul of the price structure, and a more systematic procedure for determining future changes, were both clearly needed if anything in the nature of a consistent and comprehensive price policy was to be attempted.

The 1940 Price Discussions

The opportunity for a general overhaul came in June 1940. Its occasion was the decision to establish a national minimum wage for agricultural workers in place of the minimum rates imposed county by county under the existing wage-fixing machinery. This decision—ostensibly taken in order to secure what might have been recognized as an impossible result, the immediate recruitment of 80,000 to 100,000 additional regular workers for farms in Great Britain—set the new national minimum at 48s a week for adult male workers, which meant an average increase of about 8s. a week in existing minimum rates and of about 14s. over those in force before the war. The Government undertook that prices would be adjusted to take full account of this and of other increases in costs.

The task of determining the price revisions needed to meet this change proved, however, to be exceptionally difficult and protracted. The new minimum rate of wages was estimated to add about £15 millions to the farmers' annual bill for labour. But it was calculated that the increases in prices since the outbreak of war were already sufficient to give farmers an aggregate increase in their profits of £27 millions a year after meeting all wartime increases in costs except the new rise in wages. Further price increases were, however, now conceded which were estimated to be equivalent to an additional £20 millions a year over and above the full annual cost of the increase in wages. The new prices, moreover, largely preserved the price relationships resulting from the rough and tumble of the first months of the war. They were announced at the end of June and were to be paid for the crops about to be harvested in 1940 and for the livestock products to be marketed during the summer—thus incidentally reimbursing farmers for a year's increase in wages of which only a few weeks would yet have elapsed. But prices had also to be settled for the harvest of 1941 and for the livestock products to be marketed from September onwards. The Government at first reserved its decision on these prices, and another two months elapsed before they were made known. At length, on 30th August, it was announced that the 1940–1 prices for oats, feeding barley, cattle and pigs would be reduced below those previously announced for 1940, but that there would be further increases in the prices of milk and potatoes. These changes had been decided on in an endeavour to bring the incentives for different products into closer conformity with wartime production requirements, while maintaining farmers' receipts at the aggregate level already fixed. The Government promised, in the formula which was becoming customary, that the prices now fixed 'would be subject to review in the event of any substantial change in costs of production'.

The estimates on which these decisions were based, though the best available at the time, were calculated at short notice from data which were inevitably imperfect, and they do not now appear to have been very accurate. They considerably exaggerated the effects of the rise in the prices of feeding-stuffs, which was actually more than offset in 1940–1 by the fall in supplies, and in consequence they somewhat overstated the total increase in farmers' costs. But the significance of the decisions lay not in the figures, but in the questions of principle which had now been faced for the first time since the beginning of the war. The time and effort which the Government found it necessary to devote to these discussions, during a summer not free from other preoccupations, are evidence not only of their intrinsic importance and difficulty, but of the divided state of official and Ministerial opinion. On the one side it could be argued that the increased output now required of farmers, and the changes in farm practice involved, for instance, in the increase of crop production at the expense of grass, would necessitate additional working capital; that pre-war farm incomes were altogether too low to provide a basis for judging what level of rewards was adequate for the effort now demanded; and that crop prices sufficient to give generous profits to established growers on productive soil might barely remunerate the large number of new growers whose contributions were now needed. All these arguments had some force, but it was at the same time possible to doubt whether they justified the addition of £20 millions a year to an income already increased by £27 millions since the outbreak of war. Stress was laid on the need for creating confidence among the farmers in their ability to meet their increased costs and to embark successfully on the production of unfamiliar crops. But arguments of this nature removed the discussion outside the range of the measurable and calculable. By any quantitative assessment the final decisions, although they were received with strong protests by the National Farmers' Union, whose leaders complained that they had not been consulted and unsuccessfully appealed to the Prime Minister to reconsider the new prices, were in fact generous to the farmers.

However their outcome is to be judged, the 1940 price discussions mark a definite stage both in the wartime history of prices and in the evolution of price-fixing procedure for agricultural products. They destroyed any hope that the increase in agricultural prices could be kept within moderate limits, or that a substantial rise in retail food prices could be avoided without large expenditure on food subsidies. On the other hand, they went some way towards establishing the principles, obvious enough in themselves but hitherto neglected, that the relative prices of different products and the general level of farming profits were both matters of primary importance in agricultural price policy. They did not, unfortunately, at once put an end to the unsatisfactory practice of piecemeal price revision, but they were the first step in the gradual development of a more orderly procedure for determining price changes, and the precedent for a series of general agricultural price reviews which were conducted at intervals throughout the remainder of the war.

The 1940 discussions had lasted altogether for nearly three months, and their first and most obvious lesson was that so exhausting a process could not be quickly repeated. The Government therefore decided early in the autumn to do what it could to prevent further increases in agricultural costs by stabilizing at its own expense the prices of feeding-stuffs and fertilizers. In this way it purchased a respite for over a year. A series of individual price adjustments—all of them upward—were made during the following twelve months which between them considerably modified the effects of the 1940 price settlement, but a second general review of agricultural prices did not take place until the winter of 1941–2.

Marginal Production Problems and Taxation Changes

In the meantime the Government turned its attention to a problem which the price discussions had emphasized, the problem of the 'marginal producer'. Variations in cost and profit levels are one of the perennial difficulties of price control, often necessitating a choice between a price which is inadequate to reward the high-cost producer and one which gives excessive profits to the more efficient. In agriculture the number of separate producers and the variation in the conditions under which they work are both exceptionally great, and the wartime extension of crop-growing into grass-farming areas tended to make the variation greater still. Any given price might obviously mean a very different level of profit to an Eastern Counties arable farmer and to a new grower in the West attempting an unfamiliar crop in an unfavourable climate and obliged at the same time to incur the cost of new implements and machinery.

The low-yield producer was assisted by the practice, adopted for potatoes in 1941 and extended to wheat in 1943, of remunerating crop growers in part by 'acreage payments'. But there were other aspects of the 'marginal production' problem not capable of being dealt with in this way. There were many farmers in the remoter upland areas who were prevented by their situation from profiting through the wartime extension of crop and milk production and faced, in addition, a shrinking demand for their output of store cattle and sheep from lowland breeders and fatteners. Such enterprises often barely paid their way before the war, and the low output per worker which tends to characterize them made them especially vulnerable to the big wartime rise in labour costs.

The search for methods of assisting these producers without further adding to the profits of those more favourably situated is reflected in a series of measures which began with the hill-sheep subsidy inaugur-ated in 1940. This was followed two years later by a hill-cattle subsidy and in 1943 by the provision of £1 million to be expended in 'marginal production grants' under the supervision of County War Agricultural Committees. These measures have their postwar successors in the provisions of the Hill Farming Act of 1946 and other legislation. They did not perhaps go very far towards solving the problems against which they were directed. For these are in many respects long-term problems whose solution falls outside the range of wartime policy, though war-time changes, especially the rise in labour costs, accentuated many of their difficulties.

Meanwhile, in addition to these efforts to assist the less prosperous farmers, the Government also took steps to limit the gains of the more successful by modifying their liability to taxation. Before the war farmers were, in general, assessed for income tax under Schedule B; that is, on the assumption that their profits were equal to their rent. In announcing the price decisions of June 1940 the Minister of Agricul-ture intimated that since prices fixed to encourage crop production on inferior land would be likely to give high profits to producers on better land, the Government intended to make such producers liable for income tax, in the same way as other traders, on the basis of their actual income as assessed under Schedule D. This change was carried into effect by the Finance Act of 1941, which applied the new method of assessment to all farmers except individuals or partnerships occupy-ing land of a rental value not exceeding £300. In the following year the exemption limit was lowered to a rental value of £100, and at the same time the basis of Schedule B assessments for those still below the limit was raised to three times the annual rent. These changes materi-ally increased the tax liability of the more prosperous farmers, the larger of whom were, of course, already liable like other traders to excess profits tax. They were later completed by the total abolition, in 1948, of the Schedule B assessment, which meant that for the first time in the history of the British income tax the methods of levying taxation on farmers were wholly assimilated to those applied to other traders.

The Later Wartime Price Reviews

At the close of 1941 the National Agricultural Wages Board decided to raise the minimum weekly wage from 48s. to 60s. and thereby pro-vided the occasion for a second general review of agricultural prices. This was followed by a third in the autumn of 1943 and a fourth in

February 1945, each of them again occasioned by further increases in the minimum rate of agricultural wages, which by the spring of 1945 had reached 70s. a week. These reviews, of course, took account of all changes in agricultural costs, of which wages were not the only item, though they were the most important. The rate of increase in agricultural prices, however, slowed up considerably after 1941–2. In that year the official agricultural price index number was 80 per cent higher than before the war, but during the next three years it rose only by 8 per cent. Prices had risen considerably faster than wages at the beginning of the war, but wages now began to overtake them.

Profits, however, depend on the quantities produced and on the expenditures necessary for production, as well as on prices. The calculations made for the second price review showed that the actual increase in farmers' profits since 1940 had been considerably greater than was expected when the prices were fixed. This was largely due to the series of price revisions which had been sanctioned during 1940–1 without regard to their effects on the price level as a whole—a practice which, in spite of considerable pressure, was henceforward consistently resisted. But the Government had promised to revise prices in the event of a 'substantial' change in costs, and it could hardly be denied that a 12s. increase in the minimum wage, even though many farmers were already paying more than the minimum, was a 'substantial' change. The County Wages Committees, in the exercise of the power which they retained until late in 1942 to fix local minimum rates above the national minimum, had in some cases coupled their findings with the recommendation that the Government should reimburse farmers by raising prices. But the Government's decisions, reached in February 1942 after discussions even longer than those of 1940, recognized the need for curbing the further growth of farming profits and deliberately kept the price increases somewhat below the calculated increase in costs, with the object that this should in part be met out of the unforeseen increase in profits. These decisions were not popular with the farmers, and in response to their complaints concessions were given on the prices of a few articles, but the Government stated in return its intention to control the price of malting barley from the next harvest. The farmers' leaders, though expressing dissatisfaction with the actual prices, were persuaded to accept these decisions as fulfilling the Government's pledges 'in the letter and the spirit'—an attitude which contrasted with the feelings of 'gravest apprehension' with which they had professed to regard the 1940 decisions.[1]

[1] N.F.U. *Newsheet*, 23rd February and 5th March 1942; 2nd September 1940.

The Government's firmness, however, was again tested at the third price review in the autumn of 1943. For in spite of the care which had been taken to prevent individual price revisions in conflict with the decisions of February 1942, it was again found that the future level of farmers' receipts had been seriously underestimated at the time of the 1942 decisions. But the Government now refused to permit any further general increases in prices, holding that they were already sufficient to meet the rise in wages and other costs, and it balanced an upward revision in the prices of milk and fat cows by reducing the price of barley.

Evolution of Price-review Procedure

The procedure of the later price reviews differed in one important respect from that of 1940. In the 1940 discussions the Minister of Food and his officials had played a central part. This was natural, since it was by his authority that food prices were controlled, whether in the shops or in the agricultural markets. But food subsidies had already made their appearance on a large scale in 1940, and the stabilization policy announced in 1941 would obviously throw the burden of future increases in agricultural prices on to the Exchequer rather than the consumer. As long as this policy continued the Minister of Food could take the view that his main concern with agricultural matters was to be assured of the supplies on which his programmes depended, and that given this assurance he did not need to claim any major voice in questions of agricultural policy or farm prices. This view, at any rate, was accepted as governing the relations between the Ministry of Food and the agricultural departments after the definite adoption of the stabilization policy in 1941, and it necessarily meant that the part taken by the Ministry of Food in agricultural price discussions was henceforward comparatively inconspicuous.

Further important changes in procedure occurred just before the close of the war. Dissatisfaction on the part of farmers with the decisions resulting from the second and third price reviews, and the scepticism they professed regarding the 'four-year plan' for agriculture announced in the summer of 1943, led the Government in the following January to offer to discuss with the farmers' representatives both the future policy as to guaranteed prices and markets—so far promised only for one year after the close of hostilities—and the principles and procedure of price fixing for agricultural products. As a result of these discussions the Government announced in May 1944 its intention to continue the system of guaranteed prices for four years; that is, up to the close of

P

the agricultural year 1947–8. In December it made known its decisions on price-fixing procedure. During the four-year period the Government undertook to carry out an annual price review, to be held in February of each year, and in addition to hold a special review at any time of the year should unforeseen changes make it desirable. It promised, further, that representatives of the farmers would be invited to take part in these reviews with officials of the government departments concerned. These developments, later made permanent by the Agriculture Act of 1947, transformed what had begun as a system of government control of prices into a system of collective bargaining. The first review of the new series took place in February 1945. It was the fourth, and last, to be carried out during the war.

Changes in Agricultural Prices

Let us now turn to the statistical record of agricultural price changes during the war. Between 1938–9 and 1944–5 the agricultural price level, as measured by the official index number, practically doubled. The movement from year to year is indicated in the accompanying diagram, which also shows the changes in the official import price index for food, drink and tobacco, and in the retail food price level. The rise in the agricultural price level soon outstripped the increase in prices of food imports, and though the gap narrowed towards the close of the war, the subsequent further rise in the home agricultural price level has prevented it from being overhauled even by the high post-war cost of food imports. The retail food price level, thanks to subsidies, shows little relation to the movements of the other two series.

Changes in the prices of individual products are summarized in the table on page 216. Among the main groups of products the prices of crops rose during the war more than those of livestock products; this was logical in view of the wartime emphasis on crop production, but it was partly due to the earlier and more effective control exercised over most livestock products. The rise in crop prices was outstripped by that of vegetable prices, which with poultry, eggs and barley were strongly affected by scarcity. At the other extreme, the price of potatoes failed to profit in similar fashion from wartime scarcity and rose comparatively little, but it was already relatively high before the war and the favourable wartime yields seem to have made the crop profitable to most growers.

From what has already been said as to the circumstances in which the successive price decisions were made during the war, it will be clear that the individual price changes cannot be expected to fall into a

CHANGES IN FOOD AND AGRICULTURAL PRICES

Agricultural Prices ———
Import Prices (Food, Drink and Tobacco) ------
Retail Food Prices — — —

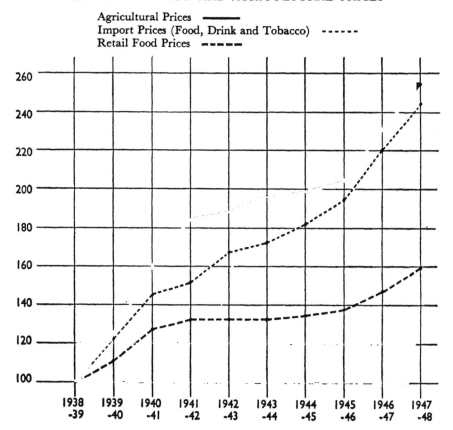

Agricultural Prices   Official index number including Exchequer payments.
Import Prices   Official index numbers of import prices for food, drink and
                      tobacco in December of each year.
Retail Prices   Index derived from data published in the White Papers on
                      National Income—figures for successive calendar years
                      averaged.

completely logical pattern. Each set of decisions was to some extent a compromise, a resultant of conflicting influences. Thus we cannot take the individual price changes as conforming in any consistent fashion to official estimates of changes in costs of production, or to cost changes modified by appropriate 'incentives' for different products. A considerable and growing volume of information on costs of production and on the financial results of farming was, and is, collected for the purpose of the price reviews. But even in the most favourable circumstances the regulation of agricultural prices in accordance with cost

Table III. *Agricultural Prices in England and Wales* (1936–7 to 1938–9=100)
(including Exchequer payments)

	1940–1	1941–2	1942–3	1943–4	1944–5	1945–6	1946–7	1947–8	1948–9
Wheat	148	154	171	189	198	200	183	229	247
Barley	201	352	323	264	241	237	234	254	263
Oats	195	195	208	210	224	209	227	272	281
Potatoes	131	149	148	148	152	160	168	196	203
Sugar beet	154	161	204	201	192	211	215	263	257
Fruit	201	218	196	196	196	178	220	249	219
Vegetables	177	226	243	259	246	239	343	272	223
Glasshouse produce	284	235	192	201	192	191	219	281	300
Fat cattle	138	145	154	154	159	166	178	213	223
Fat sheep	134	147	157	158	171	181	194	253	261
Fat lambs	125	136	141	144	156	164	175	223	229
Bacon pigs	159	183	190	190	191	209	240	283	300
Milk	154	173	180	188	193	201	218	237	241
Poultry	160	177	184	176	178	193	294	278	288
Eggs	187	217	205	205	206	219	240	266	261
Cereals and farm crops	153	187	194	195	195	203	202	236	247
Livestock and livestock products	151	169	173	180	185	195	216	244	251
Fruit, vegetables and glasshouse produce	204	223	215	223	216	206	275	263	233
General Index	158	180	183	191	195	202	225	249	251

changes cannot be a precise or purely arithmetical operation. It is rarely, if ever, practicable to base official prices directly on ascertained money costs of production. The usual procedure, with agricultural as with manufactured products and distributors' margins, was to estimate the relative changes in costs from a datum period in the past and to use this estimate as a guide to the permissible increase in price. But costs, and cost changes, vary from producer to producer according to the nature and situation of the land, the productive system used, and the efficiency of its management. Wartime changes, especially the big decline in imports of feeding-stuffs, necessitated changes in farm practice which themselves made pre-war cost data obsolete. Moreover, the actual amount of the change in costs per unit, if estimated in this way, often depends very largely on the period chosen as the datum level of the calculation, and as to this there may be much room for disagreement. In practice the determination of prices is further complicated by the need for encouraging some products and discouraging others, by the varying bargaining pressure exerted by different groups of producers, by the uneven incidence of scarcity and, finally, by the purely technical difficulties of control, which make it impossible in some cases to enforce a controlled price much below the equilibrium level.

Price control is, however, not by any means the only instrument by which the wartime changes in production were brought about. Propaganda, persuasion, the pressure exerted by the conditions enforced under the feeding-stuffs rationing scheme, direct financial inducement (for example, the ploughing-up subsidy) and, lastly, compulsion, were all employed. The existence of these latter alternatives indeed sometimes served as an excuse for a rather timid and limited use of the first. They reinforced the natural tendency to err on the side of generosity in fixing prices, and the inevitable reluctance to balance the inducements offered for some products by high prices with discouragement to others by low prices.

The Wartime Increase in Farm Incomes

The story is, of course, incomplete without an assessment of the effects of the wartime price changes on the incomes of farmers. The following official estimates of the total income from farming in the United Kingdom have recently been published (Cmd. 7933, *National Income and Expenditure of the United Kingdom, 1946 to 1949*, Table 8):

1938	1946	1947	1948	1949
		£ million		
60	190	205	258	283

Of these totals about £3 millions in 1938 and £10½ millions in 1949 are estimated to have gone to 'spare-time' farmers. Since there are about 360,000 full-time farmers, their average income per farm would be about £160 before the war, and £540, £690 and £760 respectively in the three latest years. These figures, it should be noted, relate to the net income from farming (defined in the White Paper as 'the reward of the manual and managerial labour of farmers and their wives and the return on their capital'), and this is not quite the same thing as the net income of farmers. The latter will include farmers' income from land ownership and other non-farming activities, which might increase the total by perhaps £20 to £25 millions a year, and the average per farm by £55 to £70.

The official figures cover only the years shown in the table, and they do not provide an analysis of the distribution of the net output of agriculture between the three participants, farmers, workers and land-lords. But other information makes possible a rough calculation for the three years 1943–4 to 1945–6.

The following are official estimates of gross and net agricultural output in the United Kingdom:[1]

(£ millions)

	Average 1936–7 to 1938–9	1943–4	1944–5	1945–6
Gross Output	284·9	597·9	579·7	615·1
Less:				
Feeding-stuffs	71·2	29·5	30·8	41·8
Imported store animals	15·0	20·0	20·0	21·5
Imported seeds	4·0	15·0	16·0	15·0
Net Output	194·7	533·4	512·9	536·8

From the net output as calculated above certain further deductions have to be made. Farmers' expenditure on fertilizers is estimated to have amounted to £8·4 millions in 1938–9 and to £28·0, £27·3 and £28·3 millions respectively in 1943–4 and the two following years. The cost of machinery, fuel and repairs, contract services and miscellaneous charges has been put at £22¾ millions for 1937–9 and £67 millions

[1] *Agricultural Statistics, United Kingdom*, Part II, H.M. Stationery Office, 1949, p. 27.

for 1943–4;[1] in default of later estimates we may perhaps reckon it at £77 millions for the three years 1943–4 to 1945–6. Subtracting these figures from the official estimates of net output we are left with £163½ millions for the pre-war period and £423 millions for 1943–4 to 1945–6, which represent to a rough approximation the sums available for payment of rent and wages and for the remuneration of the farmers themselves.

The agricultural wage bill has been officially estimated at £154 millions in 1945 and £171 millions in 1946.[2] Allowing for differences in wage rates and in numbers employed and for the cost of prisoner-of-war labour, the pre-war and 1943–6 totals may be put at about £65 millions and £163 millions respectively. The average rental value of agricultural land in England and Wales in 1941 was 24s. an acre; in Scotland (in 1946) it was 7s. 3d.[3] On this basis the pre-war gross rental (including the rental value of owner-occupied land) would be about £40 millions for the United Kingdom. The wartime increase was moderate, and the 1943–6 figure would be perhaps £45 millions. On this basis the remaining item, the net farm income, must have risen from something like £59 millions before the war to something like £213 millions in 1943–6. The following table brings these figures together:

(£ millions)

	Pre-war	1943–6
Net output as published	195	528
Further deductions	31	105
	164	423
Agricultural wages	65	165
Gross rental value of agricultural land	40	45
Farm income (by difference)	59	213

These estimates, though they only claim a rough accuracy, suggest that farm incomes in 1946 may have been somewhat below the level reached during the immediately preceding years. They show that the increase in farm incomes was greater both absolutely and relatively than the increase in the farm labour bill, even though the latter covers

[1] J. H. Kirk, 'The Output of British Agriculture during the War', *Proceedings of the Agricultural Economics Society*, Vol. VII, No. 1, June 1946.
[2] National income White Papers, Cmd. 6784 and Cmd. 7099, 1946 and 1947.
[3] *National Farm Survey of England and Wales, Summary Report*, H.M. Stationery Office, 1946; *Scottish Farm Rents and Estate Expenditure*, H.M. Stationery Office, 1948.

Table IV. *Farm Management Survey Results, England and Wales*[1]

Farming Type	No. of Farms	Net Income per Farm		Net Income per 100 acres	
		1945–6	1946–7	1945–6	1946–7
Types with low income per farm:		£	£	£	£
Mainly Dairying (Kent and Sussex)	53	350	173	224	112
Upland Mixed Livestock:					
(Yorkshire Dales)	24	504	291	509	287
(Wales, cattle and sheep, poor land)	67	211	158	237	178
(Wales, sheep and cattle)	77	437	229	226	118
(South-West Shropshire)	22	375	253	300	194
Lowland Mixed Livestock:					
(Kent and Sussex)	19	307	−64	182	−37
Types with high income per farm:					
General Mixed Farming:					
(East Shropshire and South-West Staffordshire)	14	1,123	1,460	432	563
(Northamptonshire)	13	1,313	1,174	459	415
Corn, Sheep and Dairying:					
(Chalk uplands)	63	1,366	903	291	189
Arable:					
(North Essex)	40	1,553	1,093	787	555
(Lindsey and Kesteven limestone)	36	1,386	1,355	558	543
(Isle of Ely)	34	1,009	1,507	726	1,094
Specialist:					
(Kent, hops, fruit and vegetables)	21	2,740	1,144	1,557	857
All grass types	1,094	555	460	378	312
All intermediate types	549	836	721	399	340
All arable types	590	1,004	1,013	533	533
All specialist types	62	1,487	820	1,830	1,240
All farms in sample	2,295	763	674	447	393

[1] These figures are based on an identical sample of farm records collected by the Provincial Agricultural Economists and summarized by the Ministry of Agriculture and Fisheries, by whose permission they are published. Net income represents the return to the farmer and his wife for their manual labour and management services and interest on farm capital other than that invested in land and buildings.

a larger number of workers in 1943-6 than before the war. Farm incomes and the agricultural labour bill both rose much faster than the national income as a whole, whose increase between 1938 and 1946 was about 75 per cent. Both were at a very low level before the war, and the wartime increase in farm incomes is, of course, to some extent offset by the change in farmers' liability to taxation and by the need for new investment, which must have absorbed large sums. The increase received by the farmers was none the less exceptionally great, and it is doubtful whether any other group of comparable numbers enjoyed so great an improvement in its fortunes.

There are, nevertheless, wide variations between the income levels realized on farms in different areas and of different types. These are illustrated by the figures in Table IV from the Farm Management Survey of England and Wales.

These figures have been purposely selected to show the extremes of the variations, which are, of course, to some extent merely a reflection of the differences in the size and capitalization of the farms in different groups. Some of them, especially those relating to the group of specialist farms in Kent, may not be representative of more than the comparatively small number of farms comprising the type-group from which they are drawn. But the extent of the variations and the consistency with which poor results are found on the upland livestock farms illustrate problems to which some reference has already been made, and suggest that if wartime changes resulted in a less unequal distribution of the national income between agriculture and other occupations, the distribution between farmers of these wartime gains has not itself been equal.

RETAIL FOOD PRICES AND FOOD SUBSIDIES

The Search for a Policy

Although the payment of subsidies to prevent increases in retail food prices actually began before the close of 1939, the food subsidy and stabilization policy did not emerge in clearly defined form until Sir Kingsley Wood's budget speech of April 1941. Similarly, the extent to which the Government would make use of its powers to control retail food prices by orders and regulations also remained uncertain until the early months of 1941. During the first few months of the war, although the Government became the owner of the stocks of the more important foods and determined the prices at which they were released, control of retail prices was limited to a small number of major articles. It was not at that time clear that its extension outside a comparatively narrow range was either possible or desirable. As late as the end of June 1940, after ten months of war, the number of foods whose retail prices were controlled were fewer than twenty, and although these were sufficiently important to represent about half the total expenditure on food, the list did not include bread, flour, fish (except herrings) or tea. The Government's evident lack of concern over possible increases in the retail food price level at the outbreak of war is shown by the fact that one of its first actions after war was declared was to increase the rate of taxation on sugar.

It was soon disillusioned. Oversea suppliers asked for higher prices, freight charges rose, the exchange value of the pound fell, and home agricultural prices began their rapid ascent. The food price index number used in the cost of living index rose by 14 per cent between 1st September and 1st December 1939, although the Government was already incurring large losses on the sale of imported cereals and meat. It thus found itself obliged to consider whether the bread subsidy adopted after three years of fighting during the first world war should be introduced almost at the outset of the second. It decided to subsidize not only bread and flour, but also milk and home-killed meat. The loss on imported meat was eliminated by the new prices fixed in January 1940, but a subsidy on bacon, whose price had risen by 30 per cent since September, was shortly afterwards introduced, and the ration increased, in order to avert a threatened accumulation of stocks.

These subsidies, which were explained and defended in the House of Commons on 31st January and 8th February 1940, kept the food index fairly stable for a few months, but it took a violent upward jump of ten points on 1st July 1940. This was mainly due to the unfortunate coincidence of a rise in the price of milk, when the subsidy to the ordinary retail price was withdrawn on the introduction of the National Milk Scheme, with a seasonal increase due to the high price of new potatoes, which in 1940 were scarce and expensive owing to the sudden loss of the Channel Islands supply by the German occupation. But it was in any case clear that new decisions of policy would soon be needed. The comparative steadiness of the food index during the first half of the year had not stabilized the index as a whole, for other items, particularly clothing, had continued to rise. The new agricultural prices fixed during the summer substantially increased the cost of home-produced food, and further increases in freight charges and insurance on imports were in prospect. It was calculated that the cost of maintaining food prices at their existing level would shortly rise to £110 millions a year, or double the rate of expenditure incurred during the first half of 1940.

If discontent and injustice were to be prevented it was clearly necessary to ensure adequate supplies of essential foods at prices within reach of the lowest-paid workers. If the upward movement of wages was to be restrained, careful attention would need to be paid to the movements of the cost of living index, unless some better measure could be devised to replace it in wage negotiations. If the cost of these measures was to be kept within reasonable limits, subsidies would have to be limited to those necessary to achieve the first two objects. Such were the chief constituents of the problem.

A large part of its difficulty centred round the cost of living index number. This index had been introduced during the first world war and its weights were based on the results of a household budget inquiry carried out in 1904. The standard of consumption whose cost it purported to measure corresponded neither to the consumption habits of the twenties and thirties nor to the changed habits of wartime. The foods included in the index represented about two-thirds of total working class food expenditure in 1937-8, but the selection and weighting of the non-food items was badly out of date. The need for a revision had been officially recognized before the war and statistical material for the construction of a new system of weighting had been collected by the Ministry of Labour in 1937-8. But this material was, of course, useless for the purpose of bringing the index into conformity with wartime conditions.

There were a number of obvious and weighty objections to any attempt to stabilize this index by subsidies. Although it covered most of the major foods, several whose importance were now emphasized by nutritionists—for instance, green vegetables, pulses and oatmeal—were not included. Subsidies to their prices would have no effect on the index, however desirable on other grounds. But other foods which were inevitably becoming scarce and dear had a comparatively large effect. Two which gave particular trouble were fish and eggs, responsible between them for a twelve-point rise in the food index between June and December 1940. Both were administratively very difficult to control and both were bound to remain scarce throughout the war, however necessary they might seem in peacetime. If it were possible to disregard their prices for the duration of the war much money might be saved to the Exchequer and much administrative effort to the Ministry of Food.

It was, moreover, arguable that subsidizing the prices of any commodities, however carefully selected, was a comparatively ineffective and expensive method of safeguarding nutrition. Such subsidies would lower prices to all consumers, rich and poor alike; whereas schemes like the National Milk Scheme, or a system of family allowances or special grants to particular groups of persons, would direct assistance to those genuinely in need of it and might achieve much more, in terms of public welfare, at a much lower cost to the State. In spite of higher taxation, rising incomes were giving many people the means of paying higher prices for food even if they did not reduce their expenditure on other things. Yet if prices stayed at their existing levels consumers would be obliged in the future to spend less on food, since the supplies would not exist to enable them to spend more. From this point of view it seemed desirable that prices of the less essential foods should be deliberately raised, either by taxation or by increasing the Ministry of Food's selling prices, in pursuance of the principle applied to other commodities in October 1940 by the purchase tax.

The possibility of revising the cost of living index or abandoning it altogether received a good deal of discussion in the first years of the war. The Scientific Food Policy Committee, a group of distinguished scientists appointed by the Government in May 1940, produced a plan for stabilizing the cost of a daily ration of 2,800 calories, whose constituents would be chosen in accordance with the supplies available from time to time, but predominantly from the proposed Basal Diet which the scientists had put forward as a basis for wartime food policy and which consisted largely of wholemeal bread and potatoes.[1] Reports were circulating in Whitehall from a group of experimenters at Cambridge who had voluntarily subsisted on a similar diet of this kind for several months in the interests of science. Lord Keynes[2] and others suggested a new index number, to be confined to a narrow range of basic necessities, and the Government itself went so far as to call for an official report on the possibility of constructing a wartime cost of living index.

The 1941 Stabilization Policy

But in reality all these proposals were far removed from practical possibility. If the Government was to embark on a policy of stabilization, it must stabilize something. There must be some symbol, some more or less objective and acceptable standard by which its performance

---

[1] Scientists, however, did not endorse the views of the persistent crank who wrote to the Ministry of Food advocating the inclusion in human diets of large quantities of grass.

[2] *How to Pay for the War*, 1940, p. 57.

could be measured against its promises. The old cost of living index, with all its imperfections, was an established institution. No new or revised index would have any chance of taking its place unless it was equally acceptable to the trade unions. But Labour opinion demanded equality of sacrifice, and distrusted the talk about calories and vitamins. It was likely to look askance at any list of necessaries drawn up for it by the Government. There could be no certainty that any new index which the trade unions could be persuaded to accept would not offer even greater difficulty than the existing index.

The view that prevailed, therefore, was that no practical alternative was in fact available to this index. If so, it was obvious that its move-ments would have in future to be carefully controlled. Its influence on wage levels was growing more and more important, not only because it was the only available measure of price changes, but because the number of wage agreements linking wage rates to changes in the index number was rapidly increasing. Stabilization of this index might be costly, but if it was effective in stabilizing wages the Government might save more, in lower prices for the goods it needed for war purposes, than it would have to pay out in subsidies.

Thus the stabilization policy announced in the budget speech of 1941, and further explained in the White Paper on *Price Stabilisation and Industrial Policy* issued in July (Cmd. 6294), had the control of the index number as one of its main objectives. 'I propose', said the Chancellor, 'to continue and extend the policy of stabilisation in an endeavour to prevent any further rise of the Cost-of-Living Index number, apart from minor seasonal changes, above the present range of 125–130 in terms of the pre-war level. . . . It will also be my aim, in conjunction with my right hon. Friends the President of the Board of Trade and the Minister of Food, to try to prevent substantial increases in the prices of other articles in common use.'[1] These measures, to-gether with the rationing of foodstuffs and clothing and the imposition of severe additional direct taxation, constituted a threefold policy aimed at checking inflation. The Chancellor expressed the hope that condi-tions would thus be created which would 'enable the wages situation to be held about where it now is'. The various voluntary organizations and tribunals concerned with wage regulation were left free to reach their decisions in accordance with their estimate of the relevant facts, which might properly include the need for adjustments both among low-paid workers and in consequence of changes in the form, method or volume of production. But the Chancellor gave warning that

[1] 370 H.C. Deb., 7th April 1941, Cols. 1323–4.

'persistence of the tendency towards rising wage rates . . . would compel abandonment of the stabilisation policy'.

These decisions marked the end of the experimental stage of price-control policy. They coincided, as already mentioned, with the measures adopted by the Ministry of Food to bring within the range of price control the wide variety of minor foods hitherto exempt. A larger number of price-control orders was issued by the Ministry in the first six months of 1941 than in any other comparable period throughout the war. With the extension of price control from the major foods to the innumerable branded articles in tins and packets, many new administrative problems were, of course, encountered, and a great deal of detailed investigation was necessary, including in some cases the issue of individual licences covering the separate brands of each manufacturer. Moreover, price control tended to intensify the apparent shortage of goods in the shops and to emphasize the need for a wider extension of rationing. To meet this need the points scheme was launched, after much discussion and not a little hesitation on the part of the Ministry of Food, in December 1941. Price control was further extended during 1942, and with the issue in January 1943 of the Green Vegetables Maximum Prices Order the only considerable group of foods still remaining free was brought within its scope. Uncontrolled goods now represented less than 10 per cent of the average housewife's food expenditure.

The tentative policy, endorsed in August 1940 by the War Cabinet, that 'luxury foods' should be allowed to find their own price level, was thus abandoned, and with it the attempt to find means of recovering part of the cost of the food subsidies by raising the prices of less essential foods. Considerable savings might have been realized by raising the prices of such articles as sugar for manufacture, chocolate and sugar confectionery, cocoa, canned fruit and China tea. In a few instances this policy was actually put into effect; the price of manufacturing sugar was raised in December 1940, and the Ministry secured a profit on rice and imposed a levy on raw cocoa. But these possibilities were pursued no further. They were given up in face of growing shortages, the egalitarian trend of popular opinion, and a widespread if irrational feeling that a Ministry engaged in preventing traders from 'profiteering' ought not itself to profiteer.

The Ministry's policy henceforward had three objectives. The first was the general application of price control. The second was the safeguarding of nutrition, which necessitated maintaining low prices for the really important foods, especially those like potatoes, whose consumption it was striving to expand, and demanded an effort to protect and improve the nutrition of children, towards which measures like the National Milk Scheme, the distribution of cod liver oil and orange juice, and the expansion of school feeding were directed.

Subsidies and the Cost of Living Index

The third objective was the stabilization of the index number. Since this was by far the most costly part of the policy it could not long escape notice that the cost of lowering the index number by a given number of points depended very much on the choice of foods to be subsidized. The reason for this lay, of course, in the widely varying relation between the wartime consumption of different foods and that assumed in the weighting of the index number. If the consumption of all foods had been the same as that assumed in the weighting, or had differed from it by a uniform proportion, there would have been nothing to choose between them as vehicles for a subsidy designed to lower the index. But under actual wartime conditions articles like eggs, butter and sugar were considerably overweighted, and subsidies to their prices would lower the index number by much more per million pounds of expenditure than subsidies to liquid milk, margarine or potatoes, whose consumption had increased. According to estimates made early in 1944, for example, the annual cost of the reductions then being effected in the food index ranged from £8 to £10 millions per point in the case of liquid milk down to less than £2 millions per point in the case of eggs.

The fact that sugar was in this sense one of the cheapest foods to subsidize was first pointed out in the summer of 1940, when the ten-point jump in the food index on 1st July was followed by a further increase in the price of sugar to meet rising costs. If the stabilization of the index really had the paramount importance that current discussion was beginning to assign to it, the sugar price decision, like the extra tax imposed at the outbreak of war, was clearly a mistake from the point of view of the Treasury. An early opportunity to put this conclusion into practice arose in November when the continued advance in the index number produced something like a crisis. Thanks largely to the high prices of fish and eggs, the food index on 1st November had reached a figure 25 per cent higher than on 1st September 1939, and had risen eight points in three months, the steepest continuous increase since the beginning of the war. In addition, a further increase in the price of milk had also been authorized, which was equivalent to at least two more points on the food index. By a fortunate coincidence, however, this increase, though it came into effect on 1st December, did not affect the food index until 1st January 1941, for 1st December fell in 1940 on a Sunday, and the Ministry of Labour's practice in such cases was to base the calculation of the index number on the prices of the preceding day. During December the price of sugar was reduced by 1d. per lb., and the cost of the reduction was met by raising the price of sugar for manufacturing, which did not enter into the index number. This reduction more than offset the rise in the price of milk. The food index for 1st January 1941 duly showed a fall of one point from the level of 30th November, and the figure of 173 (in terms of July 1914 as 100) at which it stood on the latter date was, as it turned out, the highest it was to be allowed to reach until after the defeat of Germany.

Once the Government had undertaken a definite commitment to stabilize the index, these considerations of relative cost naturally played a part in determining the choice of subsidies by which it should be carried out. On 1st April 1941 the index for all items stood at 198 in terms of July 1914 as 100; the upper limit of 30 per cent over the figure recorded on 1st September 1939, which the Chancellor pledged himself not to exceed, corresponded to an all-items index of 201½. In order to give effect to his undertaking, all goods whose prices were included in the index had to be brought under effective control. Among items other than food the most important was clothing, to whose continually rising prices the increase in the general index figure had been largely due. But since the prices of clothing were likely to rise further before they could be effectively controlled, the fulfilment of the Chancellor's undertaking required that the food index should not merely be stabilized, but reduced.

This was achieved by lowering the prices of fish and by instituting a subsidy for eggs. A maximum prices order for fish was in any case overdue, but the Ministry had been deterred from introducing it earlier by the memory of the ill-starred fish control scheme of September 1939, one of its comparatively few bad administrative failures. The order was successfully imposed at the end of June 1941 with the aid of a transport equalization levy, and brought fish prices down by 20 per cent. Control of the prices of imported eggs was comparatively simple, but home-produced eggs presented awkward problems owing to the difficulty of enforcement and the variety of channels through which eggs reached the market. Canalization of the supply was necessary, however, if any attempt was to be made to control distribution, and the Ministry now issued an order requiring all producers with more than a small maximum number of birds to market their eggs only through authorized packing stations. In order to provide an inducement to observance of the law a subsidy was introduced which enabled the Ministry, through the packing stations, to purchase the eggs from the producers at a price *higher* than the legal maximum retail price, which was reduced. In terms of its effect on the index number the subsidy on eggs was, as already pointed out, extremely cheap to the Exchequer.

Care was also taken, in 1941 and the following years, to prevent a repetition of the sudden rise in the food index at the beginning of July owing to the high prices of new potatoes. The Chancellor had indeed expressly excluded 'minor seasonal changes' in giving his promise to stabilize the index, and an increase in the food index at this time of year, like the seasonal movement due to the fluctuation of egg prices, was a normal and regular occurrence. But little advantage was in practice taken of this reservation. The new prices for eggs remained unchanged throughout the year, and the prices of old potatoes were reduced by subsidy at the beginning of July so as to bring the average price of new and old potatoes together to a suitable figure. The quotation for potatoes on 1st July was in future based, reasonably enough, on a weighted average of the prices of new and old potatoes, in place of the customary unweighted average which gave undue influence to the relatively high price of new potatoes.

By these measures the food index, instead of rising as usual between 1st June and 1st July, was in 1941 actually reduced by three points, and it fell further during the autumn as a result of the seasonal decline in potato prices and a further reduction in the prices of fish. But the prices of clothing, coal and gas, and miscellaneous items continued to advance, and two further reductions in the food index were made at the request of the Treasury in order to keep the index for all items within the Chancellor's limit. In December 1941 the price of domestic sugar was lowered by a further 1d. per lb. and in March 1942 eggs were again reduced by 6d. per dozen. Both of these reductions, of course, involved increased subsidies from the Exchequer. In June 1942 the food index reached the lowest point it touched during the operation of the stabilization policy: at a figure of 159 it stood at approximately the same level as two years earlier, and fourteen points below the peak figure of 30th November 1940.

By the summer of 1942 the Board of Trade's utility clothing scheme, designed to bring about a reduction in clothing prices, at last began to take effect. Utility clothing was exempted from the purchase tax and its slowly increasing supply led to a gradual fall in the price index for

clothing during the twelve months following August 1942. But this did
not mean that the Ministry of Food's difficulties in implementing the
stabilization policy were at an end. The prospect of a fall in the cost
of living index was almost as embarrassing to the Treasury as the
possibility of a rise beyond the Chancellor's permitted maximum. If
the index fell appreciably below this maximum the Treasury would
be incurring subsidy expenditure unnecessarily and, unless wages also
fell, the inflationary excess of purchasing power in the hands of the
public would be increased. Considerable numbers of wage earners who
worked in industries where wages were linked to the index number
would find their earnings reduced if it fell, but they could hardly be
expected to accept such reductions without protests and pressure for
revision of the wage agreements. It would save a deal of trouble,
therefore, if the reduction in clothing prices, except in so far as it was
balanced by the increase of coal prices in the summer of 1942, could
be offset by reversing the recent fall in the food index.

From mid-1942 to the close of the war, therefore, the price changes
affecting the index number foods were predominantly upward, although
fish prices were further reduced and a subsidy on potatoes brought
down the retail price by about 20 per cent in 1942–3 and yet lower in
the following year. Bread, flour, bacon, butter and tea were all raised
in price between September 1942 and January 1943, and the price of
sugar went up 1d. in the following September. The food index climbed
back to 168, thirty points, or 22 per cent, above the September 1939
figure. Here it remained stabilized, apart from such seasonal changes
as were still allowed to affect it, from October 1943 until the close of
the war.

Sir John Anderson, reviewing the stabilization policy in his budget
speech of April 1944, had drawn attention to the rise in wage rates
since 1941 and stated that the Government could no longer promise
to keep the index number within the limits laid down by Sir Kingsley
Wood. He substituted a permissible maximum increase of 35 per cent
over the pre-war figure for his predecessor's 30 per cent. But in fact the
30 per cent maximum was only slightly exceeded during the lifetime
of the old cost of living index. Sir Kingsley Wood's policy in substance
survived both the close of the war and the change of Government, and
was allowed to lapse only with the withdrawal, in June 1947, of the
index number on which it was based. Mr. Dalton, though less meti-
culous than his two predecessors in ironing out the summer seasonal
increase due to new potatoes, did not, in spite of the steeply mounting
costs of subsidies, permit the general figure to rise permanently above

203, representing an increase since September 1939 of 31 per cent. The last few months of the index number's life indeed witnessed a return to the wartime policy of offsetting increases in the prices of other articles by reducing the food index, for in March, April and May 1947 there were reductions in the prices of cheese, eggs, butter, sugar and bacon which coincided with a rise in the price of potatoes, with a big increase in 'other items' due to Mr. Dalton's heavy increase in the tobacco tax, and with a rise in rates, and which left the general index figure unchanged.

Results of the Stabilization Policy

What had the stabilization policy achieved, and what had it cost? In the nature of things the first of these questions admits of a much less precise answer than the second. But in terms of its fundamental objective the stabilization policy was a failure. It did not stabilize wage rates; still less did it stabilize earnings. The money income of the community went on increasing while its real consumable income was falling. In itself this is not, of course, surprising. War renders inoperative those rules of financial policy on which the avoidance of inflation normally depends, and it puts nothing effective in their place. Stabilization by subsidies cannot by itself reverse the effects of huge budget deficits or damp down the imperious wartime demand for labour. Nevertheless, the rate of increase of wages certainly slowed up after 1940, and there is no reason to doubt that the control of the cost of living index helped in bringing this about. During the first twenty months of war, up to June 1941, the average increase in weekly wage rates amounted to 22 per cent. During the remainder of the war there was a further increase of almost exactly similar dimensions spread over a period of four years.

The cost of the stabilization policy is not quite the same thing as the cost of the food subsidies, since the latter includes certain payments unrelated to the stabilization of the index number, and excludes various non-food subsidies (e.g. on coal, clothing and leather) which at different times affected the index number. But much the greater part of the cost of stabilization was incurred in subsidizing food, and much the greater part of the cost of food subsidies was incurred in carrying out the stabilization policy. The food subsidies paid since 1939–40 are shown in Table V. Though they were never confined to articles included in the index number, the proportion of the total which should be charged specifically against the stabilization of the index must in most years have. been at least 85–90 per cent. It thus substantially exceeded the proportion of total consumers' expenditure devoted to

Table V. *Food Subsidies 1939–40 to*

	1939–40	1940–41	1941–42
A. Ministry of Food Trading Losses and Commodity Subsidies (profits shown in brackets):			
Animal feeding stuffs	(4)	(80)	1,936
Bacon and ham	723	6,513	(50)
Cereals	10,234	31,763	38,109
Dried fruits	(398)	(586)	(1,253)
Eggs	(17)	(529)	7,184
Meat and livestock	5,534	18,539	19,599
Milk	2,549	3,607	3,184
Milk products	(606)	(2,113)	(275)
Oils and fats	(1,087)	(2,265)	(4,086)
Potatoes and carrots	41	176	14,362
Sugar	(1,542)(d)	(50)	3,418
Tea, coffee and cocoa	363	(34)	977
Other commodities	(31)	(122)	(3,113)
	15,760	54,819	79,969
B. Other Ministry of Food Payments:			
Welfare Foods Service	—	7,229	12,833
Milk-in-Schools Scheme	—	607	1,884
Contribution to New Zealand	—	—	—
Bulk payments to Argentina and Uruguay	—	—	—
Bulk payment to the Netherlands	—	—	—
Other and miscellaneous payments	101	482	1,044
	101	8,318	15,761
C. Subsidies borne on Votes of Other Departments:			
Acreage payments: Potatoes	—	—	(a)
Wheat	—	—	—
Rye	—	—	—
Fertilizer subsidy	—	—	—
	—	—	—
Total Subsidies (excluding direct subsidies to agriculture)	15,861	63,137	95,750

[1] From figures kindly supplied by the Ministry of Food.

Notes

(a) Included under A.

(b) An amount of £12 millions relates to earlier years.

1948–9[1]   (£ thousand)

1942-43	1943-44	1944-45	1945-46	1946-47	1947-48	1948-49
2,771	4,613	6,542	7,961	9,114	18,292	24,229
2,074	1,645	737	2,959	7,175	14,033	16,964
33,898	52,219	44,153	59,048	57,372	89,642	133,628
(486)	(113)	2,977	3,298	3,522	(945)	(1,016)
13,996	13,888	14,762	31,470	30,859	27,385	28,183
20,508	16,179	17,460	32,409	35,857	53,968	57,521
10,791	11,491	17,282	24,438	38,427	35,502	44,294
4,795	9,116	8,272	21,810	32,417	47,872	59,797
(4,194)	(3,750)	(793)	476	(670)	(6,850)	7,413
23,485	16,324	13,216	8,289	18,748	10,416	11,619
16,335	10,204	15,150	19,639	26,375	28,927	23,768
(1,101)	(1,367)	222	1,856	3,908	7,862	16,468
289	(717)	(1,285)	(3,823)	(2,776)	(8,304)	(5,160)
123,162	129,733	138,695	209,830	260,326	317,799	417,706
13,665	16,163	15,755	16,652	22,030	26,301	27,204
4,364	4,799	4,756	4,695	5,882	7,450	8,248
—	—	16,000 (b)	4,000	4,000	4,000	—
—	—	—	—	7,700	10,000	—
—	—	—	—	—	—	250
1,430	1,097	(12,942) (c)	482	397	(437)	12
19,459	22,059	23,569	25,829	40,009	47,314	35,714
(a)	13,830	13,850	13,650	13,618	12,715	15,795
—	10,506	13,100	9,350	4,152	4,365	2,645
—	393	510	380	110	75	105
—	6,000	6,000	6,500	6,750	9,360	12,500
—	30,729	33,460	29,880	24,630	26,515	31,045
142,622	182,521	195,724	265,539	324,964	391,629	484,465

(c) Includes surplus on Insurance Fund to 31 October 1943.
(d) Ministry of Food trading profit less subsidy borne on Agricultural Departments' vote.

foods included in the cost of living index, which in working-class households in 1937–8 was about two-thirds, and in the war years was somewhat lower.

The fact that the subsidies were mainly concentrated on the index number foods meant, of course, that the prices of these foods rose less than those of the foods outside the index. Another factor which contributed to this result was the earlier and in some cases the more effective control applied to the index number foods. There is no completely satisfactory measure of food price changes during the war; indeed, the very conception of such a measure is not free from theoretical difficulty. But the estimates given in the national income White Paper provide an alternative calculation with which the official food index can be compared, although, as already explained, they under-

FOOD PRICES AND WAGE RATES

Food Price Index
    (National Income White Papers) ───────
Cost of Living Food Index - - - - - - -
Wage Rates (June of each year)━ ━ ━ ━ ━

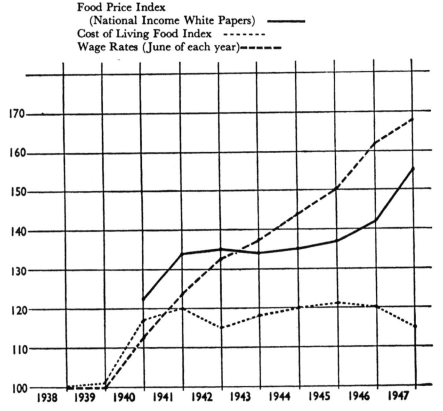

For the Cost of Living Food Index the figures are annual averages, except that for 1947, which relates to 17 June.

state the actual rise in prices. The diagram opposite shows that although the increase in the general retail food price level slowed up after 1941, its magnitude, when measured from 1938, was in the later war years nearly twice that shown by the official index. Moreover, the two sharp downward movements in the official index, from 1941 to 1942 and from 1946 to mid-1947, correspond to no similar change in the general price level, which in the latter instance indeed moved steeply upward.

One consequence of the stabilization policy, therefore, was that it deprived the cost of living index, and its food component, of much of their validity as representative measures of the general change in retail prices. This fact has itself been construed as a criticism of the policy.[1] But any policy of subsidizing food prices, even one based solely on considerations of nutrition, would have been almost bound to produce this effect in greater or less degree. Even if the index number had been disregarded altogether, and the subsidies used to stabilize the cost of a diet of basic necessities, a larger proportion of the foods covered by the index would have received subsidies than of those outside it. The bias introduced into the index by the use of subsidies to control its movement could only have been completely avoided if the subsidies had been distributed at random over all foods without regard to their nutritional or psychological importance. But a random distribution of subsidies, however attractive to a statistician, is not an idea likely to appeal to a Chancellor of the Exchequer.

In practice, however, the movements of the food index were determined not only by the large proportion of the total subsidies which was devoted to the foods included in it, but in some measure by the fact that subsidies paid on the overweighted items lowered the index by more than the same expenditure differently distributed would have done. They reduced the index proportionately much more than they reduced the cost of food to consumers. But if there was something spurious in the reduction in the index number brought about by these subsidies, was not this also true of the increase which would have resulted if the subsidies had not been paid? Other subsidies, moreover, had the opposite effect: apart from the expenditure devoted to foods outside the index (e.g. dried fruits, condensed milk, canned fish, pulses and oatmeal) a substantial expenditure was incurred on underweighted items like milk and potatoes, and no account was taken in calculating the index (though it legitimately might have been) of the cheapening of milk to mothers and children by the National Milk Scheme. And

[1] e.g. by J. L. Nicholson, *Bulletin of the Oxford Institute of Statistics*, Vol. 4, No. 17, pp. 319–25.

in the case of both the two principal overweighted foods, eggs and sugar, there were special considerations: the egg subsidy facilitated the control of distribution, and the sugar subsidy was in effect no more than a partial remission of taxation, for customs and excise taxes on sugar continued throughout the war to yield considerably more than the cost of the sugar subsidies.

There is an inescapable paradox in any attempt to use an index number of prices to regulate wages at a time when real standards of consumption have to be reduced. Any index number which in such circumstances fails to show a rise of prices in relation to earnings necessarily gives a false measure of the general purchasing power of money. If wage changes must be linked to the movements of an index number, no index which is accurate from a statistician's point of view will satisfactorily serve the purpose. In this respect the old cost of living index was better suited to war conditions than the revised calculation which has now superseded it: the latter would have been far too much affected by the purchase tax and by the wartime changes in the duties on drink and tobacco.[1] The wider scope of the new index may at some future time facilitate a policy of removing food subsidies and reducing indirect taxation, since the rise in food prices will tend to be offset by the fall in the prices of the taxed commodities. The large expenditure on food subsidies which resulted from the decision to stabilize the old index no doubt contributed to the need for restricting the demand for other goods by heavy taxation. But the use during the war of an index number which fully reflected the effects of increased commodity taxation would have been a serious embarrassment to wartime finance.

CONCLUSION

To reach a fair verdict on the policies we have been discussing it is not sufficient to ask whether they failed or succeeded. The attempt to control wartime inflation could not expect to be wholly successful. What we have to ask is whether any practicable alternatives would have succeeded better or failed less badly.

Certain obvious criticisms suggest themselves, particularly in regard to the treatment of agricultural prices in the early stages of the war. The Government entered the war with no clear idea of the policy it intended to pursue towards the farmers' claims for higher prices, and instead of facing the issue and defining its attitude it allowed the initiative to pass out of its hands by making a series of ill-co-ordinated con-

[1] cf. Professor Sargant Florence's observations in his lecture on Industrial Change, in *The Industrial Future of Great Britain* (London, Europa Publications, 1948).

cessions which threatened for a time to make a coherent policy impossible. Some of the anomalies which were allowed to arise in this way, for instance in the relative return on wheat and barley, were the cause of trouble later on and even now have not been entirely rectified. The Government succeeded, by means of a combination of price incentives with more direct measures of control, in achieving its fundamental objectives of expanding arable production and stimulating milk at the expense of meat and eggs. But a firmer and more clearly defined attitude at the beginning of the war might not only have moderated the increase in farm prices and in the cost of food subsidies; it might also have considerably strengthened the Government's hand in dealing with other issues, including that of food prices and wages.

The food subsidy policy must of course be judged, not primarily as a food or nutritional measure, but in relation to the stabilization policy of which it was the principal instrument. The rise in agricultural prices took place in spite of the comprehensive powers of price control which the Government had acquired and which it had begun to exercise as soon as the war broke out, but the stabilization policy rested throughout on the assumption that the processes of collective bargaining for the determination of wages must be allowed to continue, and that the Government, though it was sooner or later to control the price of almost everything else, could not attempt directly to control the price of labour. It is not within the scope of this essay, or the range of the writer's wartime experience, to discuss the correctness of that assumption. But even if a more direct control of wages had been attempted it does not follow either that wages could have been effectively stabilized—for German experience shows that a wages-stop decree can be circumvented—or that food subsidies could have been avoided. It is accepted that in the circumstances no such policy could have been attempted; it is not easy to see that any course differing in essentials from that actually followed in fact lay open to the Government, unless it had been prepared to accept a much more serious risk of uncontrolled inflation. The stabilization policy can at least claim to have played an important part in preventing industrial unrest, and it is not certain that any other policy would in the circumstances have been more effective in stabilizing wages.

In this essay we have considered wartime policy only in the light of wartime circumstances, and have not tried to follow the food subsidies or the collective bargaining system for agricultural prices into the post-war chapter of their history. That chapter is still unfinished and this is not the place to attempt a verdict upon it. But it is obvious that a

permanent policy must be judged by stricter standards than it is practicable to apply to measures designed against a wartime emergency.
Wartime economic policy inevitably involves a considerable element of
makeshift, and much of it is tolerable only on the assumption that it is
temporary. It consists largely of a continued search for the least unsatisfactory methods of putting up with inflation. But in practice it is
better to avoid inflation altogether.

XIV

LOCAL ADMINISTRATION OF AGRICULTURAL POLICY

by

A. W. MENZIES KITCHIN

PREPARATIONS

When the Ministry of Food was closed down after the first world war a small staff was left in the Board of Trade to be responsible for drawing up plans for the maintenance of food supplies in a national emergency. In 1936 this staff was enlarged and became the Food (Defence Plans) Department with the task of studying Britain's potential food situation in the event of war. It was particularly concerned with (a) food stocks, (b) methods of distribution and rationing, and (c) price control. With the same general objective, Mr. Walter Elliot, who was then Minister of Agriculture, initiated, in 1935, an examination of ways and means of increasing home food production.

When war came in 1939, therefore, the Government were more aware of, and better prepared to deal with, the problems of food supply than they had been in 1914. On this occasion it was obvious that the dominant aim of home agriculture would be to save shipping space and that there would have to be a considerable reduction in the standard of living. It was also obvious that it would be necessary to produce in the United Kingdom as much as possible not only of the high-calorie foods which made heavy demands on shipping, but also of those protective foods which would be required to ensure a balanced diet.

In Britain, where the great bulk of the cultivable land was already in agricultural use, any substantial increase in food production could only be achieved by increasing (a) physical yields and (b) the proportion of crops available for direct human consumption. Basically, therefore, agricultural policy depended on converting grassland to tillage, on increasing the efficiency of existing arable land, and on reducing the numbers of those types of livestock (pigs and poultry) which competed with man for the use of cereals.

It was assumed that in the event of war the administration of home production would be undertaken by County War Agricultural Execu-

239

tive Committees on the lines of those used successfully in the first world war. Further, to offset the dislocation which inevitably occurs during the early stages of a major war, it was recommended that stocks of agricultural machinery and of certain feeding-stuffs and fertilizers should be accumulated and held against emergency.

In the few years before the war, therefore, the Government, on these recommendations, introduced certain measures to facilitate the change-over from peace to war.

The chairmen and key personnel of the War Agricultural Executive Committees were selected and briefed for their duties. Stocks of agricultural machinery (particularly tractors), feeding-stuffs and fertilizers —small, but nevertheless to prove important in the critical early days of 1940—were got together. Further, in order to stimulate a return to arable farming, grants of £2 per acre were offered in 1939 for permanent pasture ploughed up after 3rd May in that year, while grants already available for field drainage were extended in scope and increased.

But although the transition from peace to war was materially helped by these direct measures it was also to be assisted by less tangible developments. Between the two wars the growth of agricultural education and particularly of agricultural research and advisory work had created a large class of trained scientists and technicians who were to prove invaluable in operating wartime agriculture. At the same time the establishment of marketing boards for certain commodities and *ad hoc* commissions for others was to provide the controlled economy with tested organizational forms and key personnel.

But the most significant factor influencing production in 1939 was the fact that the tractor was rapidly replacing the horse as the unit of power in arable farming. Otherwise it is doubtful if the wartime expansion of the arable area could have been achieved. As it was, the substitution of tractors for horses assisted production in two directions: (*a*) by releasing to other uses roughly one and a half million acres of land required in the former war to produce food for horses, and (*b*) by providing a reserve of power which made it possible to plough up and cultivate rapidly and efficiently the heavy clay lands which had gone down to grass in the depression and which are invariably the most difficult to reclaim.

Nevertheless, although the agricultural problems with which the administrators were faced were more clearly foreseen and more adequately prepared for than in 1914, they were still sufficiently onerous. British agriculture had roughly two and three-quarter million fewer acres under arable crops than in 1914. Low cereal prices during the interwar years had resulted in a deterioration in the standard of farming and in the production of livestock mainly on imported feeding-stuffs. The industry employed less labour and probably had fewer reserves of capital and credit, while in many districts the technique of arable farming had been largely lost. Speaking generally, the standard of equipment was low and much of the land required phosphates or draining or both. Moreover, some 300,000 farmers with varying backgrounds of education, training and technical knowledge were concerned with food production. Many of them, still embittered by the repeal in 1921 of the Agriculture Act, 1920, were highly suspicious of the intention of the Government and likely to react violently to 'farming from Whitehall'. The situation therefore had to be handled with firmness and discretion. Thus in certain directions the problems which faced those responsible for implementing agricultural policy in 1939 were more acute than in 1914, and it was necessary to evolve a chain of responsibility between the central government and the farming community which would apply policy with a minimum of friction. Fortunately, the system of County War Agricultural Executive Committees provided the answer.

COUNTY WAR AGRICULTURAL EXECUTIVE COMMITTEES

These Committees consisted of a chairman and from eight to twelve members, all unpaid, appointed by the Minister and directly responsible to him. Generally they were persons of local standing, capable of making decisions in the light of varied experience and knowledge on matters affecting agricultural production in their respective counties. The appointed members were assisted by a full-time paid staff, largely recruited from land agents, agricultural organizers and technical advisers from county and university staffs, who were capable of advising farmers on specific technical problems and generally directing food production in their area.

For ease of administration each county was divided into districts, generally agreeing with the local government areas, and controlled by district sub-committees of the main executive. These were again mainly composed of local farmers selected by the main Committee and also serving in a voluntary capacity. The main Committee was further divided into functional sub-committees, each responsible for a particular aspect of the campaign, such as drainage, feeding-stuffs, cultivations, livestock, labour, machinery, and so on.

The task of the War Agricultural Executive Committees was to implement policy on behalf of the Government and to link production on every farm with the general plan prepared by the Ministry of Agriculture. Their powers, sanctioned by the Defence Regulations, 1939, were, before the end of the war, extremely comprehensive and formidable. They could control in detail the cropping, stocking, cultivation and fertilizer programme of any farm. They could dispossess recalcitrant or inefficient farmers. Further, they could exercise detailed administrative control of supplies through the rationing of fertilizers, feeding-stuffs, machinery and other agricultural requirements, and of labour by the supervision of manpower under the Military Service Acts.

Called suddenly into being in 1939, their first task was to find accommodation, staff and equipment; their second to ascertain the extent of the problem. While the Ministry of Agriculture could estimate the acreages and production required at the national level and for individual counties, local knowledge was required to obtain the optimum distribution of resources within a county, in a particular district or on a particular farm.

Certain farms and fields were more suitable for one form of production than another. Some farmers lacked knowledge, others had adequate knowledge but were short of capital. In certain districts and on certain farms production was limited by inadequate drainage, by lack of labour, by impoverished soil, or by combinations of these and other factors. In others farmers were reluctant to plough up centuries-old pasture of outstanding feeding value, and lacked the knowledge, skilled men, tractors and ploughs required to do so. It was evident that to ensure success, War Executive Committees had to acquire as soon as possible a detailed and intimate knowledge of the farms in their respective counties. To provide this information a farm-to-farm survey was made in 1940 and repeated in greater detail with the assistance of the advisory economists in 1941, when it became known as the National Farm Survey, or more popularly as the 'Second Doomsday'. This survey provided a valuable record of conditions on individual farms. With the 4th June returns it gave, among other things, details of: (a) the cropping and livestock on each farm; (b) information on the condition of buildings, fences, water supply and roads; (c) the quality and condition of the land; (d) whether the use of fertilizers had been adequate in the past; (e) the personal capacity of the farmer.

This basic data enabled Committees to attack the problem of the individual farm with greater competence and to concentrate their energies on increasing the output of the less productive farms. To this end the activities of less efficient farmers were supervised in detail.

They could be ordered to put into effect specific cropping, cultivation and manuring programmes, and if they refused to do so could be dispossessed and the land either re-let to suitable tenants or farmed by the Committees themselves. As a result of this supervision the general standard of farming improved, and by the end of the war the lowest pre-war grade of farmer had virtually disappeared.

Besides farming cropped land which they acquired by dispossession, the Committees were also responsible for reclaiming considerable areas which had gone derelict between the wars. They also were responsible for supervising drainage schemes and in certain cases for carrying them out. In consequence, they became farmers and employers of labour on a substantial scale. By the end of 1942, for example, they had taken possession in England and Wales of some 200,000 acres, of which 83,000 acres had been re-let—generally after extensive reclamation and draining—but the remainder was still in hand. During the next two years the area in possession increased and in March 1944 the Committees controlled 385,000 acres and farmed 215,000 acres. For these operations they naturally required a great deal of labour and large quantities of machinery and equipment. By the end of 1941 they were employing in England and Wales some 8,600 men and women, and by the end of 1943 the number had risen to over 30,000. The county of Essex alone, for example, employed 2,000 workers. Employment on this scale introduced new problems of labour organization and management and in this connexion the Committees worked at considerable disadvantage. In the first place they had been warned not to compete with farmers for labour and much of their work was done by gangs of land girls and conscientious objectors, with a stiffening of regular labourers. This force was later augmented by prisoners of war. The difficulty of adequate supervision and of finding suitable foremen as the number and size of the gangs increased made the process a somewhat wasteful one. Efficiency was also reduced by the lack of suitable labour officers to control and direct the work of the gangs and to arrange rates of pay and payment. Moreover, the land farmed by the Committees was generally scattered. It had often to be reclaimed from scrub or marsh at a distance from a regular labour supply. Further, as the war progressed the best of the reclaimed land gradually found tenants, while the worst remained in possession.

In spite of these difficulties, however, much food was grown on land farmed by Committees, although, perhaps inevitably, it was produced at a high cost in resources.

But the Committees were faced with other problems. Much of the grassland coming under the plough was heavily infested with wireworm which, if sufficiently numerous, could virtually destroy the following crop. Fortunately, the losses which had occurred from this cause in the 1914–18 war had been remembered, and in December 1938 the advisory entomologists at the provincial advisory centres had begun to examine the relationship between the wireworm population and crop yields on freshly ploughed grassland. Consequently, a technique of soil sampling was developed which made it possible to estimate the wireworm population of any field with reasonable accuracy and, as certain crops were less susceptible to attack than others, to adapt cropping plans on the basis of the wireworm content. Thus the crop failures which had been a common feature in the 1914–18 war were largely avoided.

A further instance of the practical application of scientific knowledge occurred in the allocation of fertilizers. The bulk of nitrogenous fertilizers is home-produced, but the raw materials required for the manufacture of phosphatic and potassic fertilizers were, before the war, mainly imported from Germany and France. When these supplies were finally lost after the fall of France in 1940, it was evident that great care would have to be exercised in the use of the limited stocks available. Potassic fertilizers were, therefore, reserved for those crops— mainly potatoes and certain vegetables—where yields were likely to be limited by potash deficiency. At the same time the use of phosphates on grassland was banned. The situation was also relieved by the fact that the advisory chemists at provincial centres carried out, on behalf of the Agricultural Committees, many thousands of soil analyses on grassland scheduled for ploughing and so enabled partial soil deficiencies to be made good in the subsequent manuring.

Other problems arose with the supply of small seeds, particularly that of herbage, sugar beet and certain vegetable crops which before the war had been mainly imported. But here again the situation was quickly appreciated and the difficulties surmounted. In this connection the National Institute of Agricultural Botany, in conjunction with the Seeds Production Committee, played an important part in developing stocks and maintaining standards, with the result that by the end of the war the loss of imports had largely been made good by home production.

Scientific research and guidance was also provided in other directions. The Agricultural Research Council had for some time been a State department responsible for fundamental research. In June 1944 an analogous organization entitled the Agricultural Improvement Council was created to stimulate the application of the results of scientific investigation to farming practice, and in the same year a Technical Development Committee was set up to assist in demonstrating new farming methods through county sub-committees. Both these new organizations, in conjunction with the County Committees, did much to increase technical efficiency.

The difficulties of wartime farming were inevitably intensified by shortage of labour and from June 1940 the Restriction on Engagement Order made it illegal for employers in other industry to engage agricultural workers. Further, in October 1941 the age of reservation in the main agricultural occupations was raised to twenty-five and, later, individual deferment was substituted for block reservation. Here again, however, as a result of better appreciation, the labour situation was very much easier than in the previous war. The position was also alleviated by the very great development in the use of power equipment which occurred during the war. Not only did the number of tractors on farms in Great Britain increase from just under 52,000 in 1938 to nearly 173,000 by 1944, but the introduction of combine harvesters, straw-balers and large-scale tractor equipment did much to reduce the time required for individual operations and to increase output per man. Using a tractor and a gang roll, for example, it became possible under certain conditions to roll forty to fifty acres per day compared with ten acres by horse, and similar results could be obtained in other operations. At the same time the need for cultivations was reduced by the development of the chemical control of weeds.

But these technical developments, important as they were, would, even when supported by the varied and substantial powers of the War Agricultural Executive Committees, have been insufficient to guarantee the success of the food production campaign. It was also essential to ensure profitable prices.

AGRICULTURAL PRICES AND COSTS

Agriculture was emerging from a long period of depression. Farmers' indebtedness was generally believed to be high and little capital was available to finance new forms of production. The changeover from grassland to arable involved considerable capital expenditure. Tractors, implements, fertilizers and seeds had to be bought. Labour had to be hired and paid for before the new crops were harvested, while wages and other costs were rising. As the ploughing-up campaign developed in intensity, these changes were partly financed by the sale of livestock, particularly pigs, sheep and poultry, which had to give way before the

R

plough, but funds derived from these sources were by themselves in-adequate. Also, after their experience during the depression, farmers required some assurance that the new liabilities which they were being asked to undertake would bring a reasonable return. In consequence, the Government introduced at an early stage in the war a system of guaranteed prices for a number of crops and products.

At the end of 1939, however, State control over agricultural produce was still limited. The farm price of wheat was fixed, but barley and oat and fat stock prices were free. Milk and potato prices, on the other hand, were controlled at all stages from the farmer to the consumer. Control was also exercised over the prices of imported feeding-stuffs. Nevertheless, although the application of price control was still unequal, policy was beginning to crystallize along more definite lines.

It was becoming evident that feeding-stuff imports would have to be reduced and probably rationed. Emphasis was beginning to be placed on the importance of maintaining meat and milk supplies, albeit at the expense of pigs and poultry. The extent to which it would be necessary to change over to a more vegetarian diet was not yet fully recognized, except that a scientific committee[1] had drawn up, under the title of 'The Basal Diet', a list of the essential foods which would have to be grown to provide a reasonably balanced diet in the event of siege conditions. It was, however, quickly becoming apparent that the com-pulsory powers of the War Committees would have to be reinforced by a system of selective price fixing in order to stimulate the production of the more essential foods.

The need for more detailed price control was particularly evident in the case of cereals. The price of the 1939 wheat crop had been fixed at approximately 11s. per cwt., but by January 1940 oat and barley prices, which were free, had risen to 15s. 5d. per cwt. and 17s. 10d. per cwt. respectively. In consequence, it was evident that unless cereal prices were brought into line before the autumn of 1940 farmers would grow barley and oats rather than wheat, and the wheat target would not be obtained. The prices of all cereals except malting barley were therefore controlled during the year. Later, in order to assist production on marginal land and in districts where wheat and potatoes were not commonly grown, part of the price was paid in the form of an acreage payment of £4 and £10 per acre for wheat and potatoes respectively. Thus manipulation of the price mechanism, in conjunction with crop-ping directions and feeding-stuff rationing, was used to establish the pattern of production which the national interest required. Gradually,

[1] See page 224.

therefore, agricultural policy developed from the central plan. The Committees learned their task and gained confidence with custom. They also gained the confidence of the great majority of farmers. Perhaps not unexpectedly it was during this early period when they were building up their organizations that they were subjected to most criticism. Many of the farmers' difficulties and some errors on the part of government departments were inevitable. It was impossible to forecast the exact pattern of events which sometimes moved faster than anticipated and often in unexpected directions. Decisions, which to the spectator appeared unnecessary and contradictory, were forced upon Ministries by sudden changes in fortune and could not be explained for security reasons. But to the farmers orders and counter orders often appeared to succeed each other in bewildering succession.

A typical instance of this character arose in respect of animal feeding-stuffs. It had originally been intended on the outbreak of war to prohibit feeding wheat to livestock in order to conserve stocks for human consumption. But in October 1939 the decision was deferred because of the shortage of animal feeds. Six weeks later imports of animal feeds had to be cut because of wheat shortage. The extent to which livestock numbers would have to be reduced had not been fully realized either by the Government or by the farming community, and when it was announced farmers were taken by surprise. A similar example occurred when instructions to increase sheep flocks were closely followed by a direction to plough up additional grassland.

But the outstanding feature of the early days of the war was not the errors or omissions of government departments, but the speed with which both the staff of the two food Ministries and the War Executive Committees and the farming community became adjusted to their wartime tasks. In this connexion the government departments received valuable assistance from the scientific committees who outlined the essential food pattern and, as food shortage developed, advised on food import policy and rationing.

Misunderstandings between the Ministry of Agriculture and the War Agricultural Executive Committees on the one hand and the War Agricultural Executive Committees and the farmers on the other, were also reduced by the appointment in June 1940 of liaison officers acting between the Minister of Agriculture and the War Agricultural Executive Committees. These officers, each in charge of a group of counties, were responsible for explaining and guiding Government policy in their particular areas.

Inevitably as Government policy became more precisely defined the direction of agricultural production became more apparent, and as the administration improved most of the difficulties which were experienced in the early days of control disappeared. One grievance, however —the delay in formulating cropping programmes—persisted well into the war. Here again, it was the result of the Government delaying until the last moment a decision on a rapidly changing situation. But to the farmer it often appeared as a failure to understand the long-term nature of agricultural production and the need for laying plans well ahead. This cause of criticism was, however, eventually removed by the introduction of the February Price Review, where prices and production targets were fixed for at least a year ahead.

LESSONS

Considered in retrospect it is evident that the food production campaign was carried out with enterprise and efficiency. During the war, with a very moderate increase in labour force (much of it unskilled), the pattern of the English countryside underwent a striking change. Ditches were cleared, large areas were drained and grassland gave way to tillage. This transformation was the visible result of the efforts of the farming community in co-operation with the County Committees. Under the aegis of guaranteed prices farmers were able to make good out of profits at least part of the capital depreciation of the interwar years and to find the money to finance the purchase of large numbers of new machines and other equipment. In consequence the general standard of farming improved.

In physical terms the results were impressive. Between 1939 and 1944, when agricultural production reached its peak, the arable area in the United Kingdom rose from 12·91 to 19·27 million acres and that of tillage from 8·81 to 14·55 million acres. In the same period the acreages of wheat, barley and potatoes were roughly doubled and the acreage of oats increased by approximately 50 per cent. As a result, in 1943 home-grown wheat and potatoes together provided 45 per cent of the total calorie intake of the British wartime diet and by 1945 half the wheat in national flour was grown in this country. In addition, the production of vegetables for human consumption and of home-grown fodder crops was substantially increased; while milk production, after some initial difficulties, was well maintained. On the other hand, in order to offset a reduction of imported feeding-stuffs from 8¾ to 1¼ million tons, it was necessary between 1939 and 1944 to reduce the number of pigs, poultry and sheep by 58 per cent, 26 per cent and 25 per cent respectively.

Nevertheless, in spite of a smaller livestock population, it has been calculated that in 1942–3 the net output of agriculture in the United Kingdom measured in food values (calories and proteins) had increased by 70 per cent, while the net output in money values at fixed prices (i.e. the quantitative output) had increased by about 30 per cent.[1]

What, then, were the main reasons for the very real success of the food production campaign? Essentially it was due to four fundamental factors. First, that in the peculiar circumstances of war the problem of food production could be attacked with singleness of purpose and without counting the cost; secondly, that the overall production plan prepared at the centre was sound; thirdly, that the execution of the plan was decentralized and was undertaken by groups of individuals who in the aggregate not only had a thorough knowledge of the science and practice of farming, but also understood the psychology of the farmers; and fourthly, that farmers were anxious to co-operate to the limit of their powers. The smooth transition was also assisted by the fact that (a) the Committees had behind them the experience of the former war; (b) tractors and power equipment were available in sufficient quantity to deal with the additional plough-land; (c) a general advance in scientific and technical knowledge had occurred since 1918; and (d) prices were guaranteed at reasonable levels.

Initial difficulties and some differences of opinion could not be avoided in so complex an undertaking. To the onlooker it may some-times have appeared that the *tempo* of operations could have been increased, but the fact remains that maximum agricultural production was obtained at the period of the war when it was most urgently required. If one were so ungrateful as to criticize a highly meritorious achievement, it might be suggested that resources could, in certain cases, have been more usefully applied in increasing yields on existing farm land than in reclaiming lands which under normal conditions are unlikely to repay the cost of cultivation; and secondly, that when, in the event of war, the farmer is asked to undertake obligations which may in certain cases be against his interest, he should, wherever possible, be clearly informed why the course of action concerned is essential to national policy.

[1] J. H. Kirk, "The Output of British Agriculture during the War", *Proceedings of the Agricultural Economics Society*, Vol. VII, No. 1, June 1946.

INDEX

Notes: n = note; t = table. Keywords of special significance are printed in small capitals.

For EU product safety concerns, contact us at Calle de José Abascal, 56–1°,
28003 Madrid, Spain or eugpsr@cambridge.org.

www.ingramcontent.com/pod-product-compliance
Ingram Content Group UK Ltd.
Pitfield, Milton Keynes, MK11 3LW, UK
UKHW012159180425
457623UK00018B/281